CATF

Pat Nixon of Texas

Pat Nixon of Texas

AUTOBIOGRAPHY OF A DOCTOR
BY PAT IRELAND NIXON

Edited with an Introduction by
HERBERT H. LANG

Texas A&M University Press
College Station and London

Library of Congress Cataloging in Publication Data

Nixon, Patrick Ireland, 1883–
    Pat Nixon of Texas.

    Includes bibliographical references and index.
    1. Nixon, Patrick Ireland, 1883– 2. Physicians—
Texas—San Antonio—Biography. 3. Medical historians
—Texas—San Antonio—Biography. 4. Public health—
Texas—San Antonio—History—20th century. I. Lang,
Herbert H., 1921– II. Title. [DNLM: 1. Physicians—
Personal narratives. WZ100 N736]
R154.N66A34   610'.92'4 [B]   78-65575
ISBN 0-89096-072-0

Manufactured in the United States of America
FIRST EDITION

Contents

List of Illustrations

Preface

❦

IT IS UNFORTUNATE, but understandable, that few Texas physicians have told their stories in print. Some doctors are too busy to write about themselves; others are too modest or lack literary talent. There are exceptions. And the best of these few personal accounts demonstrate that the events of physicians' lives make rewarding reading, for each doctor's story is, in microcosm, the story of man's long epic struggle to prevail over his two most persistent foes, disease and death.

One Texas physician who left an articulate written record of his career in medicine is Pat Ireland Nixon. Born to a farm family in Guadalupe County in 1883, Dr. Pat attended first the University of Texas and then Johns Hopkins Medical School, where he also did his internship and residency. Returning to Texas in 1911, he opened an office in San Antonio and practiced medicine in that city for more than half a century. He assembled an outstanding library of rare medical books and was a well-known and highly respected collector of Texana. A skillful writer and an exceptionally competent researcher, he is recognized as the preeminent historian of Texas medicine.

After Dr. Pat's death in 1965, there was discovered in his office desk a lengthy but incomplete and unpolished autobiographical account. Incorporated in this manuscript are a sketch of his youth and education, excerpts from hundreds of letters to his betrothed from medical school, a diary he maintained while at Baltimore, a discussion of the establishment and first difficult years of his medical practice, notebooks, correspondence with friends and patients, speeches and radio addresses, a detailed account of his battles to reform San Antonio government and to bring about improvements in public health, much about his family and his personal life, and other material on a wide variety of subjects. Through the courtesy of Dr. Pat's eldest son, Dr. Pat I. Nixon, Jr., these memoirs have been made available for publication.

The manuscript has both the virtues and the faults of a first draft. On the one hand, the memoirs are enriched with the verve of spontaneity. On the other hand, they lack organization, skip back and forth in time and place, are far too repetitious, and are sometimes awkward in style. There are errors, mainly typographical, and there are troublesome inconsistencies in structure. Part of the fault stems from the circumstances under which the manuscript was produced. It was composed in spare moments, internal evidence indicates, over a long span of years. Part of the manuscript is missing—most significantly, the first few pages—and there are other gaps in the narrative. Large sections were written by Dr. Pat during his final illness, from remembered events long past.

In the course of editing, pains have been taken to preserve the writer's words, style, and meaning; however, because the manuscript is a rough first draft, the editor has taken the liberty of standardizing punctuation, capitalization, and spelling and has corrected obvious typographical errors. Bracketed italic additions are the editor's; bracketed Roman material was added by Nixon himself. Wherever possible, names Dr. Nixon mentioned have been identified by the editor in footnotes. For the convenience of the reader and for the sake of physical appearance, the memoirs have been divided into chapters that differ somewhat from Dr. Pat's arrangement. Parts of the manuscript have been shifted about to maintain continuity and flow.

The most difficult editorial decision entailed determining which parts of the manuscript to omit or condense. Deleted passages were omitted because they are repetitious or extraneous or to protect the privacy of certain individuals.

I am deeply indebted to Dr. Pat I. Nixon, Jr., for permitting the publication of his father's memoirs and for reading and criticizing the manuscript; to Frank Wardlaw, former director of the Texas A&M University Press, who initiated this project; to Ann Coiner and her able staff at the Trinity University Archives for graciously granting access to the Nixon Papers and for providing a pleasant working environment over the course of several weeks; to Dr. David A. Kronick, treasurer of the Friends of the P. I. Nixon Medical Historical Library and librarian at the University of Texas Health Science Center at San Antonio, for his many courtesies; to Mrs. Brooks B. McGimsey for sharing her memories of Dr. Pat; to Dr. Nena Harris for assistance with medical terminology; to Lynne Ricketts, librarian of the Bexar County Medical Society, for the use of elusive published works and manuscript documents; and to Betty Afflerbach, librarian of the Texas Medical Association in Austin, for her kind assistance in locating copies of Dr. Pat's published works.

HERBERT H. LANG

Pat Nixon of Texas

Introduction

~~~~~

In 1883 Texans had good cause for optimism. Symbolic of anticipated future achievement was the massive pink granite capitol slowly rising on the crest of a hill at the head of Congress Avenue in Austin, a structure destined to become the largest and most handsome statehouse in the nation. On the open prairie a short distance to the north stood the first building of the new state university. Although the school had only recently admitted the first students, its founders already talked of academic excellence and were determined to create an educational edifice of the highest order. The population of Texas had nearly doubled in the previous decade and now totaled more than one and one-half million. Texas, which had entered the Union only thirty-seven years earlier, could now boast that only ten other states exceeded it in population. The economy, resting soundly on cattle and cotton, was booming. Governor Oran M. Roberts, whose term had just ended, had adopted a pay-as-you-go policy, thus inaugurating an era of governmental fiscal responsibility in Texas for the first time since antebellum days. Railroads, which had entered Texas only thirty years earlier, now operated on a regular basis over more than six thousand miles of track, stimulating commerce and tying a population still 90 percent rural to the new, burgeoning cities. The frontier era was fast drawing to a close. Nomadic Indian raiders were no longer a serious threat to isolated farms and ranches, thanks to the cavalry and the Texas Rangers. Although the fence-cutting war was at its peak of violence, even the most obdurate cattle barons realized that the heyday of open-range stockraising was over and that a new era of prosaic ranching had dawned. The new state constitution, adopted when Reconstruction ended, had been in operation long enough to demonstrate that it was adequate to the needs of a vigorous, healthy young society ready at last to assume a position of leadership in the family of states.

For Robert Thomas Nixon of Guadalupe County and his wife Fannie, the year 1883 was significant for a more personal reason. On November 29, Pat Ireland Nixon, their first son, was born into a large family that already consisted of their four daughters and numerous offspring of Robert's previous marriage.

Even in his early years, Pat was made conscious of the heritage his forebears had bestowed upon him, and he determined to be worthy of their gift. He knew what sacrifices his parents had made, he respected them for their many admirable traits and their strength of character, and he was proud of the position they had achieved in the community. As was only natural for a young boy in a large family, in order to win the approval and affection he hungered for, he tried to pattern his own life on that of his father.

Robert was an excellent model for Pat to emulate. Ambitious to improve himself, he had migrated to Texas out of his native North Carolina in 1852. A pioneer settler of the Guadalupe River country, he was one of that small group of sturdy men who had tamed the South Texas wilderness and introduced into that savage land the essential amenities of civilization. He had earned a reputation for integrity and concern for the welfare of the community, and with the coming of the Civil War his neighbors looked to him for leadership. Robert Nixon raised a company of troops and for the remainder of his days was referred to as Captain Nixon in deference to the rank he had held in wartime. Neither a slave owner nor a defender of the "peculiar institution," he, like so many other men, served the Confederacy out of an ingrained conviction that the preservation of states' rights was essential to the survival of individual rights.

A devout Methodist, he accepted unquestioningly John Wesley's admonition, "Earn all you can, save all you can, give all you can." Willing to try anything that held promise of honest profit, he worked as drayman, farmer, stockman, and cotton ginner. Starting with little capital, he eventually put together a large estate.

But all this had been accomplished at great cost. Robert's first wife, Laura Wood Nixon, had been worn out by the physical task of building a home in a new land and by continuous childbearing. She had died in the summer of 1872 giving birth to her eleventh child. Five months later Robert married Frances (Fannie) Amanda Andrews, a woman sixteen years his junior. By the time Pat was born, the Captain was already fifty-six years of age, and he died prior to Pat's fourteenth birthday.

Fortunately for Pat, he had older half brothers who sensed his need for guidance and attention. At first it was the ebullient Sam Houston Nixon who tried to fill the void left in the young boy's life by the Captain's death. Sam was one of those rare free spirits who exult even in the normal daily course of ordinary events. His carefree attitude was contagious. Naturally kind and fun loving, he cheerfully tolerated the presence of an adoring Pat on many an escapade. Sam was a cowboy, and by definition he could ride and shoot and throw a rope right on target —just the sorts of accomplishments that would impress a Texas boy. Until a certain young lady came along to domesticate him, he and Pat were inseparable.

Thereafter Pat came under the powerful and perhaps more desirable influence of the eldest son of Robert's first marriage, James Wesley. A competent physician and a man of stern visage and demeanor, he took seriously his role as titular head of the family. He had neither time nor sympathy for the frivolity that Sam exemplified. Life was not a matter to be taken lightly, in Dr. Nixon's opinion. He stressed to Pat the need for frugality and the rewards of hard work, and, consciously or not, he instilled in the boy a determination to follow in his footsteps. Thus it was that at an early period in his life Pat made a most important decision—the decision to become a medical doctor.

Guadalupe County in the last decade of the nineteenth century was a good place for a boy to grow to manhood. Lying just east of the thirty-inch rainfall line, the county possessed a climate and blackland soil ideally suited to the production of upland cotton, the basis for the prosperous local economy. Few other areas of the state possessed a native beauty surpassing that of the Guadalupe River country. Nutritious native grasses, especially the little blue-stem and golden-headed Indian grass, nature's bountiful gift to the stockmen who first occupied the area, grew in profusion in the gently rolling countryside. Groves of deciduous hardwoods, with post and blackjack oaks, pecans, walnuts, elms, and hickories predominating, dotted the landscape. A short distance to the west was the domain of the mesquite and chaparral. Originally ranching country, during Pat's boyhood the county was undergoing transition into a major agricultural area.

Although he lived in this rural environment until his teens, Pat did not fit the mold of the average farm boy, nor, for that matter, were the Nixons a typical farm family. During an interview in 1960, Dr. Pat told a newspaper reporter, "I was reared in an atmosphere of hard work."[1] But in truth, this statement was somewhat misleading. There were always plenty of hired hands available for the really strenuous tasks, and furthermore Pat was small in stature and never enjoyed robust health during his childhood, so he was not given too heavy a load of work. This is not to suggest that Robert Nixon pampered his children. Pat and the others had a reasonable number of chores to perform on a regular schedule—enough work, apparently, to teach them the value of work. But they were not exploited, and they were even paid for at least some of the work they performed.

Pat and other Guadalupe County youngsters always enjoyed a wide choice of wholesome outdoor activities that helped them to develop physically and mentally and, for the more sensitive among them, such as Pat, to develop spiritually as well. Farm tanks beckoned irresistibly on sultry summer afternoons. Squir-

[1] San Antonio *News*, February 17, 1960.

rel-hunting forays led them into oak thickets on spring and fall days; many nights were consumed hunting the elusive coon. Pat and his companions devoted many summer days entirely to fishing the pools of meandering Smith Creek where fat perch, buffalo, and catfish waited to test a boy's skill. And then there were moments when a boy, taking up the challenge of a rival, demonstrated his courage by daring to shoot the rapids of the treacherous San Marcos River, an experience that once came perilously close to costing Pat his life.

Pat was especially close to his younger brother Zeb. The two had much in common. They both were lively, mischievous boys who loved the outdoors and all wild things, and they shared a mutual infatuation with baseball. In their teens, the Nixon brothers played on semiprofessional neighborhood teams that traveled far in search of worthy competition, and they gained a loyal following among sports enthusiasts across much of South Texas. The left-handed Pat was blessed with inborn ability. Possessed of an easygoing nature, he often sat quietly in the outfield grass, patiently awaiting the outcome of a heated dispute over some close call, while Zeb joyfully took on the umpire and the entire opposition team if necessary to win the point. Later Pat played on both the University of Texas and Johns Hopkins teams, eligibility rules being rather lax in the early 1900's. Many who saw Pat Nixon in action on the baseball diamond were convinced that had he not opted for a career in medicine he could have become an outstanding professional baseball player.

The Nixon children attended a country school that seems to have been far superior to the average of its type. In a single classroom Major Lee Russell, a former Confederate officer and one of Fannie Nixon's brothers-in-law, dispensed alternately book learning and discipline. But even good country schools do have their limitations. Unlike most of their neighbors, the elder Nixons were troubled by the quality of education their children were receiving and made up their minds to provide the best training family circumstances would permit. Most of their thirteen surviving offspring attended college; three of these, Jimmie, Pat, and Zeb, went on to professional schools. Fannie Nixon had early recognized that something in Pat set him apart from the ordinary, and a fierce determination burned in her that her firstborn (and favorite) son would be given every opportunity to develop to his full potential. She waged a relentless campaign to convince her doubting husband that he should move the family into town before Pat reached high school. Ultimately that strong-willed woman prevailed over all Robert's sound and logical arguments to the contrary, and in 1895 the Nixons settled into a newly constructed home in nearby Luling.

In the eyes of Pat and the other younger members of the Nixon household, bustling Luling, with its population of twelve hundred, was a metropolis. The children were excited by the prospect of life in a city but soon learned that acclimation to their new home would require a good deal of adjustment. The sudden, unexpected death of Captain Nixon in 1897 made the transition from farm to town even more difficult, and, for Pat, a prolonged bout with typhoid fever created additional problems. In time he won the respect of the town boys, who at first had been openly hostile, and he was accepted as an equal into the social milieu of the youth of the town. After graduating in 1900—to Fannie's intense gratification, salutatorian of his class —Pat at seventeen faced his first prolonged separation from his family.

He had already decided he would attend the state university and was eager to head for Austin. But Fannie, fearing that her son lacked the necessary background and maturity to do well in a rigorous premed program, decided after consultation with kinfolk in North Carolina that Pat should attend the Bingham School at Asheville. There, it was expected, he would acquire additional knowledge and smooth off his rough edges. For Fannie, the decision to send Pat to North Carolina could not have been easy. She still had three young children at home, completely dependent on her, and she had had to take on the demanding, time-consuming task of supervising the family farm and other property. Also, because of the drop in the price of cotton after the Spanish-American War, money was scarce in the Nixon household, especially money to send a boy to a distant, exclusive academy where most of his classmates were scions of wealthy Southern or New England families. Somehow Fannie managed, and Pat spent two happy and productive years at Bingham School. In 1902, having graduated *maxima cum laude*, he returned home and enrolled in the University of Texas.

Pat was not really happy during his student days at Austin. Because of his extra preparation at Bingham School, he entered the university as a sophomore rather than as a freshman, and he never did feel that he belonged to his class. He complained that he had difficulty satisfying the demands of some of his professors. Yet he earned respectable grades, and the sound grounding he received in the sciences helped him excel in his later work at medical school. At first the mere size of the student body awed him, but he soon adjusted and forced himself to participate in extracurricular activities. He lettered in baseball two years, and he pledged Alpha Tau Omega fraternity. Although he found it difficult to overcome his shyness, he succeeded in making lasting friendships with young men who had come out of backgrounds entirely different from his own. More important, at a church social during his junior year, he met his future wife, Olive Gray Read. By the time of his graduation in 1905, Pat had acquired a much broader perspective and a degree of sophistication he had lacked when he first arrived at the university three years earlier.

It had been assumed that Pat would attend the University of Texas Medical School at Galveston. In his college work, he had concentrated on courses prescribed by that school, and his application had received a favorable hearing there. However, his brother's partner, Dr. W. J. Hildebrand, sold him on the innovative program at the Johns Hopkins Medical School. Pat found the prospect of studying under the great medical educators at Baltimore exciting, but tuition would be considerably higher than in Texas. That problem was solved when Dr. J. W. Nixon agreed to lend enough money to supplement the income Pat received from his share of a family-owned farm. But the question of whether he could meet the strict entrance requirements at Hopkins still remained. His failure to take French in college was the chief stumbling block. In an exchange of letters, Pat made the common error of addressing his first inquiry to "John Hopkins University." In subsequent correspondence, he listed Dr. Nixon as his guardian and stated that he read Latin, had taken three years of German, and had credit for courses in physics, chemistry, and biology. At last came the eagerly await-ed favorable response; he had been accepted with the under-standing that he would make up his deficiency in French at the Berlitz School in Baltimore.[2]

By the time Pat Nixon entered Johns Hopkins, he had reached a level of emotional maturity that gave substance and direction to his existence. He had a clear image of what he wanted out of life, the route he must follow to achieve his goals, and the cost in physical and mental effort. But what forces gave him the strength and self-confidence that sustained him in moments of professional disappointments, family tragedies, and a debilitat-ing and ultimately fatal chronic illness?

Certainly paramount were the influences of home and family during his youth. The Nixons formed a self-sufficient household; its members always supported one another in time of adversity. Each person clearly understood his obligations and responsi-bilities to the others and knew exactly what responses he could count on from them in return. This tacit understanding fostered a sense of security, of belonging, and of personal worth. In such an atmosphere, Pat learned early to bear his share of the load. He knew that an education was worth striving for because it was the ultimate key, not merely to economic success, but to personal happiness and fulfillment. He was taught to accept and respect the rights and opinions of others, how to sense the nuances of conflicting interests, and when to compromise. He came to understand that there were times when he must sac-rifice personal pleasures and desires for the sake of more imme-

2 Letters of September 18, 22, and 30, 1905, in Pat Ireland Nixon Folder, Registrar's Office, Johns Hopkins University.

diate family needs. He learned to be frank and open, candid and fair, loyal and unselfish.

A second influence that made a permanent impact on Pat and helped to shape him was the spirit of the age in which he lived. His formative years coincided with the peak period of the Progressive Era. It was only natural that he should be caught up by the tenets of progressivism because much of its program drew inspiration from the Jeffersonian agrarian tradition in which the Nixons had their roots. The Progressives' program was humanitarian; it appealed to the idealist and the optimist; in the young, it fostered a craving to serve. And the ambitious goals it hoped to achieve were to be accomplished in an orderly manner through the democratic process. Progressive ideals fostered in Pat the sense of stewardship that was to manifest itself, later, in his professional work.

Progressivism, in conceiving of the ideal society as a Christian commonwealth, comported well with the profound religious faith of the Nixons and with the religious training Pat received under Fannie's tutelage. Staunch Methodists, the Nixons instilled Protestant values in their children. It was the social gospel to which they subscribed, whether or not they actually called it such, and they were certain that its precepts afforded the only acceptable solution to society's dilemmas.

Although Pat grew up at a time when the new science and the old-time religion were in anguished conflict, he himself saw no serious contradiction between traditional Christian dogma and the new revelations of scientific rationalism. Many of his professors at medical school, renowned scientists, were sincerely pious men. Several of them conducted informal religious services and encouraged the medical students to attend. Pat seldom missed Sunday school in Baltimore, and he was active in the religious programs of the local YMCA. When studies and ward duties permitted, he attended revivals led by famous evangelists of the day. It is significant that, although Pat had been a churchgoer from childhood, he did not formally join the church until he entered medical school. His letters fail to reveal why he took that step, a most serious decision for him, at that particular time. Doubtless it was the culmination of many factors, but perhaps chief among them was his experiences in the charity wards of the Johns Hopkins Hospital. There for the first time he saw and tended the suffering victims of immoral society in their most pitiable forms—the diseased, the deranged, the corrupted. This experience, too, led him to recognize a responsibility as a physician to fight to correct the abuses of society. Here was the beginning of an awareness that later culminated in his struggle to wipe out the diseases that ran rampant through the *barrios* of San Antonio.

Thus several disparate elements focused in young Pat Nixon, elements that, when crystalized, permanently altered his world outlook. Among them were the demanding standards of morality instilled at home, the teachings of his religion, and an emerging social consciousness (in which the medical profession played no small part) that was reshaping America into a nation ever more responsive to human needs.

The initial decade of the twentieth century, which coincided with Pat's student days at Johns Hopkins, witnessed tremendous advances in medicine and allied fields that revolutionized the treatment of disease in the western world. And in many ways, Baltimore functioned as the heart that pumped the flowing life stream of progress. Time-honored techniques of the profession became obsolete almost overnight. Nearly every issue of the leading medical journals reported imaginative new methods of surgery or new drugs that conquered at last age-old afflictions that had previously resisted all treatment.

It was during this period, at the turn of the century, that Pirquet first stated his theory of allergy and developed a cutaneous test for tuberculosis. Leonard Finley was demonstrating the relationship between dietary deficiencies and crippling rickets, Wassermann was developing his serum test for syphilis, Theobold Smith was urging the use of toxin-antitoxin in combating diphtheria, Lenhart and Marine perfected the iodine treatment of goiter, Casimir Funk launched the study of vitamins, and Pavlov investigated conditioned reflexes. Other major developments included passage of the Food and Drug Act, the

Introduction

organization of the National Council for Industrial Safety, the establishment by Adelaide Nutting of the first course in public health nursing, and the founding of the first course in public hygiene.

The medical profession, awakened to the deplorable state of medical education and, consequently, of medical practice, had begun to reform the antiquated ways of training doctors. Medical schools raised admission standards, drastically revised curricula, and devised imaginative new instructional methods. In this effort, the Johns Hopkins Medical School took the lead, and by the beginning of the new century it had become a mecca for a cadre of outstanding educators and bright young students. Abraham Flexner, who made a landmark study of medical training for the Carnegie Foundation, wrote of the Hopkins program, "Dr. Welch has created, in so far as it goes, the one ideal medical school in America."[3]

In order to provide students an opportunity for practical training, as well as more traditional classroom work, the Johns Hopkins Hospital was totally integrated with the medical school as a teaching facility. Dr. William Osler, Hopkins' premier professor of medicine, did his most effective teaching in the hospital at the bedside of the patient. Third- and fourth-year students were employed in the wards as clinical clerks and in the operating rooms as surgical dressers. Students received additional practical experience in the Phipps Psychiatric and Tuberculosis clinics and in the Harriet Lane Pediatric Hospital. All this constituted innovative teaching and in the long run proved most effective.

Johns Hopkins was also the first major medical school to admit women, the first to offer postintern training in areas of specialization, and the first to experiment with the concept of a full-time faculty. Hopkins professors, deeply concerned with the social implications of illness and hospitalization, instituted a program of social services for patients and for their families

[3] Alan M. Chesney, *The Johns Hopkins Hospital and The Johns Hopkins University School of Medicine: A Chronicle,* 3 vols. (Baltimore: Johns Hopkins University Press, 1943–1963), 3:135.

and began a follow-up program after the patient had returned to his home. Especially novel was a course in forensic (legal) medicine. And, in 1909, through the generosity of William A. Marburg, one of the trustees, Hopkins acquired in England the outstanding Warrington Dispensary Collection of rare medical books. These volumes became the nucleus of a major medical library. A member of the staff, Dr. John Shaw Billings, became the acknowledged dean of American medical librarians.

Johns Hopkins had a superb faculty-student ratio. Flexner's study reported that in 1909, the year Pat Nixon graduated, the medical school had a teaching staff of 112, of whom 23 were professors; there were 297 students.[4] From the beginning, four towering giants dominated the faculty: William H. Welch in pathology, William Osler in medicine, Howard A. Kelly in gynecology, and William S. Halsted in surgery. But in the lower echelons of the faculty hierarchy were younger instructors who, in time, achieved prominence in the medical fraternity in their own right. Two of Pat's teachers, Joseph Erlanger and George H. Whipple, won Nobel prizes in neurophysiology and pathology respectively. Lewellys F. Barker made his reputation in medicine; J. Whitridge Williams, in obstetrics; Clemens von Pirquet, in pediatrics; William S. Thayer, in cardiovascular studies; Harvey Cushing and the Texan Hugh H. Young, in surgery; Frederick H. Baetjer, in radiology; John J. Abel, in pharmacology; and Florence Sabin, in histology.

During his six years at Baltimore, Pat sent, by actual count, 373 letters to Olive Read back in Texas. He estimated that he wrote to her at least half a million words. These letters Olive carefully preserved in chronological order. Some of the letters were lengthy, detailed, carefully structured, while others obviously were dashed off during a few precious free moments between duties. At first this correspondence was formal and restrained, at times almost cold, but, as the Hopkins years slowly passed, Pat became much less inhibited. His letters contained

[4] Abraham Flexner, *Medical Education in the United States and Canada: A Report to the Carnegie Foundation for the Advancement of Teaching* (New York: Carnegie Foundation, 1910), p. 234.

more intimate expressions of endearment. He also began to discuss his daily experiences in the classrooms and laboratories, his plans and his ambitions, his attitudes toward the medical profession, and his candid assessment of the school, its faculty, and his fellow students. In addition to the letters, a diary survives for all of 1906 and for the first half of 1907. Hardly a day passed without an entry. Most of his comments were terse, lucid notations dealing with his studies, his recreations, the books he read, church attendance, the letters he wrote and received—in a word, a record of his daily experiences, some exciting and interesting, others prosaic and predictable. Thus in letters and in the journal, Pat revealed some of his innermost thoughts and gave a picture of medical-student life at Johns Hopkins in the first decade of the twentieth century.

In many of Pat's confidential letters to Olive, he analyzed the Hopkins faculty as teachers and as men. His frank assessments were, in the main, highly complimentary but occasionally blunt and scathing. Some of the Hopkins faculty he found to be surly and capricious. In letters summing up his feelings toward these he used such terms as *asinine, condescending,* and *obsequious.* But Pat reserved his sharpest barbs for one of the "Big Four" of the medical faculty, the distinguished gynecologist Howard A. Kelly, whom he termed "the smallest big man I ever knew." Kelly was brilliant, but in Pat's opinion he was also vain, pompous, and self-serving.

The man who ranked highest in his estimation was Sir William Osler, who had resigned his position as professor of medicine and physician-in-chief at Johns Hopkins the year before Pat entered medical school to accept an appointment as Regis professor of medicine at Oxford. It was one of Pat's greatest disappointments that he never had an opportunity to study formally under this great man. However, Osler returned to Hopkins periodically and, whenever he was there, visited the wards and laboratories and lectured the students. Pat admired and esteemed other great physicians, but his feelings for Osler approached veneration.

In general, Pat found the atmosphere at Johns Hopkins congenial and stimulating. However, the demands and tempo of medical school jeopardized his frail constitution. His weight fell to only 130 pounds. There were frequent illnesses, and an ever-present threat of tuberculosis, at that time the great scourge of Hopkins medical students. During Pat's second year, student health conditions deteriorated to such a degree that the students petitioned for "investigation and action regarding the prevalence of tuberculosis." Within only four years, eight students had become infected.[5]

Pat came to realize the danger of becoming too immersed in work. As the pressures of medical school continued to mount, he sought new outlets for his tensions. As frequently as possible, he headed for the tennis courts, and from time to time he donned the uniform of the Hopkins baseball team and took his accustomed place in the outfield. There were also precious stolen moments for solitary strolls along Baltimore's busy streets or in the countryside just beyond the city limits. The municipal botanical gardens were always an attraction. One day he discovered there a lone specimen of the common Texas prickly pear cactus; the unexpected sight of this familiar friend brought thoughts of a distant home rushing into his consciousness. He confessed to lingering long at the spot. While at Hopkins, he wrote that he "had learned something about the grandeur of solitude," and his letters reveal a deep appreciation of nature: "The woods are most beautiful at this season of the year with their variegated colors." On another occasion, he spoke of seeking out "a place where I could hear only the singing of the birds and the soughing of the winds in the treetops."[6] Whenever he was granted more free time than usual, Pat headed for the Virginia or New Jersey seashore beaches, where a swim in the warm ocean waters or a strenuous day spent pulling the

[5] Chesney, *Johns Hopkins Hospital*, 3:52.

[6] These comments and some other material in this introduction and elsewhere in the book's notes are taken from Dr. Nixon's unpaginated manuscript in the possession of Dr. Pat I. Nixon, Jr., San Antonio; hereinafter the manuscript is cited as Nixon Ms.

oars of a rented skiff invigorated his body and soul. He especially enjoyed the theater and lecture halls—concerts, far less.
Letters to Olive are crowded with titles of plays and names of
prominent actors of the day. But above all there were books
and more books. Voraciously he devoured novels, histories, biographies, works on medicine, of course, and *belles lettres*. The
avid reading regimen he developed while at Baltimore remained an ingrained habit throughout his life and was one of
his greatest sources of pleasure.

Pat felt uncomfortable and out of place at most college social
functions, but, for the sake of his career, he had no choice but
to accept invitations, at least occasionally. He was bored by the
small talk and gossip at these gatherings, and he shunned alcohol. However, like any student on a tight budget, he made the
most of the free food at these affairs.

Examinations held no great terror for Pat. He took his studies
seriously, and he knew that he was giving the best he had in
him. He was realist enough to know that there was nothing
more he could do and that he would simply have to accept the
consequences of his efforts without anguishing over the situation. Besides, since Hopkins thoroughly screened candidates
before admission, very few students failed.

Pat took special pride in his diagnostic skill, especially once,
after making what he termed a "brag diagnosis" of an acute
dilation of the stomach of a woman who had undergone surgery
for removal of an ovarian cyst. "I'm really very proud of my
diagnosis," he informed Olive, "because only about 200 cases
have been reported in the literature and of these only a small
percent have been diagnosed correctly."[7] On another occasion,
when one of the interns insisted that a patient in the wards had
chicken pox, Pat challenged the diagnosis; the disease, in his
opinion, was unquestionably smallpox. Subsequent tests proved
Pat correct. A frantic staff vaccinated the other patients, the

[7] Pat Nixon, Baltimore, October 10, 1909, to Olive Read, Box 1 Folder 1, Dr.
Pat I. Nixon Papers, Trinity University Archives, San Antonio; hereinafter this
collection is cited as Nixon Papers.

doctors, the nurses, and everyone else who had made contact with the infected patient. Pat's talents did not go unnoticed by the faculty. The Johns Hopkins staff each year chose ten third-year students to work during the summer break in areas of specialization. To be selected for this additional experience was considered a distinct honor, at least by those students ambitious enough to forego the usual vacation period. In 1908, Pat was elated that his name was posted for one of the summer appointments in obstetrics.

In his initial distaste for surgery, Pat was certainly not unique among medical students. During his second year the long-dreaded moment arrived for him to draw his "first real blood." After successfully removing a small cancer from a patient's face, he wrote that "this experience has not inspired me with any greater love for Surgery than I had before; at any rate it hasn't caused me to choose Surgery as my specialty."[8] Within three years, however, he had overcome his original dislike for the scalpel and performed his first major operation with excellent results. He was pleased to note that he had required only five minutes longer than the resident gynecologist took to perform the same surgical procedure. In one more year, Pat had become so skillful that he was asked to fill in at the Hopkins hospital for staff surgeons on leave. "I have gotten a good deal of operative work to do," he wrote, "and, more important, I have overcome the natural trepidation that comes to one when he first has a knife in his hand and a little responsibility on his shoulders."[9]

"I had my first real struggle with the 'grim monster' Friday night and he won." In these words Pat summed up the sense of futility he had experienced in waging a battle that he knew was lost before it began. A young girl had been brought to the hospital wracked with peritonitis. The patient was in an almost moribund condition when first examined, but Pat had struggled

8 Pat Nixon, Baltimore, November 25, 1907, to Olive Read, Box 1 Folder 3, Nixon Papers.
9 Nixon Ms.

hour by hour to save her life, only to see it ebb slowly away. A few weeks later he wrote of the experience: "I spoke of 'final defeat' a while ago; I didn't mean that. I will not confess myself defeated; the odds were against me, and I did as much as anyone else could have done with this same case. Usually our hindsight is better than our foresight, but in this instance as I look back over the case I can't see how I could have changed my handling of the case in any particular." This treatment seems to sum up, as well as any words can, the credo Dr. Nixon lived by in the unending struggle to overcome disease: "I will not confess myself defeated."[10]

As graduation approached, Pat gave a great deal of thought to his forthcoming internship. He knew that his excellent record guaranteed him an appointment at Johns Hopkins. There he was known, and there he would feel comfortable. But he realized that there were distinct advantages in going elsewhere to work under a new set of mentors. He was offered, but rejected, positions at a Maryland tuberculosis sanitarium and at a Macon, Georgia, hospital. Perhaps the most enticing possibility was a chance to intern at the University of Pennsylvania Hospital, one of the more prestigious institutions of the day. But a conflicting semester calendar would have required him to leave Hopkins prior to graduation and would have forced him to forego a long-anticipated and much-deserved vacation in Texas.[11] Even though he would have preferred to do his internship in New York or Philadelphia, after weighing alternatives, Pat decided to remain in Baltimore.

Doubtless one factor that had made Pat reluctant to continue at Hopkins was a regulation denying internships to married doctors. His marriage to Olive had been postponed through his student years for financial reasons, and now the wedding would have to be delayed for at least two more years. But there were

---

[10] Pat Nixon, Baltimore, November 12, 1909, and December 5, 1909, to Olive Read, Box 1 Folder 1, Nixon Papers.

[11] Pat returned home to Texas on three occasions while a student at Johns Hopkins—in 1906, 1907, and 1909.

mitigating factors that weighed heavily in favor of remaining where he was, so the young couple philosophically accepted prospects for a longer engagement. On March 25, 1909, Dr. Pat Nixon took charge of one of the female wards of the Johns Hopkins Hospital and began his post–medical school training.

Pat was fortunate in being called upon to substitute when one of the senior men, Dr. Cecil Vest, made a prolonged trip to Europe. Then, just about the time Vest was due to return, Dr. John Sperry took a leave of absence, and Pat filled in for him also. The effect of this was a considerably heavier work load but also an unparalleled opportunity for learning and for more practical work. Pat gained additional experience when one of his faculty friends, Dr. T. S. Cullen, associate in gynecology, began to take him on out-of-town trips to assist in surgery. Some of these operations were performed in the patients' homes, invaluable training for the time when Pat would have to face similar challenges in private practice back in Texas.

Although he frequently commented to Olive on the strain of the regimen, he seldom complained. His position required that he visit patients in their homes after they had been released from the hospital. "It would not be so bad if it required only one visit," he wrote, "but I call for ten days afterwards, and the cases are scattered all over this section of the city." Not having access to an automobile, he had to trudge along on foot or travel by trolley. In one letter, after spelling out the demanding schedule of the previous day, he wrote that, even after he had finally collapsed in bed, Baltimore's oppressive heat made sleep impossible.[12]

During his final year at Hopkins, Pat was given the post of second assistant surgeon; only two men on the surgical staff outranked him—a fine compliment to his abilities. Again, to use his words, he got "a great deal of useful experience."

When his internship ended, Pat was ready, as he put it, "to

---

12 Pat Nixon, Baltimore, August 12, 1908, to Olive Read, Box 1 Folder 4, Nixon Papers.

shake the Balto. dust from off my feet." He was impatient to return to Texas to begin his practice. On July 2, 1911, he could announce at last to Olive that he was "no longer connected with the J. H. Hospital."

In the summer of 1905, Pat had arrived in Baltimore still in certain ways an immature youth, naive in many respects, awed by the Hopkins staff and its reputation, and harboring some serious doubts about his own capacities for a successful career in medicine. When he left the campus six years later, he departed knowing that he had received the finest medical training available this side of the Atlantic. He now possessed a thorough grasp of the science of human medicine, he was skilled in surgical technique, he had acquired self-esteem, he was confident of his future, and he looked forward expectantly to a long and satisfying career of service. For all this, he felt indebted to the Johns Hopkins Medical School, and until the end of his life he revered that institution and took immense pride in being a product of its outstanding teaching program.

Armed with cards of introduction, Pat returned to Texas via Philadelphia and New York, thence through lower Canada, and on to Chicago and Rochester, Minnesota. The trip, with stopovers at leading hospitals, consumed many weeks. Pat met renowned physicians and surgeons, discussed technique with them, and observed their skills in the operating room. Once again he resumed his earlier habit of maintaining a diary. In comparison with Hopkins, most hospitals he saw seemed outmoded, even primitive; most surgeons, in comparison with the master teachers under whom he had studied, appeared awkward and amateurish. Only the Mayo hospital and staff came up to the standard he believed existed at Baltimore. Lacking the perspective that only time permits, he was perhaps too harsh in his assessment of many of the doctors he observed on his grand tour. Later he became more realistic in his expectations.

The fall of 1911 found Pat back in his beloved Texas. The long period of study and preparation had at last ended. He was now twenty-eight years old and eager to apply his hard-earned knowledge.[13] The time had come for him to strike out on his own. Earlier Pat and Olive had jointly decided to make their home in San Antonio. That city was evolving into a major metropolitan area and, as such, offered splendid opportunities for a young, ambitious doctor.

On October 1, 1911, Dr. Pat I. Nixon opened his office and prepared to receive his first patients. That first day in his new office turned out to be a lonely one; no patients called. The second day he made a fifty-mile drive to Yancy in Medina County to treat Dora Nixon, the wife of his half-brother John. In due course other patients found their way to his door. One elderly Mexican woman picked his name out of the telephone directory; she was searching for a doctor who was "a good Catholic" and assumed that anyone named Pat would fit that criterion. Other patients were referred to him by country doctors he had assisted in Caldwell and Guadalupe counties.

The customary charges at the time were one dollar for an office visit and two dollars for a house call within the city limits. Larger fees were an exception and not easy to collect. For months Pat lived on the brink of poverty. On one occasion he was humiliated when his landlady returned his check, a check the bank had sent back because of insufficient funds in his account. Only by borrowing from a sympathetic brother-in-law was he able to remain solvent. To a Hopkins classmate, Dr. William L. Estes, Pat wrote, "I have been practicing here for two months and have managed to keep away from the wall so far. My experiences have not been very numerous, but I have learned that the practice of medicine is not as altruistic as we

13 He must have been a youthful-looking twenty-eight-year-old. To Olive he had complained earlier, "I don't know what I am going to do about this youthful appearance of mine; a lady across town the other day guessed that I was eighteen or possibly nineteen years old. I must either grow a mustache or get married." Later he gleefully reported, "Would you believe it, I accidentally discovered a gray hair in my head the other day? And it was a genuine gray hair, the kind old men have." Pat Nixon, Baltimore, January 30, 1910, and December 4, 1910, to Olive Read, Box 1 Folder 6, Nixon Papers.

have been led to believe."[14] Of course Pat knew that it was not very realistic to expect to be overwhelmed by work immediately. He kept up his courage, cheerfully waiting for improvement in his financial condition. By June of 1912, he felt financially secure enough to inform Olive that at last he was capable of supporting a wife. The wedding took place in Olive's hometown of Mineola, Texas, the following month. After a brief honeymoon in Colorado, the couple returned to San Antonio.

Pat received an enthusiastic welcome from the South Texas medical community. In time he was invited to join the staffs of San Antonio's Nix Memorial, Baptist Memorial, and Santa Rosa hospitals. He was a congenial colleague and was more than willing to carry his share of the work load. In recognition of his many contributions to the medical profession and of his outstanding accomplishments as a physician and surgeon he was elected president of the Bexar County Medical Society in 1926 and of the Texas Surgical Society in 1956. He also edited *Southwest Texas Medicine*, the journal of the Southwest Texas District Medical Society and the Bexar County Medical Society.

One of Dr. Nixon's most important contributions to the progress of the medical profession in San Antonio, and for him a source of special pride, was his role in the founding of the Bexar County Medical Library Association. The idea of a library originated with Dr. Nixon and a few other young physicians who organized a Journal Club in 1912, assessing themselves ten dollars to launch the venture. This was the nucleus of a true medical library, which was born seven years later. Pat's tremendous regard for Sir William Osler provided the impetus for the library. Osler, an ardent bibliophile, had constantly urged his students to read and collect books. In an address delivered in 1903, Osler had stated what might very well have been the *raison d'être* for the Bexar County Medical Library: "The organization of a library means effort, it means union, it means

---

[14] Pat Nixon, San Antonio, December 8, 1911, to Bill [Dr. William L. Estes], Box 2 Folder 7, Nixon Papers.

progress. It does good to men who start it, who help with money, with time, and with gifts of books. It does good to the young men, with whom our hopes rest, and a library gradually and insensibly moulds the profession of a town to a better and higher status."[15]

In 1919, Dr. Pat was instrumental in inducing the medical society to establish a Library Association, and the following year he became its chairman. The association sold stock at $100 a share and used the money to purchase a home for the rapidly growing collection. By 1933, when the library holdings had reached fifteen thousand volumes and long runs of more than two hundred journals, larger quarters had to be found. At this time, perhaps in part as a consequence of the depression, only four county medical societies in Texas maintained their own libraries, and only two of these had extensive holdings. The Bexar County Medical Library was a working library, and it was used extensively by local physicians, but the pride of the association was its collection of rare books illustrating the history of medicine. Some of the volumes had been purchased with association funds, but most had been acquired through Dr. Pat's efforts. Some had been donated by friends of his or by grateful patients who desired to demonstrate in some appropriate way their appreciation of Dr. Nixon's ministrations to themselves or to family members. Additional items were purchased with income derived from the sale of two of Dr. Nixon's books *A Century of Medicine in San Antonio* and *The Medical Story of Early Texas.*

In 1961 a new, larger building was erected to house the Bexar County Medical Society and its expanding library. By then the rare book collection exceeded two thousand volumes. In a fitting gesture of appreciation, Dr. Nixon was invited to give the dedicatory address at the opening of the new building. He had devoted his efforts for nearly half a century to the search for

---

[15] William Osler, "Some Aspects of American Medical Bibliography," an address before the Association of Medical Librarians, 1902, published in *Aequanimitas: With Other Addresses to Medical Students, Nurses, and Practitioners of Medicine* (Philadelphia: P. Blakiston's Son, 1932), p. 293.

old and rare books and in truth could be called the father of the library.

Because of the ever-increasing rarity of the books, it became a matter of concern to secure better protection against fire and theft than society headquarters could provide. Therefore, when the University of Texas Health Science Center at San Antonio volunteered to provide adequate housing for the collection, the medical society decided that the need to protect these rare volumes justified transferring them to the medical school. There they now reside in an attractive setting designated "The P. I. Nixon Medical Historical Library." The generosity of the Friends of the Library continues to add volumes to the collection as a fitting tribute to the physician whose foresight more than sixty years ago laid the foundation for this unique library. A note from a longtime friend and patient illustrates the way the collection grew: "As my respect and affection for you extend over a great many years, I want to aid in your efforts to secure rare books; so when the time comes, I will be delighted to have you name a book of your choice which I may purchase for the library, with an appropriate dedication to you." The following month, William Withering's *An Account of the Foxglove*, published in 1785, came to the rare book collection through the generosity of this benefactor.[16]

Dr. Nixon's fascination with books and book collecting was not limited to works on medicine. By his own admission, he had become a confirmed bibliophile while at Johns Hopkins. "I must confess with you to being 'book-mad,' " he wrote from Baltimore; "I have bought and read more books in the past six months than I have in any other six years of my illiterate existence."[17] He had looked forward to the time when his books and Olive's books (she too had become an avid collector) would stand side by side on the shelves—a marriage of books. Many of the volumes he acquired while at Hopkins were inexpensive

[16] Brooks McGimsey, San Antonio, July 26, 1960, to Pat Nixon, Dr. Pat Ireland Nixon Papers, the library of the University of Texas Health Science Center at San Antonio.
[17] Nixon Ms.

Everyman Library reprints (in those days they cost only thirty-
five cents per copy), excellent fare for reading purposes but
hardly the basis for a serious collection. But Pat also frequented
Baltimore's second-hand book shops searching for old, not necessarily rare, medical books.

During this period he began keeping a notebook at his side
for copying passages from his books, passages that held special
meaning for him. Pat was never the sort of person who reads
only for entertainment or to while away the hours. A surviving
notebook contains 224 entries and provides an insight into his
reading habits. His interests were eclectic; authors he admired
included Pasteur, Osler, Socrates, Thomas à Kempis, Kingsley,
Oliver Wendell Holmes, St. Augustine, Sophocles, Plato, Pliny,
Shakespeare, Emerson, Davy Crockett, Horace, Carlyle, Ibsen,
Theodore Roosevelt, and John Burroughs.

For the Nixons their library became the focal point of family
life. It was "as much of a gathering place as the dining room."
Books provided a satisfying outlet for tensions, a source of recreation and relaxation, and a unifying force in the household.
Late in life Pat wrote, "Olive and I have never had many close
friends. We very early realized that our spare time could best
be expended in our library. This decision to a great extent kept
us at home."[18] Mrs. Nixon's reading preference leaned toward
poetry and history; his interests were broader, including biography, religion, history and historical novels, and, of course,
medicine. But it was Texas history that most captured their
imaginations. In due course they became recognized as avid
and knowledgeable collectors of Texana.

The origin of the Nixon Texas history collection was first re-
counted in an address Pat delivered at a meeting of the San
Antonio Historical Society. Later his talk was published in the
Southwestern Historical Quarterly as "The Genesis of a Collec-
tor of Texana." After reading this charming paper, J. Frank
Dobie wrote, "Your essay on book collecting is one of the most

18 Pat Nixon, San Antonio, May 22, 1964, to Mrs. Clyde Wantland, Box 4
Folder 9, Nixon Papers.

delicious morsels I have savored in a long while. I read it to myself in the office and brought it home and read it to Mrs. Dobie; she enjoyed it as much as I did—and still do and shall do."[19] The beginning of the collection dates from 1930 when the twin Nixon boys, Ben and Thomas, were collecting waste paper for sale to a junk dealer. In a neighbor's trash they found a well-worn set of George W. Kendall's *Narrative of the Texan Santa Fe Expedition.* Mrs. Nixon salvaged the books, read them with growing fascination, and urged her husband to read them also. According to Dr. Pat's account he "had intended to skim the surface very superficially," but "then [he] too became enthralled." From this beginning, the Nixons began to frequent book shops in San Antonio and wherever they traveled. Once, while the family was vacationing in Colorado, Pat discovered a fine set of Yoakum's *History of Texas.* The price was high, and the supply of cash in his wallet was low. A family conference resulted in the decision to buy this prize find, even though the purchase would necessitate cutting the vacation short and heading for home immediately.

Important to Dr. Nixon's activities as book collector was his first meeting with that dean of Texas bookmen, Dudley Dobie. Pat placed an order for Bartlett's *Personal Narrative,* and with that step he found himself snared. "A book collector is never sane, rich, or wise after Dudley gets through with him," wrote Pat. On occasion Dobie even "feigned illness to gain admittance" to the doctor's office so that he might display some new-found treasure he believed would find a home in the doctor's library.[20]

Among the items of choice Texana in the collection were Wooten's *Comprehensive History,* Kendall's *War Between the United States and Mexico,* Sowell's *Rangers and Pioneers,* Brown's *Indian Wars,* and De Cordova's *Texas, Her Resources and Her Public Men.* But the collection was not limited to rari-

[19] J. Frank Dobie, Austin, July 21, 1942, to Pat Nixon, Box 11, Nixon Papers.
[20] Pat I. Nixon, "The Genesis of a Collector of Texana," *Southwestern Historical Quarterly* 46 (October, 1942): 179.

ties; more recent works, easily obtainable at reasonable prices, also found their way into the library.

In 1963, the Nixons reluctantly decided that the time had come to dispose of their collection, then numbering more than twelve hundred select items of Texana. Fear that the books might be lost through fire or theft and a desire to keep the collection intact prompted them to donate the books to Trinity University. To a colleague, Dr. Pat described the personal sorrow entailed by parting with these treasured possessions, "Our shelves are empty, our eyes are moist, our hearts are heavy."[21] The university dedicated the Pat Ireland Nixon Collection in formal ceremonies on June 2, 1964; the books now form the nucleus of an expanding rare book collection.

Dr. Nixon participated actively in the affairs of the San Antonio Historical Society, an organization he helped found in 1939; he served on its board of directors, and was twice elected its president. He also belonged to the History of Science Society. For years he devoted much of his time to promoting the Texas State Historical Association. He was one of its most effective presidents, and he frequently presented papers at the annual meetings and chaired its sessions. He was also an active fund raiser and recruiter of new members.

Dr. Nixon's other services to the historical profession were numerous. As a member of the Bexar County Historical Survey Committee, he was instrumental in preserving buildings of historic or architecural importance. He worked on the program committee of the Association for State and Local History and the Hearst American History Award Committee and was a sponsor of the Junior Historian movement in San Antonio high schools. He served on the advisory council for the *Handbook of Texas* and wrote perceptive articles on doctors and medicine for the *Handbook*.

Over the course of nearly twenty years, Dr. Nixon waged a fruitless campaign to bring about the translation and publica-

---

[21] Pat Nixon, San Antonio, May 5, 1964, to Robert Sparkman, Box 4 Folder 8, Nixon Papers.

tion of the Bexar Archives. He had hoped that this magnificent collection of documents, of unparalleled value for the study of early Texas, might be translated at the expense of the Texas State Historical Association and published by the University of Texas Press. However, the director of the association, Dr. H. Bailey Carroll, believed that its publication fund could be used legally only for printing Texas material by the association itself and could not be transferred to the University of Texas Press. As late as 1964, Dr. Nixon wrote to the then president of the historical association, "I am still hellbent in trying to get something done about the Bexar Archives."[22] His efforts at least did encourage university officials, custodians of the archives since 1899, to work with the National Archives to make the Bexar Archives available in microprint form.

Dr. Nixon possessed a sure sense of historical time and perspective. He cherished truth. He sought passionately after facts. He never doubted the usefulness of history in helping society make its basic decisions. Inherently a modest man, he deprecated his own considerable talents as a historian. On his succession to the presidency of the Philosophical Society of Texas in 1946, he protested that so great an honor "implies intellectual and cultural capabilities to which I lay no claim." Other persons had a much higher opinion of his abilities. Frank Wardlaw, then the director of the University of Texas Press, said at a ceremony honoring Dr. Pat: "He has a feeling for the living past. It is not the dead past, and it is never dead in his books because the people come to life and we recognize them for what they are. . . . Dr. Pat believes we have an obligation not to forget those who have gone before and what they stood for."[23] J. Frank Dobie praised Pat's anecdotal method of historical writing. Chancellor Harry H. Ransom of the University of Texas, in a 1952 article in the *Southwestern Historical Quarterly*, wrote that "every reader on early Texas medicine would

[22] Pat Nixon, San Antonio, September 21, 1964, to Fred Cotten, Box 4 Folder 9, Nixon Papers.
[23] *Celebration Honoring Dr. Pat Ireland Nixon on His Seventy-fifth Birthday* (San Antonio: Carl Hertzog, 1958), p. 18.

do well to start—and continue—with Dr. Pat Ireland Nixon's"
histories.[24]

Between 1936 and 1965, Dr. Nixon published three books on
the history of medicine in Texas and collaborated on a fourth
volume. His first book, *A Century of Medicine in San Antonio*,
brought its author the San Antonio Conservation Society Award
in 1952, "for his valuable contribution to San Antonio's recorded history."

This book, Dr. Pat said, was "truly my child of the depression." Its writing, he informed his friends, provided a kind of
escape: "When most of you were lying awake worrying about
the depression and its results, I was working on my notes. You
lost a lot of sleep—I lost very little."[25] He began his research in
1929, the dreadful year of national economic collapse; he completed his manuscript in 1936, the hopeful year of the Texas
centennial celebration. Friends paid the cost of publication;
proceeds from sales were dedicated to the Century of Medicine
Fund of the Bexar County Medical Library Association.

A Century of Medicine surveys two eras in San Antonio medical annals: Part I carries the story to the year 1900; Part II
deals with events of the twentieth century. Based on sound research in more than one thousand sources, the book in a very
real sense becomes source material itself because of its many
lengthy quotations, catalogues of names, lists of speeches delivered, and biographical sketches of the famous and obscure
men who were part of the Bexar County medical fraternity. If
the work has a failing, it is the author's inability to leave anything out. Aware of this problem, he wrote in the preface: "The
problem of cementing the fragments into a composite, readable
story has not been easy. Any lack of continuity is explained by
a desire not to omit anything worthy of record." Yet the book
is effective nonetheless and eminently readable because of the
entertaining and often fascinating anecdotes scattered through-

[24] Harry Ransom, "Sherman Goodwin—Texas Physician, 1814–1884," *Southwestern Historical Quarterly* 55 (January, 1952): 334n.
[25] "Minutes of Bexar County Medical Society," September 10, 1936, Box 13,
Nixon Papers.

out and because of the writer's delightfully witty and authorita-
tive style and his incisive observations. The book is strengthened by Dr. Pat's awareness that community history and
medical history are inseparable. The political and social history
of San Antonio looms large in this work.

Optimistic in tone, *A Century of Medicine* celebrates the triumphs of Texas medicine, and particularly of the Bexar County
Medical Society, in the hundred years following Texas independence. Three major themes run concurrently: the slow development of a professional local medical society in the face of
continuing opposition by insufficiently trained doctors fearful
of exposing their inadequacies and by the out-and-out quacks
posing as legitimate healers; the tortuous, almost interminable
struggle to establish a state board of medical examiners to bring
about a strict and effective system of licensing medical practitioners; and the continuing effort to stamp out disease endemic
in the Mexican districts of the city, an effort frequently stymied
by powerful vested interests. Dr. Nixon did not pull punches.
He exposed ignorance, malpractice, and corruption wherever
he found those abuses entrenched.

Not until 1946, a full decade after the publication of his first
book, did Dr. Nixon complete the manuscript of his second
major work. Entitled *The Medical Story of Early Texas, 1528–
1853*, this more ambitious volume was financed through the
generosity of San Antonians John and Jamie Bennett, who established the Mollie Bennett Lupe Memorial Fund in memory
of their daughter. All proceeds from sales of the book were returned to the fund to be used exclusively for the purchase of
rare medical works for the collection of the Bexar County Medical Library.

Long anticipating the publication of a book of this nature,
the Texas Medical Association had sponsored the collection of
data that might serve as sources and, by arrangement with Professor Eugene C. Barker, had placed this material in the cus-
tody of the University of Texas Archives. By the time Dr. Nixon
took up the project, sixteen bound volumes of collected documents already had been assembled. The longtime chairman of

the Committee on the Collection and Preservation of Records of the State Association was Dr. Frank Paschal, a leading San Antonio physician. A close friend of Dr. Pat, Paschal had urged him to undertake the more difficult task of preparing a full history of medicine in early Texas almost as soon as *A Century of Medicine* had appeared.

The inclusive dates in the title, 1528–1853, set the parameters of the book: from the shipwreck of Cabeza de Vaca (Texas' first white "medicine man") to the founding of the Texas Medical Association (TMA). An ambitious task spanning three and one-quarter centuries, *The Medical Story of Early Texas* necessarily covered much familiar political and social history in establishing a frame of reference in which to set the medical aspects of Texas history. An extensive bibliography included archival sources as well as published materials; it would be difficult to find many pertinent works Dr. Nixon failed to consult. The book is divided into seven parts: Indian medicine, including an account of de Vaca's efforts at healing Indian patients; the Spanish period, when curative methods were "heroic and primitive"; the French era, devoted almost exclusively to stories of Dr. Liotot, the slayer of LaSalle, and Dr. Jalot, the surgeon who accompanied the romantic St. Denis across Texas to San Juan Bautista on the Rio Grande; the Mexican period, which deals not only with trained physicians but also with the *curadera*; the era of the Texas Revolution, with emphasis on doctors who participated in the struggle for independence; the decade of the Texas Republic, which discusses early-day hospitals as well as early medical men; and, finally, a section entitled "Result and the Promise," on the beginnings of organized medicine in the State of Texas. An appendix lists physicians known to have practiced during the years of the Texas Republic.

Although *The Medical Story of Early Texas* covers a much broader panorama than did Dr. Nixon's first book, it is in important ways similar to the earlier work. In large part it is in the form of biographical sketches and contains material so elusive in the original form as to make this book truly a source in itself. Again, tangential paragraphs sometimes lead the reader away from the main theme. Yet it is a very solid book, a work of genuine merit, thorough and comprehensive. Dr. Nixon intended that this work would be followed by one or more subsequent volumes, which would carry the story of Texas medicine well into the twentieth century.

In 1953 the University of Texas Press published Dr. Pat's third book on Texas medicine, *A History of the Texas Medical Association, 1853–1953*. Commemorating the centennial of the TMA, the book might, with justification, have been entitled "A Century of Medical Progress in Texas," for its theme was the spectacular progress of the medical profession under the association's leadership.

Because Dr. Pat's earlier books had been privately printed, he had been solely responsible for their contents. Friends had suggested that he should consider hiring an editor or writing assistant; this he rejected. But when he wrote *A History of the Texas Medical Association*, he said, "In this instance, I was a sort of hired hand of the Association and the University of Texas Press." When asked how he became interested in writing this book, Dr. Pat responded humorously, "I was crowded into it by a lot of folk who thought I was the logical one to do it."[26] Speaking for the board of trustees of the TMA, Dr. Merton M. Minter wrote that they all "felt that if Pat Nixon did not write the history of the Texas Medical Association in its first century of organized work, it might never be written and would surely never be written so well."[27] As early as 1911, an effort had been made to find physicians with a literary bent who might be induced to write the association's history. The task was originally conceived of as a collective work. When it became apparent that no volunteers intended to step forward, Dr. Frank Paschal was asked to take on the job. He collected a mass of material essential to the task, but he had written very little by the time of his death. The project then lay dormant until 1949, when the TMA

[26] Nixon Ms.; "Biographical Information Sheet for the University Press," Box 15, Nixon Papers.
[27] Foreword to Pat I. Nixon, *A History of the Texas Medical Association, 1853–1953*, p. x.

created a committee of three to carry the work to a conclusion; responsibility of authorship devolved on Dr. Pat. While Dr. Paschal's notes made the task somewhat easier, it was still necessary to do several years of additional research before anything could be put on paper.

The arrangement of this book, strictly chronological, is based on the terms of office of the presidents of the association and the annual meetings. For each year there is a succinct summary of proceedings and transactions and of scholarly papers read. In addition there is material on the major accomplishments of the association. Conflict within the organization, often bitter and personal, is thoroughly aired. One of the most significant contributions of this volume is to rescue from near oblivion early Texas physicians who contributed to the advancement of medical science. Dr. Pat's skill as a writer and his inclusion of anecdotes saved the manuscript from being overwhelmed by the mass of prosaic factual data he was forced to include. In the broad sense, *A History of the Texas Medical Association* is the story of the far-reaching impact of doctors and medicine on the lives of Texans, not simply in the realm of health matters, but also in political, social, and economic affairs.

In addition to writing these three major books on Texas medicine, Dr. Nixon is listed as coauthor of a volume entitled *The Texas Surgical Society: The First Fifty Years*. His role in the making of this book consisted primarily of serving as a member of the society's publication committee in the planning stage and in contributing an essay entitled "Surgery: A Cultural Factor in Early Texas." This was his presidential address of 1956; it previously had been printed in the *Texas State Journal of Medicine*. In 1957, this essay won for its author the Clement E. Trout Award of Excellence, an annual prize given by the International Council of Industrial Editors. *The Texas Surgical Society* was the last book Dr. Nixon helped guide to completion; its publication preceded his death by only six weeks.

The two books that held the most personal meaning for Dr. Pat were a memorial to his wife of fifty-two years, entitled *In*

Introduction

Memoriam: Olive Read Nixon, 1886–1964, and a family history, *The Early Nixons of Texas.* Carl Hertzog printed both volumes. The first of these was Dr. Pat's beautiful testimonial to Olive's virtues—her traits of character, her many contributions to his own success, her role as wife and mother in the household of a busy physician. "It should never be forgotten," he declared, "that Olive had a good part in all that I ever wrote. It was she who took the lead in reading and collecting Texana." But perhaps the dedication page best sums up her role in the enduring partnership of these two remarkable people: "In memory of Olive/Instigator/Investigator/Coordinator/Collaborator."

The book that Dr. Nixon believed to be "probably the high point in our writing" was *The Early Nixons of Texas.* Designed primarily to preserve Nixon family traditions for later generations, and therefore published in a limited edition of only five hundred copies, this book nevertheless received the Summerfield G. Roberts Award. Printer Hertzog, who submitted the book to the prize committee, wrote to historian Chris Emmet, "You know Dr. Nixon and how he has supported the cause of Texas history in many ways and many places. I think he deserves recognition for past performance, but in this case the book must stand on its own feet."[28]

The Early Nixons of Texas followed the pattern of other of Dr. Pat's books in being timed to commemorate a significant event. Although he had completed his manuscript in 1952, he withheld it from publication until 1956, the hundredth anniversary of his father's arrival in Texas. A relatively short book containing only ninety pages of text, it is divided into three sections. Chapter headings indicate the nature of the contents: "Robert and Laura" is an account of the establishment of the Nixons on the South Texas frontier and of their trying early years to 1872, when Laura Nixon died; "Robert and Fannie" covers the period of Robert's second marriage, 1872 to his death

[28] Carl Hertzog, El Paso, December 11, 1956, to Chris Emmett, Box 14, Nixon Papers.

in 1897, a period of building on the earlier foundation; and "Miss Fannie," the final chapter, revolves around Dr. Pat's mother in her long period of widowhood.

An essential addition to the text is the genealogy prepared by Dr. and Mrs. Pat Nixon, Jr. This part of the book is arranged in four sections dealing with the Nixon, Thomas, Wood, and Andrews families; it emphasizes, naturally, the Nixon line, beginning with the birth of Zachariah Nixon, Jr., in Nottinghamshire, England, about 1656. More than mere lists of names and dates, these genealogies also include data on place of residence, occupation, and burial site. An original system of arrangement makes clear at a glance the relationship of each person to all others in the family, eliminating the need for complicated tables or family trees.

Dr. Pat's history of the Nixon family centers around the lives of his parents—their goals, their struggles, and their achievements. To a lesser degree, he portrays the farmers and ranchers, professional men, teachers and scholars, businessmen, and public officials who also bore the Nixon name. His pen moves with pride and appreciation over the contributions of each of them. Yet, if one person stands out above all others in his narrative, it is his beloved mother, whose life "lacking four years, spanned a century." This sturdy woman of the frontier emerges from the pages of *The Early Nixons of Texas* as courageous, high-minded, astute, able, pious, and independent.

Naturally, many of Dr. Nixon's social attitudes touched on the problems of the medical profession. His position as editor-in-chief of *Southwest Texas Medicine* gave him an ideal vehicle for expounding his views. In a series of editorials published between March and June of 1935, Dr. Pat lectured his colleagues persuasively on the dangers of socialized medicine. His approach was in no sense reactionary, nor was he intransigent on the subject. The time had come for the medical profession, he warned, to recognize that medical costs were "becoming an increasingly heavy burden." No longer could doctors afford to "believe that change was impossible or unwelcome." The an-

Introduction

swer to the dilemma, and possibly the only way to forestall state or federal imposition of socialized medicine, was for the doctors themselves to devise a plan of health insurance. It must guarantee adequate medical care, administered by a physician of the patient's own choosing, and it must compensate the doctor commensurate with the services rendered. "Prejudice [*against health plans*] based on past opinions will avail nothing," Nixon wrote. Only two alternatives were open: either the profession itself must solve the problem of rising costs of health care, or government would impose a solution that physicians would find calamitous.[29]

Continuing to develop his theme of the desirability of change, Dr. Pat took up the cause of the general practitioner. While recognizing the reasons for the trend toward ever more specialization in medicine, he also saw a continuing need for the generalist. Indeed, he pointed out, most people were likely to continue to rely on their family physician for the treatment of most of their ills. Yet the general practitioner had to understand the changing times. In the past, the tempo of life was slower, communities were smaller, society was more stable and predictable, and the local doctor "was advisor, arbitrator, father-confessor, and physician all in one." But if he was to survive, the general practitioner, for whom there was still a need, would have to become at least conversant with the new technology and methodology of the specialist; at the same time, he must not lose sight of his own limitations.[30]

In an article published in the *Medical Record*, Dr. Pat grew philosophical. The medical profession from time to time in the past had been jolted out of its complacency by iconoclasts whom he chose to label "boat rockers." These were men who possessed the imagination and the courage to break with tradition and plow new ground. Although their efforts to instill new ideas into a profession that was on the verge of becoming self-

[29] Editorials in *Southwest Texas Medicine* 2 (March, 1935): 7–8; (April, 1935): 7–8; and (June, 1935): 7.
[30] Editorial in *Southwest Texas Medicine* 2 (May, 1935): 7–8.

satisfied had the effect of moving medicine forward, these men met with open hostility and resistance. But in more recent times, now that opposition to medical progress had been all but eliminated, a new breed of boat rockers had come into their own—men who Dr. Pat suggested "should be thrown overboard posthaste." This class of boat rockers was dangerous and insidious; it did not have the best interests of the profession at heart, nor was it concerned with providing progressive leadership. The modern boat rockers included the crassly commercial, the hawkers of nostrums, the quacks, the purveyors of patent medicines, and the advocates of socialized medicine. Unlike boat rockers of old, the modern variety could only be destructive to the best interests of both physician and patient, and therefore the medical community must be alert to the dangers they posed.[31]

For most men a demanding profession, such as medicine, and a time-consuming sideline of study and writing would have left little time for other pursuits. Yet, somehow, Dr. Nixon found additional energy to wage a quarter-century-long campaign for efficient, responsible government in his adopted city.

San Antonio had long suffered from the onus of political corruption. From the days of the Texas Republic to the early twentieth century, the city had been ruled by a succession of political dynasties. During this long period, officials had done little to alleviate the deplorable state of public health. Tuberculosis, infant diarrhea, and syphilis ran rampant, particularly in the vast slum areas occupied by the depressed Mexican-American population. As a physician, Dr. Nixon became painfully aware of these frightful conditions, which were the product of a combination of poverty, greed, ignorance, and indifference. He came to realize that, however distasteful to him personally, political action against government corruption was the only sure key to reform of these appalling health problems. His concern

---

[31] Pat I. Nixon, "Medical Boat Rockers," *Medical Record and Annals* 33 (August, 1939): 193–194.

as a citizen was reinforced by his experiences as a medical student when he had come under the powerful influence of Dr. William H. Welch, a staunch advocate of public health programs. Therefore, when in 1928 he was offered an appointment to the San Antonio Board of Health, Dr. Nixon eagerly accepted the task that he felt offered an unparalleled opportunity for service in an area of medicine for which his training had prepared him. Over a period of the next twenty years he served on the city or combined city-county health boards. The experience proved to be one of the most frustrating, yet ultimately rewarding, ordeals in his half-century in medicine.

Foiled by political hirelings in his every attempt to introduce improved public health facilities, Dr. Pat became convinced that he was left with no choice but to present his case before a public forum. In an eloquent speech, he enumerated the wrongs that had been perpetrated against the people. He showed that during more than twenty-five years the disgraceful health record of the city had been exposed time and again by the health department, by independent investigators, and by the U.S. Public Health Service, all to no avail. Dr. Nixon felt that he, or anyone else who dared to uphold sound principles of responsible government, would become the victim of a political vendetta.

The chief obstacle to reform was the existing city charter, a document that gave every advantage to the spoilsmen. Dr. Pat and a group of thoughtful citizens, convinced that only a basic change—the adoption of a council-manager form of government—could rescue public health from the political arena, joined together in a battle for reform that took them into bitter political campaigns that dragged on for a dozen years.

During much of this time Dr. Pat assumed a position of leadership. Associating himself with a Better Government ticket, he spoke out forcefully at public rallies and on radio broadcasts. The long struggle took a heavy toll on his stamina and health, but ultimately Dr. Pat saw the establishment of the efficient council-manager form of government he had labored so long to help bring into existence. More important, from his professional viewpoint, many of the worst slums had been cleared, making way for more adequate housing; San Antonio's shamefully high incidence of disease had sharply declined; and the old political rings, dominant for so many decades, were disintegrating. Dr. Nixon had been a major force in achieving these progressive changes. Perhaps his greatest contribution had been to arouse the public conscience. Like the muckrakers of an earlier day, he had often overstated his case, and he had been slow to acknowledge any salutary benefits of the administrations he fought. But Dr. Pat's impact on San Antonio's health and politics had brought lasting benefits.

Throughout his life, Dr. Pat remained strongly committed in his hatred of alcohol. As a medical student he had been shocked at the large number of physicians who drank; he looked on alcohol as a dangerous habit-forming drug. His attitude toward strong drink he summed up concisely in his diary with the epigram: "Touch not, taste not, handle not." Later, even though he was well aware that "patients don't like to be preached at," he could not resist taking advantage of the special relationship that exists between physician and patient to flail away whenever he learned that a person drank to excess. Friends learned to serve Pat and Olive ginger ale or some other carbonated beverage.

One of his dearest acquaintances tells this story about him. In 1958, Dr. Nixon mentioned that he would soon be celebrating his seventy-fifth birthday. The friend expressed a desire to give him a party. "That would be nice," he agreed, and he suggested several couples who might be invited. At the party his friend asked permission to order a bottle of champagne to toast his good health. He tersely responded, "I'd rather you didn't!" She didn't, and instead of champagne, glasses of water were raised by the assembled guests.[32] One of Dr. Pat's oft-repeated sayings, "Alcohol preserves dead men and kills live ones," was not with

[32] Interview with Mrs. Brooks B. McGimsey, San Antonio, August 16, 1977.

40

him merely a catchy saying; he had seen too many of his friends and colleagues destroyed by drink. Although he knew that morality could not be legislated, he was convinced that prohibition had failed mainly because it had been imposed prematurely, before the public had been sufficiently educated to the evils of alcohol.

As a young man, Dr. Nixon had proclaimed himself a Democrat, indeed, had said he could be nothing but a Democrat. With time, however, he became increasingly conservative. He grew more and more suspicious of the motives and actions of liberals, although he never let these feelings stand in the way of friendship. Of J. Frank Dobie, he lamented, "many times he seems to have gone out of his way to show that he is a modern 'liberal,' so called. . . . And yet, I cherish his friendship."[33]

Dr. Pat doubted the efficacy of the New Deal's programs and feared the concomitant burgeoning of governmental agencies that seemed to interfere more and more in the private affairs of individual citizens. In his estimation, ever since the 1930's, a succession of dangerous and inferior men had been sent to the White House by a new type of voter, one more interested in federal handouts than in statesmanship. But the dangerous trend was not limited to the Washington scene. The corruption of local government by men he considered demagogues he had witnessed at first hand through his work with the San Antonio health department. Then the coming of the Cold War era brought charges of Communist infiltration of government and even of the churches, and these charges Dr. Pat took seriously. Perhaps a final factor in his conversion to political conservatism was his fear that an ultraliberal clique in Washington, abetted by certain medical school professors, might foist a national program of socialized medicine on the American people.

Always a man of strong opinions who never hesitated to speak out freely and openly, Dr. Pat frequently found himself in the vortex of controversy. Some of his preconceptions were deep-

[33] Nixon Ms.

rooted and at times badly out of touch with the thinking of a rapidly changing society, but he was not inflexible. At Hopkins, for example, he had been certain that women had "no business going into medicine" and he termed them sarcastically "hen medics." Yet later he was honest enough to express his respect for the ability and professionalism of women doctors like his friend Mary Harper, and he came to accept them as colleagues and as equals. While at Baltimore, he had attended a lecture by the English suffragette leader Emmeline Pankhurst. Prior to going to the meeting, he wrote to Olive, "I would just like to see what a lot of wild women will do; I'm sure pandemonium will reign and not Dr. Kelly who is to preside. If you don't hear from me you will know that some sufferers did it." But several days later, impressed by the force and logic of Mrs. Pankhurst's address, he admitted to Olive, "I came away with a better opinion of the movement than I had when I went." [34]

Similarly, he changed his opinion about blacks. Those he had known as a boy, he believed "had inherited many of the fears and superstitions out of Africa," and he thought them "primitive" in most respects. Yet he urged tolerance on a white audience at Luling in 1944—long before such sentiments had wide acceptance in Texas: "There are certain changes in attitude and certain adjustments we must make. We must lay aside our prejudices and face this [race] problem fairly. We should grant to the Negro equal political, economic, and educational advantages. They must be given a better chance." The race problem in America he saw as a malignant disease, "well-nigh beyond human solution." President Eisenhower's effort to enforce desegregation in the schools at Little Rock shocked Dr. Pat. To him a solution to a highly complex and ancient problem "at the point of a bayonet" was no solution at all. He never wavered in his conviction that social equality must come about, albeit gradually. In 1963 he wrote to Mayor Walter McAllister of San Antonio that for the Negro "to demand it [equality]

34 Pat Nixon, Baltimore, November 7, 1909, and November 12, 1909, to Olive Read, Box 1 Folder 1, Nixon Papers.

today or tomorrow or next year is going far too far and far too fast."[35]

The time had come, he felt, for Texans to abandon their historic prejudices and adopt a new attitude toward minority groups. The improvement of relations between Anglo Texans and Mexican Americans he believed to be "one of our most important responsibilities."

Throughout his lifetime, Dr. Nixon sought to maintain a sensible balance between the major facets of existence. Although from childhood a career in medicine had been his single most powerful motivating force, he knew instinctively that a physician's life devoid of family, friends, and cultural amenities would be for him shallow and incomplete. "I don't want to lose sight of the other phases of life," wrote the young medical student in 1906. He was remarkably successful in integrating the diverse aspects of his being—physician, husband, father, historian, and concerned citizen—into a meaningful pattern for living.

For him, home was a refuge, an island of tranquility, that afforded a happy respite from the tensions of professional responsibilities. There his life assumed a different, more serene, dimension. There he could function best in his "other role" as devoted husband, understanding father, and faithful friend. The house on Courtland Place into which Pat and Olive moved during Christmas week of 1912, remained their home—indeed, the center of their existence—for more than half a century. There, three of their four sons were born, and all grew to manhood in an atmosphere of permanence and stability. A letter by Pat, Jr., from camp during the summer of 1929, expresses the abiding love and mutual appreciation that had been forged between parents and children in the Nixon household. "Since I have been up here I have been thinking how much more we get

[35] Pat I. Nixon, "Christian Attitudes and Christian Adjustments in the Postwar World," an address before the Fannie Andrews Nixon Class, Luling, November 2, 1944, Box 3 Folder 3, Nixon Papers; Pat Nixon, San Antonio, October 14, 1957, to Editor, *Life* Magazine, Box 5 Folder 10, Nixon Papers; and Pat Nixon, San Antonio, June 22, 1963, to Hon. Walter McAllister, Box 4 Folder 7, Nixon Papers.

than a lot of boys," wrote Pat's eldest son; "Some boys don't have any Dad to guide them, and I have one who is a guide and a pal. . . . When we are far apart, we realize how much we really have and are lucky to have."[36] Because Dr. Pat never became a wealthy man, he appreciated that his boys were not extravagant. "They knew my financial limitations and respected them," he wrote. While they were in college, though each was given his own checkbook, Dr. Pat never had to impose restrictions on their spending.

In the Nixon household, a sense of oneness prevailed. Even with the ever-increasing demands imposed by a growing medical practice and numerous civic responsibilities, Dr. Pat learned to budget his time so that neither Olive nor the boys would be deprived of his companionship. Together the Nixons vacationed in the Big Bend and the Davis Mountains of West Texas, at Carlsbad Caverns, and on the headwaters of the Gila River in western New Mexico. Trips of shorter duration took them often to Gulf Coast fishing ports and to John Nixon's Medina County ranch. Another outlet was Fairland Hills, the 350-acre family farm, conveniently located a few miles north of San Antonio on the Bandera highway. For years Dr. Pat managed to spend two or three afternoons a week at the farm, improving the land, tending his herd of registered Jersey cattle, and, after his son Tom took over the property, helping him to develop the farm to its fullest potential. But always the center of the family's private world remained the library of the house on Courtland Place, a room that over the years became ever more crowded, not only with books, but also with trophies won by the tennis-playing Nixon twins, Ben and Tom. In 1944, for the first time since they had moved into the house in 1912, Pat and Olive spent Christmas alone, with none of their sons on hand for the holiday season. But this was because the exigencies of war had called their sons to duty posts far from home.

During the war, the first grandchild was born into the family; within a few years, a total of fourteen youngsters constituted

36 Nixon Ms.

44

a new generation of Nixons. When word arrived of the birth of his first grandchild, Dr. Pat wrote a charming letter of welcome, in which he spoke of Texas and ancestors and especially of his joy, a practice he was to continue as other new grandsons and granddaughters joined the family. As the children grew older, other letters followed. His letters, first to his own sons and then later to his grandchildren, more than anything he ever wrote, not excepting his letters to Olive from Johns Hopkins, revealed Dr. Nixon's character and personality. In these letters he appears a warm and very human man—one able to communicate with young people without talking down to them—a man possessing a highly developed sense of humor, a sure gift for relating anecdotes, and withal a remarkable facility with words.

In a surviving scrapbook now in the Nixon collection at Trinity University are carefully preserved letters from friends and patients, often one and the same. These testaments of affection and appreciation reveal clearly the high esteem in which people held Dr. Pat. Like the old-fashioned general practitioner of legend, Dr. Nixon did not hesitate to rush, without complaint and sometimes still wearing his pajamas underneath a topcoat, to the home of a patient who summoned him in the middle of the night. If hospitalization was required, Dr. Pat would frequently deliver the patient himself to save the person the additional expense of ambulance service. Often he charged only a token fee for his services or sent no bill at all if he knew the patient was having a difficult time financially. Wrote one new father, a man of limited means: "We were surprised at the extreme smallness of your charges. Such a night of toil and loss of sleep, together with the years of costly preparation necessary to do this right are assuredly worth high financial remuneration."[37] One patient, living in strained circumstances but not wishing to be thought "callously negligent" for failure to pay a long-overdue bill, wrote a detailed explanation, ending with: "You probably wonder why I am telling you these personal details. I

---

[37] J——L——D——, San Antonio, September 10, 1926, to Pat Nixon, Box 11, Nixon Papers.

would tell them to very few people in the world, but I want you, our family doctor, to understand just how thin our false front is." Dr. Pat understood and was sympathetic with the family's plight and looked upon the letter as an example of the openness and frankness that develops in the course of a long and intimate relationship between patient and doctor.[38]

Himself a generous man, Dr. Nixon found thoughtlessness in others almost incomprehensible. "I am being impressed with how easy and trite it is," he had written from Luling early in his career, "for solicitous friends to simply ask about the conditions of sick ones, and how unusual it is for any of them to offer to give a few sponge baths or get dinner, when in the latter way, they could show their interest a thousand times more forcibly."[39] Quietly and discreetly Dr. Pat did his bit by performing little acts of charity to help alleviate the misfortune of others. To a home for unwed mothers in the red light district of San Antonio, he sent milk from the dairy at his Fairland Hills farm. And when Dr. Pat noticed the threadbare condition of the clothing worn by the driver of a bus that brought children from an orphanage to weekly church services, he arranged to buy a new suit for the man anonymously through a leading men's store. He always made a special effort to make life more pleasant for the elderly.

Religion was an important part of Dr. Nixon's life. He looked on religion, more accurately, the church, as mankind's "last best hope." He believed that just as each person needs to develop a "religious kinship" with other individuals, so whole communities must work to create an environment conducive to the development of "mutual respect, mutual understanding, and mutual confidence." As a prominent physician and churchman, he tried to set an example not only by professing Christianity but by practicing it as well. Although he was a lifelong Methodist, he developed an essentially Calvinistic outlook: "I have had a conscious, unutterably assuring feeling that I am one of God's Elect

38 Nixon Ms.
39 Pat Nixon, Luling, July 12, 1909, to Olive Read, Box 1 Folder 1, Nixon Papers.

and that His protecting arm and directing eye are particularly close to me."[40]

In November, 1958, friends gathered to celebrate Dr. Pat's seventy-fifth birthday. Frank Wardlaw, who had published the *History of the Texas Medical Association* five years earlier, functioned as impromptu master of ceremonies. There were the customary appropriate accolades, speeches, telegrams, letters, cards, and testimonials from former classmates, longtime acquaintances, patients old and new, and colleagues in the medical profession. Carl Hertzog assembled and published the best of the tributes under the title *Celebration Honoring Dr. Pat Ireland Nixon on His Seventy-fifth Birthday*; the originals were incorporated into a giant scrapbook. Perhaps University of Texas Chancellor Harry Ransom expressed best the sentiments felt by Dr. Pat's friends: "I have no idea what medical schools teach doctors to be, but I should think that these learned scientific congregations might well amplify Aesculapius with Nixon. Texas medicine, and all the rest of us, are indebted to him for more than impressive history; we are indebted to him for humanity, for the grace of memory and the power of insight and the promise of vision."[41]

Dr. Nixon's half-century-long career paralleled a period of steady progress toward the professionalization of medicine in America. Dr. Pat himself was instrumental in shaping and giving direction to the practice of medicine in San Antonio. He stands as a symbol of the ideal physician—sensitive to the needs of his patients, congenial in his relations with colleagues, active in the affairs of his community, and concerned for the future of his profession. A man with an astonishingly catholic range of interests, he attained success as physician and surgeon, as amateur naturalist, as cattle breeder, and as book collector. His most lasting and important contribution, however, was as medical historian. His books and his scholarship will continue to serve as models for other writers who work in the field of medical

[40] Pat Nixon, San Antonio, August 9, 1933, to Olive Nixon, Box 1 Folder 7, Nixon Papers.
[41] San Antonio *Express-News*, March 29, 1964.

history, and the library of rare medical books he assembled will stand as an appropriate monument to his memory.

The events of Dr. Pat's final years—the tragic death of his son Ben[42] and the prolonged fatal illness of his wife, compounded by his own worsening health—put his courage to a severe test. In a letter written in 1962, he lamented, "I am an old man. My physical strength and mental processes are enfeebled. I hope I will not be remembered as an embittered and irascible old man." A year later he wrote of being "afflicted with an inexorably progressive ailment" that was making of him "a physical and mental caricature" of his former self.[43] Yet, by the strength of his character and determination, and with the cooperation of his son, Dr. Pat Nixon, Jr., with whom he shared an office, he managed to continue to see patients until only a few months before his life came to a close. Dr. Nixon died of Parkinson's disease on November 18, 1965, only eleven days prior to his eighty-second birthday.

[42] Benjamin Oliver Nixon died in the crash of a commercial cargo plane, of which he was copilot, near Houston, Texas, on January 22, 1961.
[43] Pat Nixon, San Antonio, August 9, 1962, to Robert W. Jackson, Box 6 Folder 1, Nixon Papers; and Pat Nixon, San Antonio, November 29, 1963, to John Wheeler, Box 4 Folder 3, Nixon Papers.

The Memoirs

1

Youth

⌒∿ྀ⌒

PAPA NAMED ALL HIS BOYS after his heroes. I was named for John Ireland, who was Governor of Texas when I was born.[1] The "Pat" in my name is a rather logical nickname. [*At the time of my birth, November 29, 1883,*] Laura Wood Nixon had been dead eleven years, and Fannie Andrews Nixon had become the mother of five children in ten years. By then, Robert Thomas Nixon was fifty-six years old.[2] By then, the Civil War had been over for eighteen years, and an era of calm confidence had settled over the Nixon household. Jimmie, John, Steve, Maggie, and Ella [*children of Robert Nixon and Laura Wood Nixon*] were all married. That left Viola and Sam of the older set of children at home.[3] Viola is recalled as my protector when she thought Papa was a little too rough on me, however much I may have needed the punishment. Sam stands out as a hero. He spurned books, indeed anything with a scholastic appearance. He was a horseman and a cowboy in the best tradition. There was no bronco whose kinks he couldn't curry. His six-shooter was as much a part of his gear as his rope or quirt.

The front gallery of the old [*Nixon*] farm home stands out as a place of breathless memories. Except for the dining table,

[1] Other Nixon boys were named James Wesley, Robert Lee, Sam Houston, Alexander Stephens, and Zebulon Vance.

[2] Robert Thomas Nixon, 1827–1897, was married to Laura Ann Wood, 1832–1872, and on her death married Frances (Fannie) Amanda Andrews, 1843–1939. Fannie was Pat's mother.

[3] Viola Mae Nixon, 1864–1937, was married to Harrison Garrett Wilson, a rancher; they lived at Yancey in Medina County. Sam Houston Nixon, 1868–1951, was also a rancher.

the gallery was the place of closest association. Here the grown folks and visitors would sit after supper. The youngsters, especially Zeb and I,[4] would lie on the floor and listen to the conversation, which to us was absorbing—but only for a while. We would fall asleep as we listened and would be rudely awakened at the family's bedtime, which was around nine o'clock. Then there came to us one of the greatest of punishments: we had to get up and wash our feet, or wash at them.

Family turmoil or discord did not exist, if a clear memory can be credited. First of all, Father was too stern an individual to tolerate it even if it threatened. And then, Mama always seemed to have a strange insight into what was going on about her. She possessed an unusual capacity to pacify and to compromise. It is easy to remember the ease with which she would settle the physical encounters between Zeb and me. There were many, and some of them were pretty rough. Zeb, although four years younger, soon became the stronger, and many times I was ready for the arrival of Mother as a pacifier.

Our life together on the farm was not exceptional or different from that of most large farm families. There was much [work] to do, but children were not expected to do much of it. There were always plenty of servants.[5] This does not mean that we were very rich. Nor were we very poor. We were perhaps above the average family in a new and prosperous country neighborhood. Our life revolved principally about Mama. She was the head of the house, so far as the many problems and responsibilities which arose about the home. No one, however, was permitted to forget that Papa was the majordomo of the entire outfit.

About the only regular work I did was to pick cotton, and for this I was paid fifty cents a hundred. Even yet, there comes a thrill at the thought of making one dollar or one dollar and fifty cents a day. And besides, there was the close association with

---

[4] Zebulon Vance Nixon, Pat's brother, was four years younger than he.
[5] At its maximum size Robert Nixon's property totaled some fourteen thousand acres, much of it cotton land. At the time of his death twenty-one families, both Negro and Mexican-American, lived on the Nixon farms.

the Negroes, men and women, young and old. All were in the fields before daylight. To a young boy, their competition, their "hurrahing," and their singing were a source of delight. The land was comparatively new then, and yields of cotton were high in good years. At the end of the day, there was an air of expectancy as each incoming sack found its way to the scales attached to the wagon. The day's weight for each picker was added up, and envious eyes fell on those young Negroes who could boast of four or five hundred pounds, for their financial reward was great. Along with making a dollar a day and getting to work with the Negroes, there was a third reward. This was finding volunteer watermelons in the cotton patch, even this late in the year. They had been protected from the sun by the cotton stalks, and, in retrospect, would exceed in flavor any watermelon picked up at a modern icehouse. Knives were unnecessary; one of the men would break them with his big fists. The carefree days of cotton picking stand out in clear perspective and pure delight.

Much of my early days was tied into the young Negro boys who were my daily playmates. At the same age they seemed to be wiser than the white boys. Wesley, Dannie, and Stevie McKinney were always near at hand. They lived in the backyard. I looked on Wesley, he being older, as a companion and instructor. To Zeb, four years my junior, Wesley was a nurse. He [Zeb] wanted Wesley with him all the time. When Wesley would disappear, Zeb would fill the yard with his wailing, "Where's my sweet Wessie, where's my sweet Wessie?" On childhood expeditions about the farm, Stevie and Wesley and sometimes other boys were on hand.

But Dannie rarely went with us. There were several reasons. He was interested in voodoo or "hoodoo," as we called it. He had absorbed and retained much of the superstitions and customs of his distant forefathers. He was a severe stutterer. He rarely got very much said, but, if we were willing to stay with him, he would relate some weird tales which might have been new to Uncle Remus. Love of liquor was another of his characteristics. And besides, he had epileptic convulsions. From the present viewpoint, it is difficult to explain the indifference with which we accepted these convulsive seizures. It was perhaps because we had seen them from his and our early childhood and had grown used to them. Ever so often Dannie would be found along the road or in a fence corner, sound asleep. Nobody paid him any attention. There could be no telling whether he was drunk or in the coma which always follows such convulsions. A little time, however, would tell. If he got up in a few minutes, he had had a convulsion.

These colored boys were wise in the wiles of the woods. They were inventive and imaginative. They knew the best place to set steel traps for varmints. They were expert in building wooden traps for catching birds, especially quail. They taught me how to smoke a squirrel or a coon out of a hollow tree. We always had a pack of hounds, and many a possum, coon, wildcat, fox, and coyote did we catch. This, of course, was night hunting and usually on horseback. With the varmint treed, it meant climbing the tree and jumping the animal out, smoking him out, or cutting down the tree. One winter night when the leaves were dry, we had difficulty in smoking out a varmint. Someone suggested taking some coal oil from the headlight and pouring it down the hollow tree. When a match was thrown in, a civet cat came out and like a ball of fire ran rapidly across the sandhills, leaving a line of fire which spread quickly over a large area. We were regretful about this. We didn't realize the cruelty or the hazard involved. That river of fire that night must have reminded Stevie and me of another fire which two little boys started in the hay stacks one cold day a few years before.[6]

6 Five-year-old Pat and a Negro playmate "were quite cold one winter morning, so they proceeded to the haystack near the south barn and struck a match. The Luling *Signal* of December 6, 1888, records the results: 'A fire occurred at Captain Nixon's place in Guadalupe County last Monday, destroying all his cribs, with about 700 bushels of corn, 140 tons of hay, and 2000 bushels of cottonseed. Fortunately the bulk of his corn had not been cribbed. It was only by superhuman efforts that the flames were prevented from spreading to the warehouse, office, and residence. The origin of the fire is not known.' The account is accurate except for the last sentence. Well remembered is the route traveled by these two little boys: south to the neighborhood of Dallas Warren's

We had some ordinary cur dogs which we used to hunt rabbits. They ran mostly by sight and would quickly run the rabbit into a hollow tree or hollow log, usually the latter. When the rabbit could not be reached—and we never hesitated to put our arms into the log—we used another method. It was to take a stick with a small fork at the end and twist him out. The fork would fasten itself, in the act of twisting, into the soft skin of the rabbit, and then the rest was easy. Cottontail rabbit meat was not a favorite with our womenfolk, but to the boys it was most acceptable. Certainly, as we cooked it in the woods on a wooden spit, it was delicious.

It would be interesting to know whether this method of rabbit-twisting did not follow the slaves out of the African jungle, and perhaps also another practice which we followed in taking birds. This consisted of cutting heavy wire into yard lengths. One end was bent into a short loop so that, when thrown into the air, it would rotate rapidly. The trick was to squat close to the ground and then rise up quickly and throw the wire into a passing flock of birds. This was used on ricebirds, blackbirds, and sometimes doves. This is my earliest recollection of the deadliness of my left arm.[7] How many birds did we kill in one throw by this primitive method? Memory falters and is inclined to exaggerate. Perhaps six, perhaps twice that number.

Zeb and I had a feeling of dependency on these colored playmates, even though we were highly respected by them. I don't recall that they ever did anything very bad or mischievous, nor did they help us do so, unless it was to burn down a barn. Their parents were good, dependable individuals for the most part.

---

house, east for a short distance, and then north to the big house, breathless and very much afraid. Guilt was easily to be seen. Well remembered also is the punishment: there was none." Pat Ireland Nixon, *The Early Nixons of Texas*, pp. 35–36.

[7] Pat makes frequent mention of his left-handedness, especially in connection with his baseball prowess. Later, in a letter to his young grandson Stevie, he writes: "Don't let the others kid you about being left-handed. If they do, you just remind them that Granddaddy and Leonardo da Vinci were left-handed. And if that is not enough, you can refer them to the Bible, Judges 20:16." ["There were also seven hundred picked men from Gibeah, left-handed men, who could sling a stone and not miss by a hair's breadth."]

Some few of them would drink too much whiskey when they could get it. I don't recall that anyone ever met a violent death on the farm except by accident. So these people raised their children right, and these children in turn handed down to their children good behavior. Today some of their descendants are still on the farm, and many of them are in the neighborhood. And they are good citizens.

As Zeb and I wandered through woods and fields, along with the boys of the neighborhood, white and black, we absorbed much information about nature. We developed the art of being in sympathy with all living things: flowers, trees, birds, and animals. Or nearly all: certainly we had no truck with rattlesnakes, wasps, or skunks. We came to know the call of most of the birds of the area: mockingbird, cardinal, robin, three kinds of doves, bobwhite, meadowlark, killdeer, snipe, painted bunting, several kinds of sparrows and hummingbirds, martin, swifts, thrush, several kinds of hawks and owls, two kinds of buzzards, several kinds of woodpeckers, blackbirds, and flycatchers including the scissortail, ducks and geese, several kinds of wrens, chickadee, and many others. Two things stand out in memory. The first is the beautiful nests built by the painted buntings. In the spring they were numerous about the horse lot. The hair which they wove into artistic, basket-like nests was collected from wire fences and other places where it had been pulled out, and not directly from horses' tails as has been claimed. Before it became illegal, this most beautiful of Texas birds was the favorite cage bird, especially with the Mexicans.

The other thing I recall has to do with the bad times which the scissortail flycatchers gave the hawks. When these hawks invaded forbidden territory, the scissortails would tie into them and drive them far off, part of the time literally riding on hawkback.

We were perhaps less familiar with the trees and the flowers. Our knowledge of animals was greatest in those we classified as varmints. But we knew less about the bees than the birds. Certainly we didn't know that it was the old folks which were pushed out at swarming time. After a lapse of sixty years, the sight and sound of the swarm are still clear. After leaving a tree or hive and collecting on an adjacent tree in a large bucket-sized mass, [*the bees*] then began the flight to a predetermined tree. And there they would go in spite of hell and high water and anything we might do. But we always tried to deter them. The flight of bees in swarm is like that of a cyclone, moving quite fast in rotary motion but going forward only slowly. It was this slow motion forward that gave us our chance; bells were rung, dishpans were beaten like drums, sand and dirt were thrown into the swarm. But nothing availed.

Anyway, Zeb and the rest of us did learn much from the book of nature. As I reread the two themes "The Coyote" and "The Wildcat" which I wrote at the University of Texas, it is obvious that I was calling on my early education in the woods. And to this day, the song of the bluebird by day and the call of the plover by night are reminiscent of experiences in Guadalupe County long, long ago.

To complete the wanderings of three or four boys, a river would be necessary. We had no river. The Guadalupe was three or four miles away and Nash's Creek was almost as far. The Nixon home was built on a divide, so that water off the back of the house eventually found its way into Nash's Creek and the Guadalupe, while that from the front drained into Smith Creek and the San Marcos River. Just back of the house, almost in the yard, was a small dirt tank. About a quarter-mile east was the big tank which had deep water. There was little or no fishing, except for crawfish and an occasional perch. It was in the big tank that we learned to swim. But I never learned to swim very well. Twice in later life, once in the San Marcos River and once in the Atlantic Ocean near Rehobeth Beach, Delaware, I came so near to drowning that even now I shrink from a body of water larger than a bathtub. The first experience was perhaps trivial; it was just a matter of hanging on till the rapids could carry me down to quiet, shallow water. At Rehobeth Beach, the situation was altogether serious. I had gotten beyond the ropes and was being carried out by a strong undertow. Try as hard as I could, I could make no headway toward shore. I became completely exhausted and was swallowing water by the mouthful. Every moment seemed an eternity. Just when it seemed to be all over, a redheaded boy of about sixteen caught me by the hair and said casually, "Come on out of here." He deposited me on shore, and I never saw him again. When I had coughed the water out of my lungs and was able to stand up, he had disappeared. My unexpressed thanks are as real and as deep today as they were in 1907.

School was a serious undertaking with the Nixon children. We were fortunate to have had the early inspiration of Major Lee Russell.[8] His life had not been easy. One feature of his career, prolonged confinement in a Northern prison, was to leave an indelible imprint on his life. But this experience did not dim his scholarly attainments and his ability to inspire ambition in hopeful hearts. Life without an education was to him beyond conception. I don't remember many of the details of the one-room school. I do remember one book, and that was Webster's *Elementary Spelling Book*. The "blue-backed speller," it was called. This book had been in use for over a hundred years and had been used by literally millions. The wisdom of its replacement in our schools is even now to be doubted. From it we learned the alphabet and we learned to spell, so that when the spelling bees came Friday afternoon, the competition was keen. I recall my importance when I reached *baker* in Lesson Number 26; that was getting along. And how envious I was as I saw Myrtle and Alta[9] advance through *cessation* and *ambiguity* to *immateriality*. As I hold a copy of this character-building book in my hand at this moment, I marvel at the lessons taught by the fables in the back of the book: the one, for instance, about the boy that stole apples and the moral that "if good words and gentle means will not reclaim the wicked, they must be dealt with in a more severe manner."

---

[8] Pat's uncle, Major Calyer Lee Russell, 1835–1905, was married to Mary Lizette Andrews, the sister of Fannie Nixon.

[9] These are two of Pat's older sisters, Mollie Myrtle (Mrs. Frank C. Allen), and Alta Estelle (first Mrs. James Knox Walker, and later Mrs. Joseph Edgar Fisher).

Another method of teaching was the use of copybooks. At the top of each page would appear a sentence written in accurate Spencerian hand. Embodied in the sentence would be an inescapable moral such as "Honesty is the Best Policy" and "Truth Crushed to Earth Will Rise Again." These we copied and recopied many times. Thus, we learned to read and write. With this came also a lift to the heart. This, of course, is propaganda, pure and simple, but it is wholesome propaganda.

The games we played at school were as simple as they were wholesome. We played marbles, but not for keeps. This came later in Luling.[10] Mumblepeg was always a favorite, and it was really wonderful what some of those Guadalupe County boys could do with a pocket knife. They could "shave the pig" and "spank the baby" with consummate skill. The fellow who had to root the peg found little sympathy on the school ground. But the game most enjoyed by the boys was town ball. This was the predecessor of baseball, which had not yet reached rural Guadalupe County. This game was played with a solid rubber ball, in size between a golf ball and a tennis ball. For a bat, a broom handle or hoe handle was used. It was not necessary to catch the ball, in fact it might have been dangerous to do so since no gloves were used. To get an opponent out, all that was needed was to throw the ball in front of the runner.

The most hazardous game we played was popping the whip. A long line was made by clasping hands with the small boys at the end. The line would run straight for a short distance, then the larger boys would turn suddenly and bring the tail of the whip around with great force and speed. It usually meant that the little fellows were in for a bad time. This game was played also by the girls on their playgrounds. Other games of the girls were drop the handkerchief, rope jumping, fox and geese, London bridge is falling down, and tug-of-war.

All in all, our life in Guadalupe County was a happy one. Most of what we experienced was wholesome, little was improper, and all was developmental. As a result, we achieved

---

[10] The Nixons moved into Luling in 1895.

health of body and mind. Someone has said that there is virtue in gardens and orchards, in fields and streams, in rustic recreations and plain manners that towns and cities do not enjoy.

When we moved to Luling in 1895, I, of course, did not realize what a foundation for life my twelve years in the country had built. Isolation from outside influences logically led to a feeling of shyness which has been lifelong. But as an offset, there have come many memories and many blessings that are likewise lifelong.

We cannot assess the feelings and the misgivings which our parents entertained as they made plans to move to Luling. We do know their motive: it was to improve the lot of their family. Their roots had grown deep into the life and the soil of Guadalupe County. They had created a family life where honesty, character, and loyalty had been stressed. It had been a happy home and a carefree life. As I look back on our lives together in that home, I can appreciate fully what Victor Hugo meant when he said that he conceived of heaven as a place where all parents are young and all children are small.

When the Nixon family moved to Luling, a new world opened up for me. Up to then, my approach and my attitude had been severely rural—indeed they have remained more or less the same. Of course, I had been to Luling a good many times on Saturdays. But my urban contacts were few and short. I recall that the storekeepers noticed me enough to give me a cone of *piloncillo* or a few sticks of peppermint candy. This gesture, however, was not made solely in my direction, because it was a reward for purchases made.

So the whole business was strangely new. Especially do I remember going to Maggie Stevens's home on one of these trips to Luling. Two evidences of magic were experienced. The first was the electric light. This invention was only seventeen years old, and I saw it in Luling soon after its practical application had been effected.

The second magical sight for me was iced tea. To this day, that large pewter pitcher, sweating and smoking from its cold contents, stands out as a gastronomic delight. If all the wait-resses who have looked at me so unbelievingly when I ordered iced tea for breakfast could have seen that pitcher and tasted its contents—then and only then could they have understood.

Long before 1895, Luling had made the transition [*from rail-head to permanent community*]. The houses had aligned them-selves so as to form straight streets, and the social standards and the drinking habits of the citizens had been transformed. As was the more or less universal rule in Texas, the business section was built adjacent and parallel to the railway. The same three blocks of stores that were there when I first saw them re-main today as the center of things. The main difference is that many places of business have been established on the south side of the railway, principally because the Houston–San An-tonio highway passes this way.

Fortunately, the railroad was not a dividing line in the social standing of the citizens of Luling. There was no right and wrong side of the tracks. While it is true that most of the resi-dences are located to the south, there are many worthy people who have lived and still live in the north section of town. As the town has grown, particularly since the discovery of oil by Edgar B. Davis, Luling has expanded in all directions; but here again, the main growth has been south toward the San Marcos River, about a mile away.

It was into this young and thriving town of 1,500 people that I was projected at the age of twelve. Never before had my in-nate timidity been put to such a test. Only an individual born in the country can understand the embarrassments and the in-hibitions which come to a country boy when he is taken out of his environment. I made friends slowly, all the while longing for the simple surroundings of the country with its wholesome companions. In those days, the town boys had an ugly attitude toward boys from the country; they dubbed them "hayseeds." Since I was all alone and they were many, they made life mis-erable for me for a while. One boy, Willoughby Lipscomb, was especially rough on me. But this didn't last long, and the time for revenge came. This was the first time that I used my left fist with really serious intent. One source of acceptance of me by the Luling boys was my proficiency in all games: marbles, tops, and especially baseball.

Here, as at Old Nixon, I accepted my schoolwork seriously.[11] Naturally, at first I was overawed. The mere sight of what appeared then to be an enormous school building impressed me deeply. It was made of stone and had two stories. The seats were manufactured and had an inkwell for handy use. Before this, I had seen only a few rough benches in a small, unceiled room. And as for ink, I had never used anything but a pencil.

One morning at the breakfast table, one of the girls said to me, "Oh! you've got the measles." There was measles in school, and I had broken out during the night. My reaction was to cry vigorously, because I had to miss school. This was during my first year in Luling. A more serious disease overtook me that year. That was a severe attack of typhoid fever, which brought me near to the end. This disease was very prevalent in Luling and most other areas. Why it didn't occur in decimating epidemics remains a mystery. Water was pumped from the river to the standpipe and was drunk by all except a few who had their own wells. And besides, outdoor privies were universal and sewers were nonexistent. Dr. S. J. Francis was my doctor. Of course, Dr. J. W. Nixon came in frequently.[12] The best-known treatment was used, the principal treatment of which was the withholding of food and water. Starvation was easily borne, but the unquenched thirst was a daily torture. Nurses were not to be had, so it devolved on the family to care for me during the day, and each night one of the good neighbors "sat up" with me. I waked up one night in a delirium from fever and thought an elephant was sitting beside my bed. I learned later that it was Mr. John Orchard. He was a large, wrinkle-faced man whose skin did resemble [that of] a pachyderm. After two months, my fever subsided, and I was permitted to sit up and eat a little food. I needed a lot of food.

[11] The town of Old Nixon, Texas, was established by Robert Nixon.
[12] Dr. James Wesley Nixon, 1855–1939, Pat's eldest half brother, practiced medicine at Nixon, Wrightsboro, and Gonzales.

Uncle Lee Russell, during my six years in school at Old Nixon, had pointed me in the right direction, and I had come to have a high regard for him. During the five school years at Luling, I had many teachers, but only two stand out in clear perspective: Miss Ida Hunter and Professor William M. Schofield. Miss Ida was my first teacher in Luling and the grade was the eighth. In three short months, she took a timid country boy and opened his eyes to many things ahead. Then I came down with typhoid fever.

She came to see me during my convalescence. I thought she was most beautiful. She sat and talked with me for a while and then gave me a copy of Jane Porter's *Thaddeus of Warsaw*. She inscribed it, in a hand worthy of the school copybooks, to "Pat Nixon, Luling, Texas, Feb. 9, 1895." On the back endpaper she had written this inscription: "Accept this book, which you more than merited, from one who loves you and wishes you a speedy recovery." This book was read and cherished year after year. It helped me to get a glimpse of the great world of books. Thirty-nine years later I wrote to her:

> In a copy of Porter's *Thaddeus of Warsaw*, which I ran across the other day, is the name of "Pat Nixon, Feb. 9, 1895," written in your handwriting. If you search your memory, you may succeed in recalling a most unsophisticated and very backward boy of this name, who at the age of twelve had typhoid fever, and you presented him with this book. You may recall that this boy had just moved in from the country, and a town the size of Luling, even, was no mean city to him.
>
> My object in writing is to let you know that your efforts to instill a little knowledge and a few high principles in that timid boy of twelve were not altogether in vain. I was finally graduated at Luling and then finished at the University of Texas in three years and graduated at Johns Hopkins Medical School in 1909, being chosen as a member of the Phi Beta Kappa at the latter institution. Since that time I have been practicing in San Antonio. I may not have done anything wonderful in a professional way, but I do have a wonderful family, a wife and four boys.
>
> Let this letter serve as my belated thanks to you for what you were able to do for me as a boy.

I was happy to receive a reply [*which read in part*]: "It is wonderful after all these years to find you again! And a book was the link that connected the years. I had forgotten about giving the book, but I had not forgotten the boy. I am glad I gave the book, else I might never have known all the good things that have happened to you; surely I would have missed knowing that you gave me credit in your scheme of life. These are the sweet rewards of a teacher, expressions of appreciation for *our little* services."

My contacts with Professor Schofield came later—principally during my last year in the Luling Public Schools—when some of the rural timidity had been overcome. [*I was*] a more mature individual: I was sixteen years old. Professor Schofield was principal of the high school. He was interested in such subjects as history and government. He was more than a teacher; he was friend and confidant. When the time came for the 1899 graduating exercises, it is significant that, as salutatorian, I wrote on a historical subject.[13] Of course, Professor Schofield chose the subject and probably supplied most of the material. Even so, this may well have been the beginning of my interest in Texas history.

But there was much more than school during these five years in Luling. Hunting and fishing played a big part. Every Saturday, when we didn't have to clean up the chinaberry leaves which were inexhaustible in late summer, Zeb and I would go to the river and stay all day, usually in the Josey bottom. Abe Josey was a very tolerant man to permit so many of us to impose on him. Fish, caught principally on a trot line, were plentiful: catfish, buffalo, and perch; cottontail rabbits and squirrels were easy to find. In those days, in addition to fox squirrels or red squirrels, we found cat squirrels or gray squirrels. These were a little smaller and much wilder, staying for the most part in the tall pecan and cottonwood trees. In these river bottoms there was another variety of rabbit, the swamp rabbit. This rabbit, when startled by a dog, would break immediately for

---

[13] The subject of his speech was "Disciples of Bacon." Pat is in error here; he graduated in 1900, not in 1899.

the river and swim across, thus trying to evade the dog. But, fortunately for the hunter, the rabbit was easily killed as he swam.

Boyhood friends at Luling come trooping back through the lanes of memory. The list includes a group of boys who entertained a feeling of fairness and equality toward each other, and they have carried that feeling into the serious problems of life. Here was a bunch of boys who were not reminded that there was any difference among Jew, Catholic, or Protestant. The race problem was not a problem in Luling. The Negroes of the town were respected for what they were, and they were respectful. They knew their place and were willing to let the processes of time help in the solution of their problems.

Differences of varying description and varying importance sprang up. When these were of sufficient significance, there was only one way of settlement: resort to bare fists. I bear a scar below my left eye, the result of a well-placed blow from the fist of Frank Bridges. It happened in a baseball game at Longer Park. I hit an infield fly, about which there was some argument. Frank spoke up, and I thought he called me a liar when in reality, it developed afterwards, he said he was on the line when he caught the ball. We tied into each other in a prolonged rough-and-tumble scrap. He drew the most blood; I wound up on top. We were both glad when Mrs. T. E. Cocreham pulled me off.

These boys of Luling were not bad boys—anything but. However, we did things which perhaps we should not have done, such as running a bunch of tramps out of town, throwing a scare into Julius Meyer (later official town crier of San Antonio), or engaging in petty pilfering of candy, watermelons, and even things of greater value. One hazardous thing which we did was to steal rides on the railroad to Harwood, Kingsbury, or Seguin. Riding the blind baggage of a passenger train was easy and comfortable, but hanging on to the rods of a freight car, in a constant barrage of small rocks whipped up by the suction of the wind, was so venturesome that we ignored the ever-present danger. No deep soul-searching is necessary to recall some of these escapades.

Tragedy stalked among these boys. Leslie Huff and Knox Walker were taken off by tuberculosis before their maturity had more than arrived.[14] Eugene Cocreham outlived many of the other boys;[15] he is singled out because of his dramatic rescue from immediate death. He was a diabetic, and his disease was rapidly overcoming him. And then the year 1923 came, and insulin became available. Eugene was one of the first to use this miraculous drug, and his years were prolonged. The most painful tragedy came to Claire Holcomb. In retrospect, his ailment was a sarcoma of the glands of the neck. Once or twice a year, he would go to New Orleans for surgical removal, doubtless by the great Rudolph Matas, and each time the growth would recur. With his fast disappearing strength went his voice. His whispered words could have been no more than the unrealized dreams of a boy of fourteen. His last message to his classmates was one of encouragement: "You stay in the middle of the road, while I stay in the middle of the bed."

Luling has always been a good baseball town. It accepted the game early and year after year has had an unusually large number of good players. Playing the game at Luling was the beginning of a long career in baseball for me; two years at Bingham School at Asheville, North Carolina; three at the University of Texas; three at Johns Hopkins; and then two summers of semiprofessional ball at Cuero. From this last it might have been possible to go on into professional baseball, but fortunately nothing came of this.

We played all the nearby towns: Lockhart, Gonzales, Seguin, San Marcos, and New Braunfels. We usually defeated these teams. Lockhart was our arch rival. Here the games were hotly contested and usually close. Isadore Mazur recalls that I rarely objected to an umpire's decision. While Zeb would be in the center of all arguments around third base,[16] I would be sitting on the ground in left field. Occasionally we would play some

---

[14] James Knox Walker, 1881–1905, married Alta Estelle Nixon, Pat's sister, in 1902; he died in 1905.

[15] Eugene Cocreham was later a pitcher for the Boston Braves.

[16] Perhaps this was good training for Zeb; he later became an attorney.

semiprofessional team in San Antonio. The farthest we ever went was to Richmond. Nothing is remembered about the ball game, but the great fear that was ours can never be forgotten. The feud between the Woodpeckers and the Jaybirds was well known to us.[17] A short time before, several men on each side had been killed in a street battle. We went straight to the ball park and straight back to the depot where we stayed till the train arrived several hours later. We made no second trip to Richmond.

One man did a great deal for baseball and for the boys of Luling. He was Edgar Perry, who was in the cotton business. He later moved to Austin, where he built the Commodore Perry Hotel. He called himself our manager. In reality, he was our financial father. He saw to it that we had the best equipment, good hotel accommodations, and whatever else we needed. He was making an investment in boys; and in return, he expected and received from us good behavior and gentlemanly conduct.

It is interesting as well as punishing how certain little transgressions will linger through the years—like the pinpricks of conscience. One year, we were playing Eagle Lake. On this team were two imported players who called themselves Smith and Jones. Jones was an exceptionally good pitcher and was bent on stopping a good batting streak I was having. He was succeeding, so I was equally determined. I came to bat and got what would have gone for a single into right field. But, by cutting first base when the umpire wasn't looking, I stretched it into a double. There is no better proof of my regret than that I have remembered the incident for more than fifty years.

Another time, we were in New Braunfels. Some of the hos-

---

[17] Richmond, in Fort Bend County, was the center of the notorious Jaybird-Woodpecker feud, a political struggle with racial overtones that had its origin during Reconstruction days. Although both factions claimed to represent local Democrats, the Woodpeckers had gained power under Republican auspices and had remained in office through control of Negro votes. In 1890, Governor Lawrence S. Ross intervened to end the violence that characterized the feud and engineered a settlement resulting in Jaybird control of county politics. Ill will between supporters of the two factions continued to flare up periodically, however, well into the twentieth century.

PAT NIXON OF TEXAS

pitable citizens gave a reception for us. We all went, even though we were at the age when we didn't know what to do with our hands and feet except on the baseball diamond. We were offered a glass of beer—a drink that flowed as freely as water in New Braunfels. I accepted mine and took one sip. The stuff simply spewed out of my mouth. I had never dreamed that anything could be so loathsome. I have looked back on this incident with amusement as well as gratitude on many occasions. This was my first and last taste of anything alcoholic. The experience may have been more meaningful than it appeared that night. Since I have always tried never to do anything halfway, I have often thought that, under proper conditions, I might have made a first-class drunkard.

Zeb and I had plenty of work to do in Luling, as did Myrtle and Alta. We had a cook but not all the help we had grown used to at the farm. We had a garden, chickens, two milk cows, a buggy horse, and usually two saddle horses. And there were always wood to cut, ashes to take up, and chinaberry leaves and berries to rake. Caring for the hundred or so pigeons which we had was not considered work. The wood cutting was different and very regular, as wood was used for cooking and heating. Milking the cows and caring for the horses were disagreeable chores that are well remembered, especially on cold, wet mornings. We had many cows put their feet in the bucket, but we didn't do as the little city girl did, milking for the first time for her grandmother; she was found feeding the milk to the cow. She explained that the cow had stuck her foot in the bucket and she was putting the milk through again.

Speaking of chores, it might be philosophising to ask whether youngsters of today would not be better off if there were wood to cut, ashes to take up, cows to feed and milk, horses to feed and curry. These new youngsters seem to be completely occupied, but most of their activities are supervised. Their mothers are hardly more than glorified delivery agents, madly rushing from one thing to another and shattering their nervous systems in the bargain. The only ashes their youngsters ever encounter are those that drop in the eyes of an occasional breast-fed baby.

68

These five years in Luling comprised a chapter in the life of a bashful boy. These were eventful years, years of preparation and adaptation. When on April 24, 1900, a boy of sixteen walked across the stage at the Opera House and held out his left hand to receive his high school diploma, there was a welling up of pride of accomplishment and ambition for the future. That diploma stated I was "entitled to all the honors and privileges of a graduate of this institution." The bestowal of honors and privileges on me assumes added meaning as I now look over the clearly written signatures of the members of the board of education. These men were all good citizens who were willing to give their time and talents to the cause of education. And their children and children's children are good citizens. The diploma also bears the signatures of my old friend and mentor, William M. Schofield, as superintendent, and of R. L. Adams, as principal.

The year 1900 was important. In that year, an important decision was made. I had been considered as "puny" from a health standpoint during my five years in Luling. There had been nothing serious, except the attack of typhoid fever in 1895. But I was not as sturdy as the other boys; my arms and legs were smaller and my strength less. Anything which I had done along athletic lines had to be attributed to skill and determination rather than to physical stamina. An X ray of my chest, hardly known in those days, might well have shown some reflection of the long visit of our tuberculous kinsman from North Carolina.

So, the question of where I should go to school after I graduated from the Luling High School came up. Here again, Uncle Lee Russell entered the picture, and he brought the proper answer. His old cell mate in a federal prison on Johnson's Island in Lake Erie during the Civil War, Colonel Robert Bingham, was now superintendent of the Bingham School, in existence for over one hundred years and widely known in educational circles.[18] Colonel Bingham was a gentleman of the old school.

[18] The school was founded by the Reverend William Bingham in Hillsboro,

Here, I would learn more than the three R's. The school was located in the mountains near Asheville, North Carolina, so the problem of my health would be cared for. The school was expensive. But Mama now had control of her property, and she would help out.

This trip to Asheville, with all its meanings, was an adventure into the great unknown world. Preparations were elaborate and prolonged. A trunk was purchased, something new in my career and something more important than would be indicated by the minor position which that same trunk now occupies in our attic. New clothes were bought, emphasis being on long, heavy underwear with elastic material about the ankles and down the outside of each leg; scrivens, they were called. And there were many other things; most of them were luxuries theretofore unknown to me. One item, not at all understandable at the present time, was a heavy flatiron for pressing uniforms. This thing didn't lend itself to easy transportation. It would be placed in one part of the trunk and wind up in another at the end of the journey.

To an intensely timid and wholly unsophisticated boy of sixteen, that first long train ride was unforgettable: the new country, the rivers, the Great River, the farms, the towns and cities, and the constantly changing panorama which disappeared spokelike to the rear. Then there was the wonder of the train itself: the great engine, the many coaches with their population shifting from station to station, the people themselves, the employees of the railroad—especially the butcherboys with their varied assortment of candy, fruit, and magazines. There were, of course, sleeping cars on my train, but I didn't use them. Money was too hard to come by. Food for the journey was not a difficult problem. Mama prepared a shoe box, well filled with fried chicken, cake, and such like.

I thought Bingham was a gorgeous place. In reality, the

North Carolina, in 1793. It was later moved to Mount Repose, then back to Hillsboro, then to Mebane in 1865, and finally to Asheville in 1891. The last male member of the family died in 1927, and the school was closed the following year.

buildings were extremely plain, almost drab. The whole setting —the boys, the mountains, the river, the distant view, the red splashes of rhododendrons on the hillsides—all this was absorbing to a boy away from home for the first time and allowed no time for homesickness.

Located on a shelf-like plateau, high above the French Broad River, the school commanded a view of all the surrounding area. Four or five hundred feet below flowed the beautiful French Broad, while to the west mountains of increasing height extended to the Blue Ridge. Construction of the buildings—or barracks, for this was a military school—had been carried out with two purposes in mind: utility and safety from fire.

My two years at Bingham were little less than one adventure after another. Colonel Bingham and the teachers made the classroom work attractive and beneficial, that is, for those who wanted to learn. The school had the reputation of making men out of boys. But some were failures. One of my own kinsmen, in later years, burned down the guardhouse while he was in it. The school utilized the honor system, and it was strictly enforced. Black marks in the form of demerits were given for various transgressions, and these were read out at the morning assembly. Certain acts meant confinement in the guardhouse, and there was no recourse. A certain number of demerits called for longer periods in the study hall. Demerits, however, could be erased by exposure to Doctor Black or Doctor Brown. These were two leather straps attached to a piece of broom handle, the only difference being the color of the handle. These settlements were regular Saturday morning affairs. Colonel Bingham was very fair and very generous. For each offender, he had two questions: "Will you choose Doctor Brown or Doctor Black and will you take it on your hand or your F. S. (fat sitter)?" I never did meet either of these worthy doctors, but I acted as scorekeeper on many occasions. Even now, it is easy to recall the Colonel's voice as he droned out, "There's one, there's two, there's ten," and by the time he got to ten, he was really bearing down.

There was much outside the classroom to interest a group of

young boys: the military drills, wandering about the country-side on Saturdays, pilfering neighbor Pearson's apples, trips to Asheville on Saturday afternoon, athletic events. It was here that I saw my first football game, but I never played. I had never played tennis before but reached the finals in a school tournament during my second year.[19]

There was bad blood between Bingham boys and the boys of Asheville. During a football game between these two groups, there developed a free-for-all fight. The entire field was a writhing mass of struggling boys. There were several severe injuries. I came out with a foot-long gash across the back of my uniform, but my skin was untouched. Colonel Bingham was thoroughly exercised about this unhappy episode. He called the student body together and asked each cadet about the origin of the fight and the part he played. We all faced the facts: the fight was a flare-up in a long-smoldering feud, and once it was started we had to get into it. We all faced the facts with one exception, a boy named Ott from Louisville, Kentucky. When his time to testify came, he tried to be funny. "I don't know what happened," he said, "I was in the grandstand talking to the ladies." That was too much for an aroused student body; they rode Mr. Ott out of school on a rail.

We had a good baseball team at Bingham, one of the best amateur teams in North Carolina—if indeed it could be considered an amateur team. Our coach and catcher was a man who ran the trolley car from Asheville to the school. We played and often defeated such teams as the University of North Carolina and Davidson. Our main rival in all sports was Asheville School. This was a highbrow institution to which only boys from northern states went. The rivalry between these two neighboring schools was most keen. It was almost like drawing the Smith and Wesson line [*Mason-Dixon line?*] all over again. Even some of our own boys from the north were known to speak contemptuously of "that Yankee school." But on the diamond or gridiron, they were rarely much of an opponent.

[19] Dr. Pat continued to play tennis until his seventy-fifth year.

One incident of an athletic nature should be set down. One Saturday afternoon a group of us were wandering about the country. In the group were C. C. Pardue of New Orleans and some other members of the baseball team. We came to the athletic field at the foot of the hill, where some men were having a field day. Among the events was a baseball-throwing contest, and we were asked to participate. Without warming up our arms, we took our turns. Pardue and I threw the ball further than any of the men, and my awkward, left-handed effort was the longest of all, well over a hundred yards.

Much more could be said about Bingham School, its classroom work, centered about Major Grinnan and Captain William F. Bryan, its military department under Captain Charles S. Fowler, its method of settling personal differences by way of bare fists, its gymnasium, Old Booze and the other Negroes about the place, the cakes Mrs. Fowler used to make for us for fifty cents, the twenty-five-cent oyster dinners we used to enjoy at the Elite Cafe in Asheville. All these were a part of the life of the school. Special mention should be made of the influence of Major and Mrs. R. T. Grinnan. Mrs. Grinnan was the daughter of Colonel Bingham. The students affectionately called the Major "Old Tony," but not to his face. The ministrations of these two meant much to many Bingham boys. And closely allied with them was the work of Captain W. F. Bryan. Mrs. Grinnan supplied the grace and the charm and the place of retreat for the homesick and lovesick cadet. But the real heart of the school was Colonel Bingham.

When the Civil War ended, there were thousands of Southerners, like Colonel Bingham, for whom there seemed very little left in life. Their country had been overrun, their property destroyed, their families starved, their boys lost. And yet they, heartened by the noble example of Robert E. Lee, set heart and hand to the rebuilding of their beloved Southland. Such loyalty proved to be the salvation of a discouraged and impoverished people. Prominent among this group was Colonel Robert Bingham. He had come from a long line of educators, his father and his grandfather having preceded him as head of Bingham

School. His brother William was the author of Bingham's *Latin Grammar*. Thus, his greatest contribution to his desolated country would be in the field of moral and intellectual development. He believed deeply in the essentiality of a strong foundation of a classical and literary culture. So, he devoted the remainder of his life to the building of character into the youth of the land, both South and North.

By the end of the century, hundreds of boys had sat at the feet of this great man and then gone on to become leaders in the business, professional, and political life of the country. He had two approaches to his boys, one private and one public. The conferences he held in his office, especially with those cadets who were not taking their opportunities and obligations seriously, were of inestimable value. His greatest good, however, came from his daily chapel talks and from his Sunday afternoon assemblies. On these occasions, he would discuss topics of general interest, but at the same time he would be stressing the amenities of life: love, truth, loyalty, culture, beauty, the dignity of work, honesty, integrity, and all the rest. He spoke often of the necessity of the will and the determination to get things done, often emphasizing the effect of mind over matter.

The influence of Colonel Bingham and Bingham School on me was beyond all calculation. In the first place, I thrived physically and all "puniness" disappeared. Above and beyond this, however, was the lift which came to mind and spirit. My relation to Major Lee Russell gave me immediate acceptance by Colonel Bingham, and I was early permitted to appreciate the greatness of this man. He, in turn, kept in close touch with Mama and other parents by frequent reports. These reports, yellowed by fifty-two years, are before me. Mama carefully preserved them in an envelope from the Colonel postmarked at Luling, May 1, 1901.

On November 12, [1900], came this word: "Pat is one of our most satisfactory pupils. His conduct is excellent, he is capable, is interested in his work and is at the top of his classes. I congratulate you on having such a boy." On December 22: "Pat's conduct is very good, his application is fine and he is doing well all round. We wish that we had more pupils like him." On March 19, 1901: "Pat's conduct is good and he is an excellent man all round." On May 27: "Your son is one of our very best boys. He is capable, orderly, and studious and stands at the top of his classes and at the top of the school." These reports were a source of great pride to Mama, even though she was making a financial sacrifice. The propriety of keeping me "in a school as expensive as this" was not, in her estimation, a subject for discussion. There was no discussion, either, that the school was expensive by standards of that day. The total cost for the first year was $372.40. School expenses were listed as $300.00, incidentals as $55.10, and uniform as $21.00. The last item was broken down as follows: coat $10.75, trousers $6.00, dress cap and ornament $3.00, and fatigue cap $1.25.

Cadet Nixon's report card was nothing to get excited about. On the five quarterly reports that are available, he was "kept in" from one to five times for "missing his lessons." In all instances, "his deportment in the classroom" was "good" or "very good," and he received no demerits "for neglect or breach of orders." His "report on scholarship" for December 21, 1900, is about average for all five: "soldierly appearance and bearing, fair"; "proficiency in drill, fair"; "English, fourth year, very good"; "writing, fair"; "Latin, fourth year, good"; "junior algebra, very good"; "chemistry, first year, very good." The grade of "fair" in writing was an undeserved compliment. There was marked improvement in soldierly bearing and proficiency in drill so that by May 24, 1901, he was graded "very good." It was on this basis that he was commissioned a first lieutenant at the beginning of the second year. The Colonel made this pointed suggestion on each report: "This Report, both of Conduct and Scholarship, should be made the basis of Commendation or Admonition by Parents." One recollection of Colonel Bingham must be recorded. During the summer of 1901, he visited Texas and honored the Nixon family by visiting in our home. To all who saw him in Luling, he was the very soul of all that was fine and cultured and gentlemanly.

The boy who left Bingham School in 1902 was greatly differ-

ent from the one who had timidly walked up the long hill beyond the French Broad in September, 1900. I was more mature
and more secure. Much had happened to the inside and the
outside of me. I had been much impressed and much improved
by all that I had experienced. It had been expensive financially,
and it had meant sacrifices on Mother's part. But both of us
felt that it had been worth it, physically and intellectually. My
self-confidence was greatly bolstered, and I had begun to learn
more clearly of the significance of group spirit or loyalty. From
a belief in Bingham School and its ideals, there had grown the
larger belief in Texas and the other states. Fortunately, my
patriotism for state and nation did not then, nor has it, become
chauvinistic. I knew then, and I know now, that there are other
worthy schools and states and nations. Nothing, in my eyes, is
quite so detestable as the professional Texan or professional
American.

One benefit which I derived from Bingham deserves more
emphasis. As I look back, it is rather obvious that I was not
ready for university work when I graduated from the Luling
High School. I was too immature from every standpoint and
especially from the standpoint of my scholastic shortcomings.
After a thorough grounding in how to study and in how to get
things done, I was able to enter the sophomore class at the University of Texas, where the going was never too rough.

My Bingham diploma bears the date June 13, 1902. It sets
forth that "Whereas, Patrick [sic] Ireland Nixon has completed
our regular course in English, Mathematics, Latin, and Chemistry with the grade of Ninety-Four in the same, therefore we
declare him a Graduate of Bingham School *Maxima cum
Laude* and award him this Diploma."

So, my two years at Bingham School were a venture of faith,
faith in the judgment of Uncle Lee Russell, faith bolstered by
the character of Colonel Bingham, faith confirmed by the confidence of Fannie Andrews Nixon.

My work at Bingham School permitted me to enter the sophomore class at the University of Texas. Many of my recollections

76

of this great institution are not happy. It may have been the bigness of it all; the enrollment of 1,348 seemed enormous compared to the 125 boys I had known at Bingham. This feeling of being overawed pursued me during most of my career at Austin. At Bingham, we were a closely knit group with the same interests and the same ambitions. The University of Texas seemed to be without a heart, at least without a heart that could concern itself with the welfare of the individual newcomer. As I look back on the situation that faced me in 1902, it is obvious that much of the blame lay within me. I was nineteen years old and should have been able to clear my own path and make my own opportunities. But, in self-defense, let it be said that I was still an awkward country boy. It should be said also that during the last twenty years my relations with the University have been most wholesome, through the media of the History Department, the Eugene C. Barker Texas History Center, the Texas State Historical Association, the University of Texas Press, Frank Wardlaw, and Harry Ransom. When these things have been said, however, the fact remains that few students ever went through the University of Texas so unobtrusively and so unnoticed as did I.

One other extenuating explanation might be made. When I entered, I was classed as a freshman along with 194 others. However, I went to classes with sophomores. The result was that I belonged to neither. This situation continued for two years. It was not until the third year that I was properly classed and grouped with seniors.

It should not be inferred that I considered the time spent at the University of Texas as wasted. Far from it. I had gone there for a premedical course, and I got a good course. I did get off to a bad start. During the first year, I made one *A*, four *B*'s, one *D*, and one *E*. The *D* was made in Latin and was easily corrected the rest of the way. The *E*, given in English, was a nightmare and could not have been otherwise. When I recall the circumstances—the ugly, goat-faced teacher, his master's degree from Harvard a few months before, his Harvard accent, his utter contempt for all things Texan, and his majestic name:

Arthur Llewellyn Eno—under such circumstances, the wonder is that I did as well as I did. My main difficulty in English was in writing themes, or at least old Eno thought so. In later years I did some writing, but he considered my early prospects as negligible. He would assign such subjects as the philosophy of Cotton Mather. If he had made the subject cotton picking, I could have done better. I got permission later to write on some subjects which I at least had heard of. Two of these were "The Wildcat" and "The Coyote," on both of which a grade of *B* was inscribed. One was considered "good." On the other, he scribbled: "If this is all from your own acquaintance, it is very good. I feel some bookish passages in it." To tell the truth, old Eno's ignorance of the wildcat and the coyote was in direct ratio to my ignorance of Cotton Mather.

Late in Eno's course, I unloaded some right heavy stuff on him. Such subjects as these sound threatening at a distance of fifty years: "Dr. Jekyll," "Chaucer as a Writer," "John Ruskin, His Style and Teaching," "Plot Structure in Shakespeare's *Merchant of Venice*," and "Relation of Marlowe's *Dr. Faustus* to the Earlier Drama." None of these earthshaking efforts received a grade, which in itself could be interpreted as a gesture of despair. And, in addition, it may well be that this Harvard neophyte, misplaced in Texas, had increasing difficulty in interpreting my calligraphy.

But there were offsetting compensations in the form of other teachers, notably, Dr. William James Battle, professor of Greek; Dr. Henry Winston Harper, professor of chemistry; and Dr. William Morton Wheeler, professor of zoology. Dr. Wheeler, a young man at the time, later became one of the best known of American zoologists; he became curator of invertebrate zoology at the American Museum of Natural History after leaving Texas and later became professor of zoology at Howard University. Dr. Harper, with his calm and attractive disposition, was a source of great inspiration to all premedical students. Although he had a medical degree, he devoted more than fifty years to the development of the Department of Chemistry. A student with any ambition couldn't fail to learn chemistry from him and his associates. Only two things need be said about lovable Doctor Battle: every grade I received in his class was an A and, most important, I came to know Olive in his class.[20] There may have been a direct connection between the two.

The premedical courses in science required a great deal of time in the laboratories of chemistry, physics, and zoology. It is easy to recall how patient [*the instructors*] would be with us. Many afternoons would pass into the night, and someone would be on hand to direct us. With the lights on, they would stay with us as long as we were at work. The same was true on Saturday afternoons. This was my first glimpse of experimental work. And, while I had no flair for experimentation, this experience was of basic significance. It is worthy of note that one of the men who supervised us with such painstaking care, Dr. Carl Hartman, fifty years later published a book which is the last word on opossums.[21] While I was writing in a superficial way on the coyote and wildcat, Carl Hartman was working out the intimate details of the life of the opossum.

One of the things which tinged my early contacts with the University of Texas was my experience with baseball. A man by the name of A. Caswell Ellis was coach and boss of the team.[22] At the time, there was a good deal of feeling between the fraternities and the "barbarians." Unfortunately, this feeling involved the athletic teams. I was a "barb" and remained one until my last year, when I joined the Alpha Tau Omega fraternity, mainly at the insistence of Henry Burney and Bob McMillan.[23] I didn't have a chance the first season. The boss of the team wouldn't give me a chance. Merit and ability were flaunted. This statement would not be made were it not for the fact that there were two other players in the same situation. Conditions were about the same at the beginning of the second

[20] Olive Gray Read, later Mrs. Pat I. Nixon, had enrolled in the university in 1904.

[21] Carl Gottfried Hartman, *Possums* (Austin: University of Texas Press, 1952).

[22] Later he was professor of psychology at the university.

[23] Henry Burney was Pat's roommate at the university; later he became an attorney and judge.

season. And then things began to happen. The unfairness became more and more obvious to the student body. So the boss
had to unbend a bit. By this time, a coach had been brought in
from the outside, but his attitude was influenced by Ellis's desires. His name was Ralph F. Hutchinson. This year I was
permitted to play [center field] in most of the games, although
I was classed as a substitute in the Cactus[24] and made the long
trip which the team made each year. We played, among others,
the Cleveland Indians, San Antonio of the Texas League, St.
Edward's College, Tulane, Alabama, Arkansas, Drury, Trinity,
Add Ran, Baylor, and Southwestern. Of the thirty games
played, we won twenty. The 1905 schedule of twenty-five
games, of which we won seventeen, included Vanderbilt, Mississippi, and Missouri.

My batting average on the University of Texas team has
grown with the years and with the telling to such an extent that
I hesitate to set it down from memory. I have checked with the
athletic department and find that the old records have not been
preserved, so I am safe and rather sure when I set down my
batting average for my last year as around .400. Late in the
season of 1905 a circumstance, disappointing and regrettable,
occurred. I had been accepted as a fixed asset in center field
and was playing in all the games. Jimmie had come to take an
increasing interest in my expenditures because it became necessary for me to borrow some money from him to get by on.[25] One
day a letter came forbidding me to make any of the trips. He
thought I was doing too much "frolicking." This, of course,
meant giving up the game. This experience was disappointing.
But as I look back on it, I am glad that I did not bow my neck
and refuse his demand, for I was just as stubborn as he was.
Such a refusal might have been disastrous, for I was to become
increasingly dependent on him for financial assistance.

One satisfaction at Austin—and there were many—came from
spending three years at Brackenridge Hall, B Hall as it is usual-

---

24 The Cactus is the yearbook of the University of Texas.
25 Dr. J. W. Nixon.

ly known. B Hall has been called the citadel of democracy in Texas. More accurately, it could have been called the haven of the poor boy. I paid $12 a month for room and board, only $2 of which was for the room. Ten dollars a month for board seems very cheap today but may have seemed high at the time. When the building was completed ten years before, according to J. J. Lane in his *History of the University of Texas,* a meal of soup, sirloin steak, potatoes and other vegetables, coffee, and dessert could be bought for twelve cents. This sort of economy fitted well the condition of my pocketbook. My last year at Bingham had cost $386; my first year at the university, $280. The next two years amounted to $305 and $345, respectively. To live on $30 to $40 a month, even in those days, was not easy. Clothing, books, and incidentals had a habit of rising beyond their expected figures. It was not easy when the meager income from the Denman farm—owned jointly by Jimmie, Zeb, [*Judge Leroy Denman*], and me—was at the mercy of uncertain seasons. This income did suffice, but there were no luxuries. Twenty-five cents for an occasional ticket to the peanut gallery of the Hancock Opera House, a ride on the streetcar—we usually walked the mile to town—a rare meal purchased outside B Hall—that's about all.

There were many things which might be mentioned [*about student life*]: my association with Harry Peyton Steger, our shirttail parades down Congress Avenue, our March 2nd celebrations, Carrie Nation's visits to the University, the fights on the campus after the A&M football game, our obstreperous behavior in the peanut gallery of the Hancock Opera House, and many others.

In spite of any disappointments or prejudices that may have involved me at the University of Texas, the fact remains that it was there that Olive Gray Read and I met. That happy circumstance outweighs all other considerations. The Tenth Street Methodist Church, at the beginning of the school year in 1904, invited all freshman students to a reception at the church.[26] She

---

[26] Olive was a freshman; Pat, of course, was a junior in 1904.

and I attended and were introduced by Linda Paine of Lufkin. She was seventeen, and I was nineteen. We made a go of things from the start. We had a mutuality of interests which has continued to this day. I remember now the blue dress she wore. She was never more lovely. She went home to Mrs. Kirby's and told her roommate, Linda Paine, that she had found her brown-eyed boy. I told myself that I had found my hazel-eyed girl.

Happily for both of us, we were in Dr. W. J. Battle's Greek class. She had studied the subject [*Greek*] at Mineola, but the subject was new to me. We made a habit of sitting near each other in class and could often be seen on a campus bench, but we were not always studying Greek. Her previous experience had much to do with my receiving a regular succession of *A* grades in Greek.

Our contacts in other directions were many. We played tennis, walked the Peripatus, went walking in the country on Sunday afternoon, took in an occasional show at the Hancock Opera House. We would have night dates as often as Mrs. Helen Kirby would permit, and invariably she would have to send me home with a warning voice from the stairway that it was ten o'clock. Much of our courting was done at the home of Mr. and Mrs. W. R. Long, who lived at 814 West 23rd Street. Mr. Long is a first cousin to Olive. Little Robert, aged five, was a constant source of annoyance. He even insisted on going in the Long buggy with us when we went to get ice. We tried to discourage him by forcing him to sit on the ice all the way back, but that didn't cool his desire to pester us.

So, logically, it wasn't long until she was wearing my ATO pin. This event took place on a bench in the attractive grounds of the State Hospital, which was a favorite trysting place for university students. It was not an expensive pin, and she understood why. We both thought the red rubies on the Maltese cross were beautiful and meaningful.

Our relations became more close as the months came and went. We both seemed to take it for granted that our futures lay in the same path. It was a short year for us both. I was to be graduated in June and would be going to Johns Hopkins in

September. That meant long but not uncertain separation. So our newfound happiness was tinged with sadness. It was late in May that we were visiting in the home of Mr. and Mrs. W. R. Long. We were alone on the gallery. It was about time to take her to her room. I asked her to marry me and she accepted. We both knew I would be gone at least four years, and we both accepted the situation with equanimity. We both felt that our careers were so fused that only happiness could follow our long period of waiting, although we did not dream that our wedding was seven years in the future.

When on Wednesday, June 14, 1905, the Twenty-second Annual Commencement of the University of Texas was held in the University Auditorium, the exercises were very simple. There was some music and a prayer. Then the degrees were conferred by President William L. Prather, followed by the benediction. There was no address. As a final example of the impediments that had come my way, my name was placed on the program with those receiving Bachelor of Arts instead of Bachelor of Science degrees. After graduation, someone told me that I stood eighth in the class and that, had I stood seventh, I would have made Phi Beta Kappa. Harriet Smither was number seven.[27] Unsophisticated as I was, I doubt whether I even knew about the existence of Phi Beta Kappa.

So I left Austin with Olive's promise to wait for me in my heart and an acceptance from the School of Medicine of the University of Texas in my pocket.[28]

[27] Again, Pat is in error. The first fifteen students were elected to Phi Beta Kappa; he ranked sixteenth in his class. Harriet Smither was for many years Texas State Archivist.

[28] Pat had been accepted at the University of Texas Medical School but then decided to go to Johns Hopkins instead.

2

The Medical Student

~⦿~

JUST WHEN I DECIDED to be a doctor is unclear. As far back as I can remember, the decision had been made. Even as a little boy on the farm, I observed Jimmie at his work and felt then that I would like to follow in his professional footsteps. At Austin, my course was shaped for admission to the medical school at Galveston.

Shortly after graduation from the university, I received a letter from Dean W. L. Carter saying how glad he would be to have me in Galveston, adding that students with such thorough preparation were most welcome. Certainly, I could have looked forward to four profitable years, with the main departments headed by such men as Dr. Carter, Dr. James E. Thompson, Dr. Edward Randall, Dr. Marvin L. Graves, Dr. William Keiller, Dr. A. E. Thayer, and Dr. J. F. Y. Paine.

But I didn't go to Galveston. Late in the summer, Dr. W. J. Hildebrand, who was his partner at Gonzales, urged Dr. J. W. Nixon to consider Johns Hopkins. He explained that [*Johns Hopkins*] was a young, active school which had graduated only nine classes. After an exchange of letters, my grades at the University of Texas were sent in. There were twenty *A*'s, twenty-one *B*'s, eight *C*'s, one *D*, and one Eno *E*. Word came back quickly that my grades were satisfactory and that I had been accepted on condition that I take a course in French. This I could do at night at the Berlitz School of Languages. So, again I was on my way out of the state. In 1900, it had been on the advice of Major Russell; this time, of Dr. Hildebrand. As my memory has

turned backward, my gratitude to these two men has been renewed. To me, they were real benefactors who contributed
much to my career.

The six years at Johns Hopkins determined the destiny of my
professional life. This young and virile institution was pointing
the way of medical education, and I became a part of it. There
was much that was routine and much that was tedious, but
there was nothing that was stagnant. New conceptions and new
techniques were being utilized successfully. Only the very highest type of student was being accepted, since a college degree
along with other requirements was necessary for admission.
These early graduates of Johns Hopkins became teachers in
other schools and leaders of the profession.

The heart of Johns Hopkins was located in the Big Four:
Osler, Welch, Halsted, and Kelly. In my eyes, Sir William Osler
was the greatest physician who ever lived. He was held up to
our class as the ideal physician, and he still fills that place in the
eyes of the medical world, even though he has been dead
[*many*] years.[1] Dr. Osler left Hopkins for Oxford shortly after
I arrived. Although a freshman, I attended all his clinics and
absorbed something of the spirit of the man. I recall one lecture
he gave on Hirschsprung's Disease. He had published a book on
diagnosing abdominal tumors a few years before and was still
interested in the subject. As if it were yesterday, I can clearly
recall his benign countenance and his melodious voice as he
said, "Observe the large, hypertrophied colon." Before him was
a young boy with an abdomen twice normal size.

But, more than that do I recollect about Dr. Osler, personal
recollections of the man himself and recollections gained from
reading practically everything he ever wrote and from reading
and rereading Harvey Cushing's biography.[2] To me, he was and
has continued to be a source of inspiration. His love for litera-

---

[1] Sir William Osler, 1849–1919, taught at McGill (1875–1884), at the University of Pennsylvania (1884–1888), at Johns Hopkins (1888–1905) where he held
the post of professor of medicine and physician-in-chief, and at Oxford (1905–
1911).
[2] Harvey Cushing, *The Life of Sir William Osler*, 2 vols. (New York: Oxford
University Press, 1925).

ture and history was highly contagious. Anything which I may have achieved along the line of medical history is traceable directly to the influence of Dr. Osler.

The other three of the Big Four meant far less to me. Dr. William H. Welch was a great pathologist, a great leader, a great inspirer of medical benefactions.[3] "Popsy," as the students called him, was the leader in Hopkins medical circles after Dr. Osler left. My impression of this truly great man was given to Olive in [*a letter of*] May, 1908:

> I broke away from my very attractive book on the above subject [clinical microscopy] last night and went over to McCoy Hall at the academic department to hear Dr. Welch talk on preventive medicine. Dr. Welch is professor of pathology in the medical school and is much beloved by the students and all others who know him. He is one of the four fathers of the medical school and hospital, a man whose head is hoary white, yet he has never married—to me that is the strange and pitiful side of his life; it's hard for me to understand. It is said that in his young days the girl he loved proved faithless to him; if so, then the girl was the loser, for none of them is too good for him.

Dr. William S. Halsted was a great surgeon and a great hermit.[4] His accidental addiction to cocaine, even though it was temporary, doubtless had a bearing on the latter characteristic. He had few friends, and few sought his association, except in a professional way. Howard A. Kelly was definitely and deservedly the least of the four.[5] It is significant that no one has tackled the writing of his life, while the other three have had worthy, full-length biographies. Even after deliberation of [*many*] years, I am very sure that he was the smallest big man I ever knew. This opinion is based on personal experience. I served a year's internship in his department of gynecology. I realize that Dr. Kelly made many contributions to his specialty,

[3] William Henry Welch, 1850–1934, was a pioneer in bacteriology; his work with gas-producing bacillus led to important discoveries in the treatment of contaminated wounds.

[4] William Stewart Halsted, 1852–1922, was renowned for the development of surgical procedures for breast cancers and inguinal hernias.

[5] Howard A. Kelly, 1858–1943, developed advanced techniques for hysterectomies and myomectomies and for kidney surgery and uterine suspensions.

wrote several textbooks, invented several instruments (he was accused of pilfering the idea of some of these), brought Max Broedel,[6] the great medical illustrator, to Johns Hopkins, and was outspoken, at YMCA meetings and elsewhere, in his attachment to the Great Physician. He even liked to have it noised about that he said a silent prayer just before each operational incision. Maybe that was for the soul of the surgeon rather than the safety of the patient. But all these cannot enlarge the caliber of the man in my eyes.

Why do I say this? Why do I devote so much space to a little man like Kelly and so little to a big man like Osler? Osler's story has been told many times. Kelly's has not and the medical world ought to know.

One morning, he operated on a girl of about eighteen. This was a ward patient, and he had not seen her before and knew nothing about her except what was presented by her medical history. When he made the incision, he found a bilateral hydrosalpinx. The ovaries were normal; the uterus was normal. He began to say, "What a beautiful specimen! What a beautiful specimen!" Then he muttered to himself, "*Puella publica, puella publica*" "woman of the street, woman of the street"! Quickly grabbing artery forceps and scissors, he removed, with his usual dexterity, uterus, tubes, and ovaries. The added danger to the life of the girl and the prolonged misery of her afterlife did not enter in. He had his beautiful specimen, but he had outraged the sensibilities of all who saw and had scarred his own soul.

One other personal confirmation of the puniness of Howard A. Kelly: one day in the bacteriological laboratory, I was working through some discarded culture plates and found what I proved to be a growth of gonococcus from a specimen of urine from the kidney. I followed through on this unusual finding, made a complete survey of the literature, made photographs of the removed kidney, and wrote a paper on the subject, "Gonococcal Infections of the Kidney." This paper was accepted by

6 Max Broedel, 1870–1941, a German art teacher and medical illustrator, established the department of art as applied to medicine at Johns Hopkins.

Surgery, Gynecology, and Obstetrics and appeared in the issue of April, 1911.[7] As a terminal footnote, I added this: "I am under obligation to Dr. E. K. Cullen, in whose service the patient was admitted, for the privilege of reporting the second case. Dr. G. L. Hunner has very kindly put the bacteriological notes of the first case at my disposal."[8] To an old country boy, just graduated from medical school, this seemed like a real accomplishment.

In the meantime, my letters kept Olive informed about the progress of the paper:

> The article which I mentioned in my last letter is just about finished and it's a weight off my mind. I have had it typewritten, and to me it sounds pretty good, but you know how prone we are to think well of our own products. It remains now to see whether a good journal will publish it. I think that *Surgery, Gynecology, and Obstetrics* will accept it. . . . During the two weeks just passed I have had a plentiful lack of something to do. I'm frank to admit that I have very little to show for the time spent. I have done some studying and a good deal of reading, and I have finished the medical article which I was writing; in the preparation of this I read fifty or sixty articles, some of which were in German or French. Dr. Burnam, one of the older men on the staff, pronounced it "very well done."[9] It remains to be seen whether the publishers will have an equally good opinion of it. . . . Since I began this letter I have received word from the editor of *Surgery, Gynecology, and Obstetrics* that my article has been accepted, so I am a little proud of the first attempt of your [*future*] husband.

But Dr. Kelly met me in the corridor one day and, in a great fit of anger, told me that I had done him a great injustice. "All work from the department should be credited to the head of the department, and I am head of the department. G. L. Hunner and E. K. Cullen have nothing to do with it." Up to that time, Dr. Kelly had never spoken to me and didn't even know me by

---

[7] Pat I. Nixon, "Gonococcal Infections of the Kidney: Report of Two Cases," *Surgery, Gynecology, and Obstetrics* 12 (April, 1911): 331–341.

[8] Ernest K. Cullen was resident gynecologist; Guy L. Hunner was associate in gynecology. He also headed the Female Cystoscopic Clinic.

[9] Curtis Field Burnam, 1877–1947, was resident gynecologist. He specialized in surgery, radiology, and urology.

sight. But he made some inquiries, and he knew me that morning when we met near the elevator in the Surgical Building. His face grew red, and he became more and more violent. He gave me no chance for explanation and apology, either of which I would gladly have given. He was technically correct in his contention, even though I was completely ignorant and innocent of what I had done. But he wouldn't listen to any explanation then or later.

In reality, I might have thanked him for his tirade. I learned afterwards that I was slated for one of the assistant residencies the next year. If this had happened, my marriage to Olive would have been postponed indefinitely, and that would have been tragic. It would have meant that, by our postponed wedding, our children would have been entirely different from the four fine boys we have. So, perhaps, I should feel more kindly toward Howard A. Kelly, the little big man.

But I have gotten well ahead of my story. The six years I spent at Hopkins comprised the formative period of my professional life. I did not need to read Osler's great essay "The Master-Word in Medicine" to learn early that work, hard, unceasing work, was the lot of the medical student. In other years, I had not known how to work or how to study. Now, it had come down to an individual matter: work and survival became synonymous. But it was work of a practical, everyday variety. I spent long hours in the laboratories and hospital wards. I bought a few textbooks, but most of the work was assignments which took me to the original sources in the library. Many of these were found in German or French periodicals, through which I travelled very haltingly. The courtesy, the kindness, and the willing assistance of the librarian, Miss M. W. Blogg, is well remembered. I had the best of teachers during the first two years, the preclinical years, men like Franklin P. Mall in anatomy, William H. Howell in physiology, John J. Abel in pharmacology, Walter Jones in physiological chemistry, William H. Welch and W. C. MacCallum in pathology. These men were the very best in their subjects; all were fine citizens, likeable and approachable—all except Dr. Mall, who was irritable and crotchety. He was strictly business, no foolishness and no familiarity, but withal he was one of the most eminent of anatomists and investigators.

These preclinical years were basic and preparatory. The real test and the real satisfaction came during the two final years. These were spent mostly on the wards. These years covered medicine, surgery, gynecology, obstetrics, orthopedics, and other specialties. Teachers such as these are an unforgettable blessing: L. F. Barker, William S. Thayer, Tom Brown, Tom Boggs, and Charles P. Emerson in medicine; J. M. T. Finney and Joseph Bloodgood in surgery; T. S. Cullen, Guy Hunner, and E. H. Richardson in gynecology; and J. Whitridge Williams and J. M. Slemons in obstetrics. Much could be said about this group of unusual men, by tradition and by sequence of time secondary to the Big Four. However, men like Dr. Finney, Dr. Cullen, Dr. Bloodgood, and Dr. Richardson were secondary to few men in their line. Dr. Finney was the students' ideal, as man and as surgeon.[10] He used to tell us that it is just as important to know what not to do as it is to know what to do. To the relief of his friends, he put this negative action into practice when he declined the presidency of Princeton University. His autobiography, *A Surgeon's Life,* "reflects a man singularly free from the self-consciousness and conceits common to most men."[11]

Classroom teaching was kept at a minimum at Hopkins. Most of my time was spent in the laboratory, the ward, and the autopsy room. Laboratory work with Dr. Bloodgood or Dr. C. P. Emerson is remembered with the same satisfaction as ward rounds by Dr. Barker, Dr. Finney, or Dr. Cullen. Keenly anticipated were the weekly clinico-pathological conferences conducted by Dr. Thayer and Dr. MacCallum in the autopsy room of the old pathological building. It was to this same room that we followed our cases that died. On an autopsy performed by Dr. MacCallum on April 20, 1907, I made the following notes

[10] John Miller Turpin Finney, 1863–1942, headed Hopkins's department of general surgery. He was a president of the American College of Surgeons.
[11] Dr. Nixon did not identify the source of this quote.

in my autopsy book: [12] "Name: Louis Blahos, age twenty-seven. Clinical diagnosis: gastric tetany. There were no important lesions except in stomach. This was very much distended, extending down into the umbilical region. It was excised and distended with four liters of formalin. When opened, it showed a very much stenosed pylorus, it being only a few millimeters in diameter. This condition probably due to healing of ulcer. A fresh ulcer was found in the neighborhood of the pylorus. The parathyroids were enlarged." The notes on this case are quoted because of their brevity. Some cases required ten pages or more.

The question of expenses at Hopkins was ever-present, just as it had been since I left Luling for Bingham School. My last year at the University of Texas had cost $345.00. The first year at Johns Hopkins amounted to $700.00. For subsequent years, the amounts were $712.00, $657.00, and $918.00. When these amounts are added to previous expenditures, the total from 1900 to 1909 is $5,031.44. My sole reliance rested on my part of the income from the Denman Farm, and that was not enough.[13] For instance, by the end of 1907, I had spent $3,156.00, and my income was only $1,483.00, leaving a difference of $1,673.00. This difference and all subsequent needs were supplied by Dr. J. W. Nixon, and I gave him a note at 8 percent.

After I entered Hopkins, he practically took over my financial affairs. He wrote frequent letters, urging economy in all things. He required me to account for every cent I spent. I have before me the little notebook I kept for the purpose. Here is a sample month, which is May, 1906: baseball, 35 cents; stamps, 25 cents; shoe repair, 25 cents; board, 12 dollars; room, 6 dollars; haircut, 25 cents; medicine, iron, 25 cents; socks, 25 cents; paper, 40 cents; church, 50 cents; laundry, 75 cents; picture, 60 cents; quinine, 50 cents; suit, 15 dollars; shoes, 4 dollars; hat, 2 dollars. Such figure as these do not add up to the totals mentioned above. Tuition of $110.00 a year and railway tickets

12 The notebook is in Box 2 Folder 2, Dr. Pat I. Nixon Papers, Trinity University Archives, San Antonio; hereinafter cited as Nixon Papers.
13 The farm was owned jointly by Pat, Zeb, Dr. J. W. Nixon, and Judge Leroy G. Denman, a half brother of Laura Wood Nixon.

going and coming were the larger items. The outlay of $91.20 for a Spencer microscope, which I still have and use, was an early expenditure.

There was a tendency on my part to object to some of Dr. J. W. Nixon's requirements. This tendency came out in a letter to Olive written from Gonzales on September 12, 1906: "I am down here making final arrangements for my next year's work. To tell the truth, there are not any arrangements to make, but of course I had to come down to see them and let the Doctor tell me what he does at the beginning of each year: 'Study hard, practice economy, take advantage of your opportunities, there's always room at the top, etc., etc.' All this I have to listen to in meek submission. It's excellent advice; the rub comes in applying it at all times."

As a matter of fact, I should have been grateful to him for urging thrift on me, for the more money I spent, the more I would have to pay back. There was never any doubt about the sincerity of his interest in my welfare. He seemed to want me to be with him in Gonzales as much as possible during the summers I was at home. Whenever I would get ready to leave he would say, "You can't go home today; I haven't talked any business with you yet." He liked for me to go on country calls with him.

I played on the Johns Hopkins baseball team, most of the members of which came from the undergraduate school. I also played tennis regularly on the courts on the hospital grounds, especially during the two years I was on the staff. My entries show that I saw the Baltimore Orioles play eight times, at first for 25 cents, and then, as the high cost of living advanced, I had to pay 30, 35, and 40 cents for bleacher seats. Johns Hopkins did not emphasize football; it had a team at the time, and I saw them play one game. The institution afterwards wisely gave up intercollegiate football. I saw three Army-Navy games, two at Philadelphia and one at Princeton at a cost of $3.00, $3.50, and $5.50, including transportation.

A more logical source of culture was sought in the theater. Here are some of the plays which I saw and enjoyed: Richard

Mansfield in *Doctor Jekyl and Mr. Hyde*, Robert Mantell in *Hamlet*, Sothern and Marlow in *Romeo and Juliet*, Mrs. Fiske in *Leah Kleschna*, and Maude Adams in *Peter Pan*. No one can gainsay that such offerings at 30 to 65 cents were a real bargain. Others that I appreciated were Viola Allen, Mrs. Leslie Carter, Lew Dockstader, Grace George, Otis Skinner, Elsie Janis, William Faversham, Raymond Hitchcock, Maxine Elliott, and Marie Cahill. Some of the lesser plays were *The Prince and the Pauper*, *College Widow*, *The Clansman*, *The Virginian*, and *The Lion and the Mouse*. All these had a broadening influence on my development and, besides, they served as diversions in a busy medical student's life.

Many, if not most, of my experiences at Hopkins were communicated to Olive, who very carefully preserved the letters; there were 373 of them.[14] As an explanation of the multiplicity of the letters, I had this to offer on May 9, 1909: "I write to you not because the week is out or because I think I ought to, but because I love you and because I enjoy writing to you. Just because I'm busier than ever, I'm going to think about you all the more and obtain strength and assurance therefrom, which I cannot obtain elsewhere."

Some of these items [*discussed in my letters*] were medical, some were not. I was pretty lonely at first. In my first letter after reaching Baltimore, written on September 30, 1905, I made this observation: "Everyone lives in flats here. I have not seen an ordinary dwelling since my arrival. This is a form of life that does not appeal to me. No galleries, no yards—this can never seem like home to me." On November 11, I told her of walking through Patterson Park and finding an old friend: "I came across some Texas prickly pear. These are the only things seen here that have reminded me of home. I stood around them for quite a while, although there were other things more beautiful, but not so to me." Two months later I was expressing an early, but not permanent, opinion of the natives of Baltimore: "I am

---

[14] Typed copies of these letters are in Box 1 Folders 1–6, Nixon Papers.

beginning to long for the Lone Star State. This may be a good country, but I don't like the people here. The men never think of giving their seats to women on the cars. I can't stand to see them hanging on the straps. Perhaps the men are wise, for, after one has given his seat to a woman, she never so much as thanks him for it. It is nothing but right that she should have the seat. It is also right that she should show her appreciation by at least one word, 'thanks.' "

I repeated and enlarged for Olive an item in my diary on January 29, 1906: "Dr. Osler came in the dissecting room the other day. He put his arms around me and the student next to me and made some remark about our dissection. You can imagine how we felt with that great man leaning on us. He created quite a stir among the first-year students. He will be with us only a few days longer. Everyone hates to see him go. He is dearly beloved by all who know him, not simply because he is a great physician but because of his personality."

My social activities were few and far between. So when I "broke over," I had to tell Olive about it. The reception I attended was given on December 28, 1907, to those members of my class who were unable to go home for the Christmas holidays:

> Last night I took that contemplated step. It was a step into high society. The occasion for it all was the annual reception given to the third-year class by Dr. Thomas, professor of nervous diseases, and his wife.[15] It was a very formal affair. I along with others donned a dress suit (I borrowed it from Higgins) and broke into society. Several of this season's debutantes were there and many others with their broad *a*'s who were equally as distasteful to me. I went more because of curiosity and appreciation of the invitation than for having a good time. But I was surprised that things went along so easily. Except for slight discomfort of the formal dress, I enjoyed the evening very much. We chatted and sang college songs most of the time. Dr. Finney, who is an old Princeton man, surprised and pleased us all by singing "Old Nas-

---

[15] Henry M. Thomas, 1861–1925, headed the outpatient department as well as the department of nervous diseases.

sau." And then came the refreshments, which were by no means
light. I am awfully glad I went, though I wouldn't care for that
sort of thing every night in the week. I would a thousand times
rather sit alone and talk with you than be entertained by any or
all of this season's buds.

Although she didn't say so, Olive must have thought her prospective husband was impossibly prudish when she read this,
written in June, 1908: "I degraded myself Monday night by
going to a prize fight, and in a theater with a questionable reputation, too. Three women graced the audience with their honorable (?) presence. Everybody smoked, drank beer, and kept
his hat on. I indulged only in the last of these privileges. I
haven't much to say about the fight. The outcome was to land
the victor behind bars and to put the victim in the hospital with
a fractured skull and hemiplegia. This was my first, and I hope
it shall be my last, prize fight. I went to see what it was like and
don't care to go again."

Busy as I was and short as I was of funds, it is a little surprising how often I left Baltimore. References were made to this in
my diary. Here are three trips about which I wrote Olive.

I can't begin to tell you all that I saw in Washington. I took
in all the points of interest, including the Capitol, White House,
Congressional Library, Treasury, State, War and Navy Building,
Corcoran Art Gallery, Navy Yards, Washington's Monument, and
several national museums. I was very much impressed with the
beauty of the city of Washington. It is such a contrast to Baltimore; where our streets are narrow and irregular, theirs are wide
and symmetrical. And, too, the national parks add considerably to
Washington's beauty.

[This about the Army-Navy football game at Princeton]:
President Roosevelt and many other important men witnessed the
game. There were about thirty thousand people inside the
grounds. In spite of threatening weather, the women were out
wearing their costly silks and furs. I have never before seen such
a display of dresses and wraps. It was rather cold, all the rivers
being frozen over, but the weather was entirely forgotten after
the game began.

I hardly know how to tell you about the Exposition at Jamestown.[16] I won't begin with a long, drawn-out account of what I saw there. I met a friend just as I was starting to the grounds, and, as he was also just going out, we went together and together we covered most of the ground pretty thoroughly. We began systematically and took the buildings in order. I was very much pleased with everything. I regret that I didn't have more time to spend there. In two days we could not see thoroughly all there is to be seen. It would take a whole week to do that. There are some buildings, e. g., the history building, where we could easily spend a day or two and never get tired. In this building there are all sorts of historical relics and records. We saw many of the things that once belonged to George Washington, among them the tent that he used throughout his campaigns. I remember seeing there, too, the commission of John Paul Jones signed by John Hancock, the original Declaration of Independence, the first account of the John Smith–Pocahontas incident, and many other interesting things too numerous to mention. It was rather difficult to get something to eat on the grounds. I heard someone forcibly sum up the conditions as follows, "Ask for what you want, eat what they bring you, and pay what they charge you."

Many trips to Washington were made for one reason or another. One of these, on November 23, 1907, was notable in that the International YMCA Convention was in session:

I have seen and experienced much. I wouldn't try to estimate in dollars and cents what has been mine to enjoy yesterday and today. As I had intended, I went to Washington yesterday at noon and came home last night at midnight. I was fortunate in hearing [*William Jennings*] Bryan at the afternoon session of the convention, and by this I was repaid for the time spent and for the inclemency of the weather. To see thirty-five hundred people, mostly men, gathered in that great hall was an impressive sight, but to hear one of the great men of the country give us positive views on things eternal was an impetus to continue in the ways of right thinking and right living in spite of all arguments and temptations to the contrary. Last night the meeting was addressed by two well-known men of the country. Both made splendid addresses. This finished my day for yesterday. But this morning, I was very agreeably surprised to find that Bishop Wilson was to preach for us,

[16] This exhibition, commemorating the founding of Jamestown in 1607, was held at Hampton Roads, Virginia, April 26–December 1, 1907.

and he made a good talk. But to cap the climax of my two days, I heard Bryan again at the men's meeting at Ford's Opera House this afternoon. He delivered his famous lecture, "The Prince of Peace." I can't express in words my admiration for him and for his subject. He talked for an hour and a half, and I would gladly have listened another hour and a half. I have never before listened to a man who came so near to literally lifting me from my seat by the power of his words. This lecture along with the other things that I have enjoyed today and yesterday has meant more to me than I can tell. I feel that I have a better insight into, and hence a firmer grasp upon, life and its hereafter.

With absolute disregard for my personal welfare and, at the same time, with absurd inconsistency, I set down this remarkable journey for Olive in March, 1909. It is amusing to conjecture whether I wore an overcoat:

My trip to Washington on [President Taft's] Inaugural Day was a stormy one. From the paper I sent you, you will get a better idea than I can give about the conditions. A fierce snow and ice storm the night before made it next to impossible to reach Washington. (Strange to say the weatherman predicted "Smiling Skies for Inauguration Day.") I got up at 5:30 and had the pleasure of walking through the snow to the station, the street-car system being paralyzed. It is reported that over one hundred miles of electric wire were down in Baltimore alone. My stay at the electric terminal (for I had intended going on the electric line) was long and uninteresting; with a sleepy head and a hungry stomach, I waited until afternoon, when I went to the B&O depot where I got a train at 2:30 P.M. The road was in a frightful condition; about six hundred poles were down between here and the capital city, many of which were lying across the railroad track. From the car window I could get some idea of the fury of the storm; telegraph poles were snapped off at the ground, and the wires were bundled into a tangled network, all covered and weighted down with ice and snow. We went the distance of forty miles in three hours; we had to wait for the men ahead to cut the poles and throw them off the track. These three hours would have been more tiresome had it not been for three giggling girls near me who entertained the crowd with their antics. I got to Washington in time to see the last part of the parade. It was worth the trip over to see the crowd; Pennsylvania Avenue from Capitol to White House was one mass of humanity, made up of all sorts and conditions of men, all filled with the carnival spirit. At night, the fireworks near the Washington Monument were fine. I struck up with one of the men of my class, and we saw the sights together. We got back to Baltimore at 12:30. It was a good experience, if it was a hard one. So far I haven't suffered any ill effects, though I rather expected them, for I waited till I got my feet wet before I put on overshoes.

Seen in summary, these activities seem excessive, but they were not. They were not only educational, but they were recreational and diversionary. At the time I was at Hopkins, there was apprehension concerning the health of the medical students, especially as to tuberculosis. More than one of my own class broke down and had to withdraw, at least temporarily. So the students were urged to avoid too close application to work. These amusements off the hospital area were thus a protection against disease, even though they took something from my hard-earned funds.

Of my many visits to Washington, few were more significant than the one I made in the fall of 1908. I was about to enter my final year in the medical school, so was able to appreciate the attractions afforded by the meeting of the International Congress of Tuberculosis, September 21 to October 12. Advance programs announced the coming of the medical giants of that day: General George M. Sternberg, Abraham Jacobi, Theobold Smith, William H. Welch, Sir William Osler, A. S. Warthin, H. Noguchi, Victor C. Vaughn, William T. Councilman, and J. G. Adami; and from abroad such men as Robert Koch, A. Calmette, C. von Pirquet, and Arnold C. Klebs. A high spot in my memories is the moment the great and dynamic Teddy Roosevelt came in unannounced and began his speech in these words: "I could not deny myself the privilege of saying a word of greeting to this noted gathering." Also remembered is the heated discussion between Koch and M. P. Ravenal of the University of Michigan as to the relationship of the bovine tubercule bacillus to the human strain. The old master, with dogged tenacity, held that the bovine type sometimes caused pulmonary tuberculosis, whereas Ravenal produced confirmatory proof that bovine tu-

berculosis is practically always limited to the glands of the neck.
This is what Olive read about the congress:

As I am just back from Washington, I will tell you of my few
days there. Much of my time was spent at the meetings of some of
the sections of the congress, of which there were seven, listening
to papers on the various phases of tuberculosis. I have heard so
much of the subject that I am thoroughly saturated with it—with
the subject and not with the disease, thank goodness. Papers read
in French and German were heard about as often as those in our
native tongue; these were followed by an interpreter in a short
resumé. In addition to these sectional meetings, public gatherings
were held each night when one of the foreign delegates made an
address. Many of the countries and many of the states of this country had exhibits, presenting the pathological, sociological, and economic aspects of the problem; these were an education in themselves. And then there were demonstrations and stereoptican ex-
hibitions galore. Even the much-abused phonograph was put to
good purpose pouring forth speeches containing advice as to the
best way of avoiding and combatting "the poisonous germ." There
was too much going on for one to see it all. The social side was
not neglected; yesterday afternoon about five thousand members
of the congress, including your future husband, attended the president's reception—so-called. The reception consisted in waiting in
a three-hundred-yard-long line for two hours, shaking hands with
and smiling at the presidential couple, and then passing out into
the street again, wondering if about five thousand people had not
wasted two hours of valuable time. But I am glad I went, just for
the opportunity of seeing how such affairs are pulled off, if for
no other reason. The attraction last night was a smoker at the New
Willard Hotel. [*Many of the delegates were*] smoking cigarettes
or cigars and drinking beer or kindred beverages. Naturally, I felt
out of place. I was struck by the large number of physicians who
emptied their glasses of their alcoholic contents. I'm sure the ab-
stainers were in the minority. As I say, I felt out of place here, but
when it came to the second part of the program, the lunch, I was
perfectly at home—of that you may be sure. A photograph was
taken of the two thousand delegates present; within an hour the
finished picture was brought to the banquet hall. The farewell
meeting of the congress was held this morning, with Secretary [*of
the Treasury G. B.*] Cortelyou in the chair. The roster of nations
was called, and the head of the delegation from each country replied with a few words of thanks for the kindness, hospitality, etc.,
received here. Scarcely was the roll call completed, when amid an

uproar of applause the President was unexpectedly escorted to the platform by a body of soldiers. All rose to their feet cheering, and the Marine Band struck up "The Star Spangled Banner," after which the President made a short speech lauding the courage and unselfishness of the physician. I have never seen a meeting so electrified as was this one by his sudden appearance and as sudden departure.

So, it is seen that my six years at Baltimore were full years. It is true that I had to live cheaply, but that was neither new nor difficult. My room at 1711 Fairmount Avenue was small and in the rear. The price was six dollars a month. The students in the front had larger and better-furnished quarters at about twice the cost of mine; one of these was James Russell Stewart of Indiana, who was a close friend.[17] I took my meals at Mrs. Little's boarding house on Broadway, about two blocks from my room. The medical school and hospital were about eight blocks to the north. That seemed like no distance in those days, as we walked it two or three times a day. It got quite cold in Baltimore, and the rainfall was heavy. I don't recall that I ever wore an overcoat or raincoat there, just as I have not here in San Antonio. Somewhere along the line I must have owned an overcoat, but I don't recall it. To me, an overcoat is as useless as a vest.

Some of my letters to Olive throw light on my last two years as a medical student. There was an obligation and a pleasure in keeping her informed of my progress, and often I was proud:

> I made my debut before the class this week by presenting to it one of my cases. In alphabetical order, we take our turn in getting up before the class and giving the history and symptoms of the case before us. I suppose I got along all right, but can't say for sure, since my memory was rather vague about that time. It was an easy case, and Dr. Barker asked me only a few questions about it. It was a case of exophthalmic goiter. Rapid pulse and excitement are two of the symptoms; at this particular time both the patient and the student showed these two symptoms. Now that the ice has been broken, it won't be so hard the next time. This experience demonstrated to me the fact that a fellow isn't half so

---

[17] Stewart graduated in the class of 1909 and later maintained a practice at Colorado Springs, Colorado.

wise when he is standing before the class as he is sitting back in one of the seats.

I saw a neat operation this morning. To gradually accustom you to matters medical, I am going to tell you about it. The patient, a woman of about twenty-five years, had fallen in the fire when a child and burned her chest, neck, and arms. The scar had contracted and drawn down her lower lip, so that she was continually wearing a sardonic grin. This contracting scar tissue was excised and a flap of skin taken from the arm to fill into the wound on the neck. The arm was bandaged up to the neck where it will be kept till the skin flap begins to grow into the neck. The flap will then be cut loose from the arm and fixed permanently into the neck. This girl will have to lie in this position for several days with her hand up to her face and her eyes bandaged. On seeing the uncomfortable position of the girl, one of the fellows remarked today, "What won't a woman do to improve her appearance." But she is a woman. No man, I'm sure, would submit to the ordeal in order to have a few wrinkles removed.

I've been digging away in the accustomed manner, trying to complete the work assigned for me to do. It is a sort of perpetual motion affair; no sooner do I complete one thing when another longer and larger takes its place. I am just now beginning to see clearly the magnitude of the subject which I have undertaken to master. I can see that with the completion of next year's work, I shall merely have begun the study of disease, its causes, effect, etc.

I drew my first real blood last Wednesday. A man came in with a small epithelioma (cancer) on his face, and it fell to my lot to remove it. I had always dreaded the time of my first operation, for there are always a lot of onlookers who are anxious to notice any awkwardness or error in technique. However, I went ahead, injected some cocaine into the growth, removed it without any trouble, and finished with a decently closed wound. This experience has not inspired me with any greater love for surgery than I had before; at any rate, it hasn't caused me to choose surgery as my specialty.

Medicine has its humorous as well as its serious side. I read tonight about a certain disease, that "it begins in the child by a gradual increase in the size of the calves of the legs, which are at first subjects of pride to the mother, but soon awaken her apprehension because of being out of proportion," etc. Again, "whistling, blowing, or kissing is impossible"—a deplorable state of affairs. How glad I am that you—but I won't say it.

I don't know whether I have told you that there is a typhoid epidemic here at the present time. Two of the members of our class are in the hospital and are suspected of having this disease. We had a very peculiar case of it at the clinic the other morning: this man had been delirious all throughout the course of the disease, but at this particular time he was convalescing. He said someone had put in the Philadelphia mint for him $150,900,000. When questioned on the subject, he said he didn't care to tell how the money came to be his, though he was perfectly sure the money was there. The typhoid had left him with this one delusion; otherwise he was all right. This was one of the so-called psychoses which are so common in typhoid. It is one of the many manifestations of the disease and does not signify any mental degeneration, as is popularly believed among laymen. I had typhoid fever when I was in my teens. I am hoping that that attack has rendered me immune to any future attack. I don't feel that I am any too safe for I am eating nothing that is likely to infect me, nor am I drinking any water that has not been boiled.

I had only one examination and that was in obstetrical pathology. The exam consisted of one slide which we were to describe and diagnose. I made my description all right, but, when I came to the diagnosis, I was not over sure. When I handed in my paper, I said, "Dr. Slemons, you will tell us what the section is, won't you?"[18] He opened my paper and looking at my diagnosis replied, "I don't have to tell you; you are right." This reply eased my uncertain mind and now that it is all over I am wondering how it happened.

In my regular scientific work, I am always on the lookout for peculiar things. This is my latest discovery: a man came into the dispensary yesterday with beads of perspiration (*sweat* is a more scientific word) on the right side of his face and none on the left. He could go in the hottest months of the year without perspiring on the left side, whereas, in the coldest months, he perspired profusely on the right. He said he could wear a collar two weeks on the left side of his neck and two minutes on the right without soiling it. I won't give you a technical explanation of the condition, will merely say that it is nervous in origin.

[18] Josiah Morris Slemons, 1876–1948, was associate in obstetrics.

Olive and I had hoped that I would get back to Texas in 1908. However, since this was the end of my junior year, I felt that I should stay in Baltimore and take advantage of opportunities that had presented themselves.[19] On May 31, I explained my plans to Olive:

> My card has probably already informed you that my examinations are all over. Tonight I tell you that I am highly pleased with the result of all of them. Had I written you last night, I would have said that I was satisfied with all of them except obstetrics, but today unexpected things have happened: each year ten men are chosen by their standing in this particular subject to work during the summer. These ten places are looked upon as prizes and are aspired to only by those who are very ambitious. To my great surprise, and consternation almost, my name was posted along with nine others for summer obstetrical work. All along I had known of these appointments but had not looked upon them with an envious eye, because I didn't care to be disappointed in case I was not among the chosen few—and, to tell the truth, I did not expect to be. Feeling as I do about all my examinations, I think I am safe in considering myself a fourth-year man, but there is a possibility of some of my instructors disagreeing with me, so congratulations are not in order yet.
>
> I have a most profitable summer's work planned. I am spending my mornings in the medical dispensary and my evenings in skin work and gynecology. When I get tired of these, there are plenty of other things which I can do. I expect to do some surgery, though this subject doesn't attract me as much as straight medicine. The work that I am doing requires no studying and but little mental effort, so it is quite a relaxation after the regular schoolwork is over. What I am doing now is what I expect to do all my life, except that at present I have an overseer whom I must give up when I get out on my own resources.

That obstetrical experience was pretty rugged, as set out in a letter of August 2, 1908, Olive's birthday, and in another ten days later:

> Night before last I was out from two to six-thirty. Last night I was called at twelve and got back at three. Hardly had I closed my eyes when I received a second call which kept me out till five-

---

[19] This was the only summer prior to his internship that Pat did not return to Texas.

thirty. I spent the solid morning looking after convalescent patients. This afternoon I tried to sleep, but it was so hot that I didn't have much success. As a result of this rather strenuous run, I am tired and sleepy tonight; my eyelids are heavy, my hand is unsteady.

This morning at nine o'clock I turned over my patients to my successor, Mr. Baetjer.[20] As a sort of farewell, I was kept out from twelve to five last night. My service has been full of new experiences. It comprised twenty-seven cases in all. I have paid dearly in physical capital for it, but I feel that it has been worth it. On my final visit yesterday, one woman in her generosity offered me a dollar bill. I very magnanimously refused to accept it with the remark that "we hospital doctors" have plenty of money.

The reputation of Johns Hopkins was well known in Texas. From time to time, patients from my state were in the hospital. Once I mentioned the name of Burke Baker of Houston and told of going over to Ward B to see him.[21] Great concern about another Texan was expressed in two letters of 1908. I was correct in my opinion about the gravity of the operation, but the patient did recover, although his convalescence was prolonged for many weeks, during which many fine silk sutures sloughed out. This was the only time I ever saw Dr. Finney work under great tension.

You knew Joe Brown, did you not, an ATO from La Grange?[22] He is in the hospital and is to be operated on next Tuesday. As a result of splenic anemia, he has almost bled to death a couple of times. Although he is in good health, it is considered wise to have his spleen out before it gives him any more trouble. I saw him yesterday, and he told me he was ready for the ordeal. The operation is a serious one, serious enough to cause great apprehension. [Two weeks later] Joe Brown was operated on last Wednesday. The operation was to have been done a week previously but was postponed because he had a rather severe gastric hemorrhage. The operation consisted in removing the spleen, which was forty or fifty times as large as it normally should be, so large in fact that,

[20] Walter A. Baetjer, of the class of 1909, returned to Hopkins as an assistant professor. In 1915 he invented the term *infectious mononucleosis.*
[21] Pat had known him at the University of Texas. Later Baker became a director of Banker's Trust Company in Houston.
[22] Joe C. Brown, Jr., another friend from the University of Texas, took his degree in engineering.

to get it out, it was necessary to make a twelve-inch incision along
with a six-inch cross incision. Several times there was danger of
his bleeding to death on the table, but he pulled through all
right, and the operation itself was a success. I have never had an
operation so try my nerve as did this one; I suppose my personal
interest in the patient had something to do with the anxiety. To
make up for the blood he lost, an artery from another patient
was connected with one of Joe's veins, and blood passed from one
to the other—in other words, a transfusion was done. Since the
operation, Joe has just about held his own, and since he has done
so I believe he is going to get well.

In a letter of May 10, 1908:

It fell to my lot on last Monday to talk to the class on the
action of digitalis. Well, you know my shortcomings on talking on
any subject. In spite of these, I buckled down to it and relieved
myself of the painful duty without a hitch and without a glance
at my notes (which were in my pocket, by the way). I think I'll
send you these notes, which I jotted down, for your criticism.
They will be of interest to you because the heart is mentioned
several times, and, where the heart is concerned, I know you will
be interested.

It is just twelve days till my first examination. I have worked
almost continuously and still have much ground to cover. I suppose I shall be ready when the time comes. Even though I had an
unlimited time, I could still find something else to look up. After
the strain of this strenuous year is over, I am certainly going to
take things easy. I am glad to say that I am bearing up under the
strain better than I had expected to. A short three weeks will end
it, and then comes vacation with its joys, the greatest of which is
the hope of seeing you and enjoying the pleasures which your
presence always brings to me.

In a letter of February 2, 1909:

We have resumed our psychiatric clinics at Sheppard-Pratt
Hospital this term instead of Bay View Asylum. We saw quite an
interesting old man out there yesterday; he was a prominent lawyer of good family. In his younger days, he was a courier in the
Confederate Army. For several years, he had been the victim of
spells of unconsciousness, between which he would have perfectly
lucid intervals. He told us of a battle where he lost one of his toes
by a bullet. Some days after the battle, he told a friend of his experience, who said, "Then it was a *notorious* affair for you." Since

this time, the old fellow says he has been called Notorious George Savage. He said a lawyer was a man to whom you paid "a retainer, a reminder, a refresher, and a fee," which I was able to appreciate after being told that these words were all used synonymously. He defined a physician as a man "who puts medicine, about which he knows little, into a body about which he knows less, to cure a disease about which he knows nothing"—a good definition, no doubt, in many instances.

Three items of passing interest are recorded on one page of a letter written in May, 1909:

> We had our last meeting but one at the YMCA tonight. In the absence of the president, it fell to my lot to lead the meeting, introduce the speaker, etc. It's gotten so I can do such things without much embarrassment—something I couldn't do a couple of years ago.
>
> Our group dined with Dr. Barker Thursday night; [23] Dr. Barker is Dr. Osler's successor, as you probably know, and is a wonderful man in many respects, considering the fact that he is just a little older than forty years. He encouraged us by saying that we should not expect success too early; that sudden success is likely to be short success.
>
> I lost my first patient a few days ago. It was a case of carcinoma of the liver and of course was hopeless from the beginning. There was some disagreement between the ward doctor and myself as to the presence of a coexisting pneumonia; I believed that it was present, and he not. Post mortem examination revealed that I was right.

In a letter to Olive under date of May 9, I wrote:

> Olive, the year is drawing rapidly to a close. Just sixteen days from today, I have my last examination, and one month from yesterday is Commencement Day. These few days, which will be the last of my student days, will have come and gone before we realize it. The days from now to the end will be happy days in spite of the fact that they will be busy days. It is a pleasure to work when the goal is so near, when the prize is almost won. My feelings are not unlike they were when, after a long journey from here

---

[23] Lewellys F. Barker, physician-in-chief at Hopkins, is credited with bringing the first electrocardiograph into the United States. The research division which he created in the department of medicine became the model for similar divisions in medical schools throughout the nation.

to Mineola,[24] the last few miles seemed so short because I was soon to feel the pressure of your loving arms about my neck and of your lips to mine. From this comparison, you may know that my feelings are anything but disagreeable. From my vantage point, gained with no little difficulty, I like to look back over the ground covered and see what has been accomplished, noticing where mistakes have been made, how I might have done a little differently here, and how I might have made an improvement there. It's a pleasure to feel that something worthwhile has been accomplished, to know that I have something to show for my four years' work—not something material—but something real, nevertheless. From this same vantage point, I can look a short ways into the future, and there the prospect is bright. In the midst of it all, in all and above all, there stands the figure of a lovely girl, my girl; she has stood the test of the years, she has proven herself true. About her all my future is interwoven; our lives are one and inseparable, even though our bodies are separated for a season. Her life has been the inspiration of mine; to her I owe all that has been accomplished. It will be the happiest day of my life when I can lay all at her feet, giving credit to her to whom credit is due.

My last two years at Johns Hopkins were just as full and as satisfying as the first two. The work was practical and pleasant. No grades were given in our work. All we knew was that we were getting along all right or we were not. A few days before graduation in 1909, I was told that I had been chosen as a member of Phi Beta Kappa. At the time, I didn't know that medical students were eligible. As it was, I was glad to receive the honor in medicine rather than in academic work. In a 1909 catalog of the medical school, I have marked the standing of the first ten men out of the class of fifty-three; Dr. Charles R. Austrian of Maryland, first; Dr. Walter A. Baetjer of Maryland, second; Dr. Thomas P. Sprunt of South Carolina, third; Dr. William L. Estes, Jr., of Pennsylvania, fourth; Dr. Charles R. Kingsley, Jr., of New York, fifth; Dr. Charles R. Essick of Pennsylvania, sixth; Dr. Pat Ireland Nixon of Texas, seventh; Dr. Montrose T. Burrows of Kansas, eighth; Dr. Arthur B. Cecil of Maryland, ninth; and Dr. Solomon W. Schaefer of Mississippi, tenth.

[24] Mineola was Olive's hometown.

The Medical Student

The letter of May 16, 1909, was one of the last that I wrote before graduation. In it I told of attending the three-day dedication ceremonies of the new home of the medical and chirurgical faculty of Maryland, at which Dr. Osler and Dr. Weir Mitchell were the chief speakers.[25] I had just spent the day, which was Sunday, in the ward and laboratory and went on to explain: "From my short experience, I can see how easy it would be for a physician to forget about Sunday and everything connected therewith. I have already determined to fight against this temptation." I closed the letter with a trivial incident: a ball game between the seniors and the interns. "Our team played in hospital orderly uniforms and nurses' caps. The superintendent of nurses got so indignant that she wouldn't let the nurses watch the game, much to our amusement." But the burden of the letter dealt with the closing days as a medical student:

> Naturally the thing uppermost in my mind—excepting, of course, the time when I shall see you—is the closing of the year, and the closing of this year is more significant than that of any other year. It is hard for me to realize that there are only six more days of regular work. During those days, I have three practical examinations in addition to the routine work. And then on Monday and Wednesday of next week come the final examinations in medicine and surgery. I haven't allowed myself to be uneasy about this somewhat formidable array. I have my last practical in surgery tomorrow and don't expect to lose any sleep over it tonight. From May 26 to June 8, we are free to do what we choose—at least supposedly so, but for me there is no alternative but to study in preparation for the State Board examinations, which I hope I shall stand in Cleburne [Texas], June 22. Such will not be a very pleasant way to spend commencement next week, but I'm willing to do it if I can get this burden off my mind. Anyway, there is little or nothing going on here except a reception on the night of June 8. Wouldn't it be great if we could repeat commencement week of 1905, with its buggy rides, its moonlight picnic, and its never-to-be-forgotten heart-to-heart talks.

The senior student, soon to be a doctor, grew a little boastful on May 23, 1909:

[25] S. Weir Mitchell, 1829–1914, was one of America's first great neurologists.

My written examination in medicine comes tomorrow, and that in surgery two days later; this will finish up the year's work. I have had fair practical exams and am satisfied with the result of all of them. From one of them, I was dismissed with "That's all right, Mr. Nixon; first-rate. Call the next man in." After I handed in my diagnosis in another, the examiner said, "Good work, a hundred spot." I had hoped to use the time between now and June 8 in studying for the State Board examinations, but don't suppose I'll have much time for studying at the hospital.

The final act of my life as a Hopkins medical student came on the afternoon of June 8, 1909, when I received my diploma, signed by R. Brent Keyser, president of the board of trustees; Ira Remsen, president of the university; and W. H. Howell, dean of the medical school. This occasion meant much to me, more than I could have realized at the time.

The class of 1909 were pioneers in modern medicine, but little did we realize it. We were the thirteenth class to graduate from this new institution, but this was not particularly significant to us at the time.

We sat at the feet of such men as Osler, Welch, Halsted, Cullen, Kelly, Brown, McCrae, Howell, Mall, Bloodgood, Abel, Thayer, Barker, Finney, Williams, Hunner, Slemons, Cushing, Young, and MacCallum. The medical world, up to that time, had never seen such a galaxy of medical teachers, and in all likelihood never would again. Here again, we were so close to this remarkable situation that we were unable to assess it properly.

As the years came and went, most of us became aware of the good fortune that had been ours. Slowly we came to the realization of the fact that more and more of these early Hopkins graduates were heading departments in other medical schools or were standing out in some other capacity.

This exceptional situation continued for a generation, and then there was a lag. This may have been because there were so many other good medical schools, but this was not the whole story. There was a definite falling-off in teaching capacity.

But this was not for long. The twelve of us who attended our fiftieth class reunion in connection with the biennial meeting of the Johns Hopkins Medical and Surgical Association were thoroughly convinced that Johns Hopkins is again a leader. One proof: on the second day of the meeting, eight men from the classes of 1933 and 1934 presented short papers on research work they were doing. The important thing is that every one of these eight men were heads of departments elsewhere or were in some equivalent position.

Our reunion was a thrilling experience. The accumulated reports and accomplishments of fifty years were varied and worthy, as was to be expected. In all of us, there were differing degrees of decay and dissolution. Most of us were average in such changes. But two stood out. One boasted that he still skied with his granddaughters. The other, with whom I played on the Johns Hopkins baseball team for three years, had difficulty with his memory. Several times each day, he would ask, "Where are you from?" Each time I would tell him San Antonio, he would ask, "Did you ever run across a man down there named Pat Nixon?"

In a letter to Bill Estes,[26] I tried to set down some of the emotional and personal factors that affected us:

I am on a train, far enough away from Baltimore to assess, partially at least, the heartwarming experiences that have been ours. To me, and doubtless to you, our reunion was not a mere desire to get together, not just a homecoming. More, it was the fulfilling of an obligation incurred fifty years ago, a sort of reckoning, a stocktaking, as it were.

Fifty years ago we went forth in youth and enthusiasm. We took our talents and applied them to the fullest. Some of us may have faltered for the moment. Some fell early by the wayside. Most of us pushed forward and finished the race with heads high and consciences clear. Surely, in our mind's eye we can hear the applause of our Alma Mater: "Well done!"

Everybody in the hospital and medical school—nurses, students, doctors, employees—all shepherded us as though we were

[26] William L. Estes, Jr., of the class of 1909, later practiced surgery in Bethlehem, Pennsylvania. He was a president of the American College of Surgeons.

their very own. It was good to be cared for so tenderly and yet so understandingly.

Through the mists of fifty years came the faces of Baetjer, Cole, Dimon, Estes, Gentry, Harvey, Kingsley, Nixon, Schaefer, Stick, Wyatt, and Youmans. We missed the other nine. We missed, perhaps more, that larger number who had finished their course. In the words of Osler, we paid them silent homage in unspoken thoughts. Together we talked, and we asked questions. We recalled, and we forgot. We repeated our questions and varied our answers. As we recalled those dim distant days, there was no word of disagreement, discouragement, ugliness, or failure. We recalled and were content.

The inexorable ravages of time were upon us in mind and in body. We shall not pass this way again.

But, surely, somewhere out there in the eternities of time and space, we shall meet again. There, decrepitude and decay will have passed away.

At the banquet of the Johns Hopkins Medical and Surgical Association, we were each given a beautiful medallion commemorating our fiftieth anniversary. On one side there is a replica of Johns Hopkins' monument with our name below. On the reverse side there is the Johns Hopkins seal with its motto, *Veritas vos liberabit*. This medallion is a tangible reminder of our reunion. But above and beyond, is the assuring conviction of the worthiness of our Alma Mater.

3

The Diary

~ჟ~

Up to now, much of what I have set down has come from memory, prompted by a few notes. Now I want to record the entries from a journal which I kept from January 24, 1906, to June 18, 1907. Here will be found some of the more trivial as well as some of the more intimate details of my first two years at Hopkins. Keeping a diary is monotonous and time-consuming, but it is rewarding. In my case, the greatest reward came on the first page: my hero touched me.

January 24

Took out sternum and part of ribs from our subject today. Did fairly well in both anatomy and histology. Good letter from Callaway tonight.[1]

January 25

Cut out lungs from Jim Johnson. Dr. Osler came around to dissection room. Put his arms around Drinkard and me, remarking about our dissection. Letter from Zeb. Went with Higgins tonight to get his streetcar damage money.[2]

January 26

"That's very nice, push right ahead," says Dr. Mall, otherwise known as "Johnnie."[3]

[1] Gib Calloway was a friend from the University of Texas.
[2] William H. Higgins, of the class of 1908, later was an internist in Richmond, Virginia.
[3] Franklin Paine Mall, 1862–1917, an anatomist, did research in embryology and in blood vessels, spleen, liver, and heart.

January 27
Dissected a little this morning. Went to Dr. Futcher's clinic this noon.[4] He showed four cases of diabetes. This recalls Dr. Osler's clinic of last week: a case of cretinism and one of giant enlargement of colon, the boy having gone three weeks without a stool. No theater tonight. Stewart's gone flossying or fussing.

January 28
Went to YMCA meeting at Ford's this afternoon and church tonight at Mt. Vernon Methodist Church.

January 29
We split our head today, so Kingsley and I are over in the corner "growling."[5] Went to medical historical meeting tonight. Good talks on "The Gold-headed Cane" by Drs. Osler, Futcher, Cushing, and McCrae.[6] Letters from Mama and Sadie.[7]

January 30
Good day's work. To my sorrow, nothing doing in the mail line.

January 31
Fair day's work. Still no mail. Took walk with Partridge.[8] Got note from Mr. Coy: "due $100."

February 1
Worked all day in anatomy. And still no mail. Looks like I will never get *that* letter.

February 2
Read *Hamlet* tonight. Still no mail except a foolish letter from L—— H—— in H—— V——. Got called on in physiology. Did pretty well, only thing: I didn't know exactly what caused osmotic pressure.

---

[4] Thomas Barnes Futcher, 1871–1938, was professor of clinical medicine.
[5] Charles R. Kingsley, Jr., of the class of 1909, later practiced obstetrics and gynecology in Staten Island, New York.
[6] The "gold-headed cane" was a symbol of medical preeminence in seventeenth-century London. A cane ceremony still exists in some medical schools and medical societies. The term is taken from a book by William Macmichael, *The Gold-Headed Cane* (1827).
[7] Sadie Epstein was a childhood friend from Luling.
[8] Carroll D. Partridge, of the class of 1908, practiced as a roentgenologist in Cudahy, Wisconsin.

The Diary

February 3

Saw Robert Mantell in *Hamlet* this afternoon. Pretty good. Letter from Olive today.

February 4

Went to Mt. Vernon Methodist Church this morning and united myself with that congregation.[9] Went to men's meeting at Ford's Theater this afternoon. Mr. Morris P. Fykes of Penn. spoke. Good talk. Based his talk on story of "Buck," a dog, by Jack London. Heard a good practical talk by Dr. Howard Kelly at YMCA tonight.

February 5

"Johnnie" told us today we would be through with our head in two weeks. Hope we will. Took my first French lesson tonight. Very cold going over.

February 6

Eight degrees above zero today: too cold for a Texan. "Push right ahead." Paid all my debts, including board and room rent.

February 7

"Oh! That looks nice. That mylohyoid is good," says Mall. Had our picture made in the laboratory today. Letter from Alta.[10]

February 8

Ground covered with snow; still falling. Went to French. Fletcher of Georgia went for his first lesson.[11] It must have gone to his head, for he could not stand up very well after the operation.

February 9

Sloppiest day I ever saw: rain after snow on a surface sewerage system. Dissected eye in both anatomy and histology. Dr. Howell: "Have you studied the spleen in histology?" Miss Child of Philadel-

---

[9] "Much could, and perhaps should, be said in connection with my waiting until I was twenty-three years old before I joined the church. It was not as casual as my simple record would indicate. . . . Suffice it now to say that I, although I never had any feeling of dramatic conversion, always carried a conviction that I was really born into the church or very close to it." Dr. Nixon's unpaginated manuscript in the possession of Dr. Pat I. Nixon, Jr., San Antonio; hereinafter cited as Nixon Ms.

[10] Alta Estelle Nixon (Mrs. James Knox Walker, later Mrs. Joseph Edgar Fisher) was Pat's sister.

[11] Harry Quigg Fletcher, of the class of 1909, practiced surgery in Chattanooga, Tennessee.

115

phia: "I don't remember."[12] Note from Mrs. Sheridan, my Sunday school teacher.

February 10

Tried to dissect this morning but couldn't do much: too many fellows fussing Miss Spencer. They all have Spencer carditis. Saw my first autopsy this morning; it was not so bad. Quigg and I went to French this afternoon.[13] I guess we are pretty swift French students. Letter from Olive this morning. Wrote to Olive, Alta, Sadie, and Leslie. And now I am going to mow my beard.

February 11

Went to Sunday school and then to church where I heard a good sermon by Brother Sheridan on "Culture." Went to YMCA this afternoon. Mr. Erdman of Germantown, Penn., spoke.

February 12

Good day's work on the eye. Letters from Mama and Callaway. Picture of Callaway. Went to French tonight. Quigg and I are the best two in our class: there are only two in the class.

February 13

Letters from Mama and Nina. Saw Sothern and Marlowe in *Romeo and Juliet*. Mighty good.

February 14

Signed up for another part today. Will finish my head tomorrow. Meader[14] sneezes and takes exercise on Essick. Letter from Zeb.

February 15

Finished dissection of head, thank goodness! Had our first lecture in neurology by Dr. Sabin.[15] She beats Dr. Harrison.[16] I am getting

[12] Florence C. Child, of the class of 1909, was with the United States Public Health Service.

[13] Harry Quigg Fletcher (see n. 11 above).

[14] Fred Marlin Meader, of the class of 1909, was with the United States Public Health Service.

[15] Florence Rena Sabin, 1871–1953, was the first woman to hold the rank of full professor at Hopkins. She was also the first woman president of the American Society of Anatomists. Her fields of specialization included anatomy and histology.

[16] Ross Granville Harrison, 1870–1959, an anatomist, was the first to devise a satisfactory method of growing tissue outside the body. He also did seminal work in neurology. He was chairman of the National Research Council, and he coordinated scientific research during World War II.

anxious about that letter again. Fletcher starred in French tonight. Only thing, he insists on saying *Ya* for *Oui*.

February 16

Worked a partly dissected part today. Will get a new subject tomorrow. "Batted Howell's eye out" in physiology.[17] Began study of brain. Higgins has joined the menagerie: he has a white rag around his neck.

February 17

Couldn't work today: our subject was not brought up. French this afternoon. Olive has either forgotten me or the U.S. mail is on the bum.

February 18–22

Not much doing. Was sick in hospital with malaria. Dr. Barker came around on 20th. Good nurses, good everything. Some of my friends: Misses Cadal, O'Connor, Krause, Henderson, and Belzer. Letters from Mama and Olive on the 22nd.

February 23

Began work on a new part today. Kingsley is three days ahead of me. I'll have to hurry. Lots to do these days. Higgins is having a time with his carbuncle. He is in hospital now.

February 24

Went to French. A coed in the class now. Took a walk with Partridge of Vermont. "Ability is a man's capital. Success is what that capital earns." "If a man's success makes him unhappy, then he has failed."

February 25

Rainy Sunday. Didn't go to church, but went to YMCA at Ford's this afternoon. Heard a fine talk by C. Bayard Mitchell of Cleveland. Subject: "The Devil and a Man." Three chief temptations: money-getting, unholy ambition, and lust. Higgins is better today. Thinks he will be out tomorrow. Carstens of Iowa got back from Chicago where his father's eyes were operated on. "Every man has a world to conquer."

---

[17] "This tendency to boast . . . is hard to explain . . . probably nothing more than outbursts of temporary elation." Nixon Ms.

February 26

A fair day's work. Neurology is somewhat unsatisfactory. Fletcher made a hit with the coed tonight. "Yesterday's unanswered mail is a mortgage on today." Lewis cussed out Birdsong.[18]

February 27

Snowed all day long. A good day's work all the way around. Essick is a worker. Stewart's vaccination is taking. "Rastus" came for my clothes. Says his ancestors are about gone.

February 28

Cold day: 16° F. Took walk with Partridge. Letter from Gilcreest.[19]

March 1

Got called on in physiology. Did all right. Stewart is laid up with an infected vaccination. I am playing doctor and nurse.

March 2

Good day. Began work on abdominal viscera. Stewart went to hospital. Cecil is also there.[20] I went up there tonight and saw Misses Cadal and O'Connor.

March 3

A rainy day. Haven't done much. Went to French this afternoon. Wrote to Olive and Gilcreest tonight. Went over to the hospital to see the sick students, and incidentally the nurses.

March 4

Went to S.S. and church this morning. Both good. Went to hospital tonight.

March 5

Not much doing today. Lewis is still in N.Y. Heard he is getting married.

March 6

Good day. Letter from Sadie. Saw Stewart and Cecil tonight, doing well.

[18] Warren Harmon Lewis, 1870–1964, professor of physiological anatomy, pioneered time-lapse photography of living cells. Julian Lee Birdsong, of the class of 1909, later practiced in Hartford, Connecticut.
[19] Edgar Lorrington Gilcreest, of the class of 1910, practiced surgery in San Francisco. Pat had known him earlier at the University of Texas.
[20] Arthur B. Cecil, of the class of 1909, practiced urology in Los Angeles.

March 7

Dr. Gilcreest and Dr. Hugh of Gainesville and Denton came to see me this afternoon.[21] Showed them through laboratory. Stewart came home tonight. Letters from Zeb and Olive.

March 8

Not much doing.

March 9

Met Hancock of my '05 class today. Case of smallpox in hospital. Took a walk with Higgins tonight.

March 10

Lazy Saturday, windy, disagreeable. French. "A clean desk tonight makes a good beginning tomorrow."

March 11

Went to S.S. and church this morning. Took a walk out to Patterson Park this afternoon. Sellards and Jeans of Kansas called. Went over to Rinde and Drinkard's room a while tonight and talked anatomy.[22] They have their exam in a month.

March 12

Blue Monday. The Negro question settled by Birdsong and Kingsley in the lab today. French tonight.

March 13

Slow snow all day. Pretty good work. Dr. Lewis was on a tear. Remarked that Miss Child should be in a room to herself. She is so noisy. A new girl in the menagerie. Higgins and I matched for her and I won.

March 14

More snow. Went down to Rinde's room and then took a walk with Higgins. Letter from Olive.

March 15

A rainy, sleety day. Last lecture in neurology by Dr. Sabin. Last recitation in physiology under Dr. Howell.[23]

---

[21] Jacob Edward Gilcreest, father of Edgar Gilcreest (see n. 19 above), was president of Dallas Medical College, which later became the medical department of Baylor University. He also served as president of the Texas Medical Association.

[22] Hamilton Rinde, of the class of 1909, practiced as a psychiatrist in Middletown, Connecticut.

[23] William Henry Howell, 1860–1945, was professor of physiology and dean of the medical school. He pioneered the study of coagulation of blood.

March 16

More snow. Exam in physiology. Did pretty well. "Johnnie" came around and complimented our dissection today. Another new girl among the animals, named Peacock. She looks it when she gets on her loud, red dress. Took walk with Higgins.

March 17

St. Patrick's Day. All of us Irishmen sported our shamrocks. Saw *Clansman* tonight. True story, good play: makes one a better Southerner.

March 18

Fine day. Went to missionary service at S.S. this morning. Took walk with Wiesender of Wisconsin.[24]

March 19

Snow and slop, lots of it. First lecture by Dr. Dawson and by Dr. Jones.[25] Jones is good. Dawson is on the bum. Letter from Mama.

> Tis easy enough to smile
> When all the world flows along like a song.
> But the man who is worthwhile is the one who smiles
> When all the world goes dead wrong.

March 20

First work in chemistry. Got polite tonight: gave a young lady the right of way and fell sprawling on the ice. Newsboys are yelling, "All about the capture of Winder, the escaped murderer. Xtra edition." Alphabet of success: (A) Attend carefully to details.

March 21

First lecture on digestion and secretion by Erlanger—a pretty good lecturer.[26] Went to Grand Opera *Faust* played by Metropolitan Opera Company. Had to stand. All was great—Caruso, Eames, Plancon, Scotti, Poehlman—all good. (B) Be prompt in all things.

March 22

A pretty good day—almost like spring. Nice work in chemistry. (C) Consider well, then decide positively.

---

[24] Arthur James Wiesender, of the class of 1909, practiced medicine in Berlin, Wisconsin.

[25] Percy M. Dawson taught physiology. Walter Jones, 1865–1935, taught physiological chemistry. He later headed the department of biological chemistry.

[26] Joseph Erlanger, 1874–1965, received the Nobel Prize for his work in neurophysiology.

The Diary

March 23

The Savoy Sextette gave a recital tonight.[27] Bill carried the air. Letter from Olive. (D) Dare to do right, fear to do wrong.

March 24

Snow tonight. Next-to-last French lesson—thank goodness. "Rastus" swears he "seen" Olive's picture in two other students' rooms. "You all must love that gal." (E) Endure trials patiently.

March 25

Talk at S.S. was made by Mr. Warner of Grace Church. Brother Sheridan ably reviewed Methodism from the beginning. Took about a four-mile walk with Gundrum of California.[28] He is a fine fellow, redheaded, good-natured, jolly, sensible. His head is level on the Negro question. (F) Fight life's battles bravely.

March 26

Quigg and I graduated tonight—thank goodness.[29] Coedski was not there to witness the performance. Lewis came around today and told me that he wanted our dissection for the study room. Letters from Nina[30] and Henry Burney. (G) Go not where you would not have your friends know you go.

March 27

Split the body in two today. Fascia-throwing was the event of the day. Birdsong of Ga. got sore. Took walk with Higgins. Stopped by and saw Fletcher, Bush, and Cecil. Letters from Myrtle[31] and Callaway. (H) Hold fast to that which is right.

March 28

A spring day. Cut the body today and Kingsley and I are again over in the corner "growling." Took walk with Stewart. (I) Injure not another's reputation.

March 29

Rain, couldn't walk, couldn't do anything, so had to work. Loevenhart tried his hand at lecturing.[32] Dr. Howell accepted my French

---

[27] This was an informal student musical group.

[28] Frederick F. Gundrum, of the class of 1908, practiced as an internist in Sacramento, California.

[29] They completed their course in French at the Berlitz School.

[30] Nina Katherine Champion (Mrs. Charles L. Jackson) was Pat's niece.

[31] This was Pat's sister Mollie Myrtle Nixon (Mrs. Frank C. Allen).

[32] Arthur Loevenhart, 1878–1929, taught in the department of pharmacology and physiological chemistry.

certificate—thank goodness! Several recruits in the menagerie. Letter from Olive. (J) Join hands with the virtuous.

March 30

A pretty good day's work. Winder hanged this morning. Took walk with Higgins, Carsten, and Clark. (K) Keep your mind free from evil thoughts.

March 31

Worked in anatomy this morning. Spent afternoon in writing letters. Took walk in the snow. "Dr." White, the maker of love powders and president of the "College of Science" arrested today. His powders: 7 drops blood from black cat's tail, 3 hairs from gray mare, 2 pinches of crushed snail shell, and a prayer breathed on it all by the "doctor"—guaranteed to make the most stupid like an ardent Romeo. (L) Lie not for any consideration.

April 1

All Fools Day. Went to S.S. Mrs. Sheridan was absent. Dr. Sheridan made the talk. Went to Madison Avenue Methodist Church at eleven and heard Bishop Luther B. Wilson. He preached a fine sermon. Took walk in Patterson Park this afternoon. (M) Make few special acquaintances.

April 2

Fine spring day. Second-year students begin anatomy exams. Letter from Mama. (N) Never try to appear what you are not.

April 3

Good day all around. (O) Observe good manners.

April 4

Nothing doing. (P) Pay your debts promptly.

April 5

Worked all day in anatomy. Went with Higgins to buy some flowers for Miss Clark. Concert by the Savoy Sextette tonight. Letter from Jimmie. (Q) Question not the veracity of a friend.

April 6

Ether and separating funnels: Kingsley, Harvey, and Pretz.[33] Lots of fun. (R) Respect the counsel of your parents.

---

[33] Thomas W. Harvey, Jr., of the class of 1909, practiced surgery in Orange,

The Diary

April 7

Three Negroes came over to the anatomical building this morning, hunted up Bill Hartley and wanted to get Tom Jones out of the cold-storage room. Perhaps I dissected Tom six months ago. Higgins called tonight. (S) Sacrifice money rather than principle.

April 8

Palm Sunday. Mr. Warner taught our S.S. class. Heard Reverend Robert E. Speer preach at Brown Memorial Church this morning. Fine sermon. Gist: Manhood: there can be no manhood without character, no character without religion, no religion without Christianity, no Christianity without Christ. What is your attitude? Heard him again at night. Gist: always do your duty and something more. Keep a space between you and the marginal edge. Took long walk in Clifton Park this afternoon. (T) Touch not, taste not, handle not intoxicating drinks.

April 9

A sloppy day. We all moved into Room 76 in anatomy today. Letter and tie from Olive. Had some good music over at the Savoy tonight—Miss Myers.[34] (U) Use your leisure for improvement.

April 10

Worked all day in anatomy. (V) Venture not on the threshold of wrong.

April 11

Handed my part in to the study room—thank goodness! Finished up in chemistry. Had to manufacture 50 cc saliva today. Some of the fellows have gone home. This is beginning of Easter vacation. Miss Myers, Partridge, and Moss gave us some music tonight.[35] Letter from Zeb. (W) Watch carefully over your possessions.

April 12

First day of vacation. Walked an hour in Patterson Park this morning. Saw Hopkins-Lehigh baseball game this afternoon. Good game, gilt-edge finish. Score: 9 to 8 in Hopkins' favor. (X) Xtend to everyone a kindly greeting.

New Jersey. George Rupp Pretz, also of the class of 1909, opened his office in Lebanon, Pennsylvania.

[34] Rose Myers, an outpatient of Dr. Barker, lived temporarily at Mrs. Little's boarding house, where Pat was staying.

[35] Philip Ball Moss, of the class of 1909, practiced in Selma, Alabama, as a roentgenologist.

April 13

Good Friday. Saw Columbia-Hopkins game this morning. I put on a suit and warmed up a little. Score 5 to 1 in Columbia's favor. Fisher, an old Binghamite, played right [*field*] on C's team. Hadn't seen him for five years. Higgins and Carstens fussed two girls out at the game. (Y) Yield not to discouragement.

April 14

Lacrosse today. Hopkins, 7; Harvard, 1. Went over across to Locust Point and saw a German steamer just in. Went over it. (Z) Zealously labor for the right, and success is certain.

April 15

Easter. Miss Thomason taught our S.S. class, Brother Sheridan preaching in the morning. Many women were disappointed in not getting to wear their Easter gowns and bonnets on account of the threatening weather. Tried my hand at fussing Miss Myers tonight.[36] Had pretty good luck. We had to mail a letter; naturally we could not find a box except at a distance.

April 16

Took Miss Myers to the train this morning. A nice, lively girl. Saw Grace George in *The Marriage of William Ashe*. Good show.

April 17

Went to West Point, New York, with baseball team. Fine trip. Beautiful scenery along the Hudson. Saw Jim Marley.[37]

April 18

Took long walk about the Point early this morning. Practiced in morning and saw cavalry drill. Game this afternoon. Score, West Point 3, Hopkins 2. We should have had the game. Took two meals at Cadet Mess. Good hospitable bunch of fellows. Left at 7:30. Crossed over into New York City for a short time. Our train picked up dead man killed by train ahead of us. Got in at 4 A.M. and had to walk home. This is day of great earthquake at San Francisco.

---

36 "During the seven years of our engagement, Olive and I made no pretense at monopolizing the attention of one another; such an attempt would have been absurdly silly." Nixon Ms.

37 James Preston Marley had been a friend of Pat's at the University of Texas.

April 19

Got up at eleven and went to physiology. Too tired to do much today. Went to bed early. Short note from Miss Myers.

April 20

About over my soreness from the ball game. Am not so crowded with work since I finished anatomy.

April 21

Went over to the cage and had baseball picture taken. Saw my first lacrosse game and enjoyed it. Hopkins defeated Cornell 7 to 0. Letter from Olive.

> Look forward, not backward
> Look up, not down
> Look outward, not inward
> And lend a hand.

April 22

Miss Thomason talked to our S.S. class again this morning. Brother Sheridan on the San Francisco disaster. It is not a punishment or a judgment, but the result of a natural law. Took walk with Stewart and got some wild flowers.

April 23

Tried to get cold again today. Dawson surprised us with a quiz this morning. Heard Erlanger talk at medical meeting tonight on "Heart Block."

April 24

Studied my first cross sections this morning. Saw part of Balti.-St. Johns b.b. game at Oriole Park, and we practiced a little.

April 25

Good day's work. Letter from Mama. Had a coon hunt in my dream last night.

April 26

Saw Buffalo and Balto. play today, 6–1.

April 27

Cut out from chemistry early this afternoon. Played N.C. Score 9–3 in their favor. We outplayed them with the exception of that rotten third inning. Letter from Myrtle.

April 28
Not much doing today. Had to go over and have b.b. picture made again. Saw Balto.-Buffalo game. No good.

April 29
Heard Dr. Patton, president of Princeton, preach this morning. Stewart and I went out beyond Wallbrook this afternoon and got some violets. We stayed too late for supper and we were both broke, so we stopped downtown and got a 20¢ lunch.

April 30
Not much doing. Letter from Miss Myers.

May 1
May Day. Went to Bishop McDowell's Bible class over at surgical building. Letter from Mama.

May 2
Finished up my work in anatomy for the year. Letter from Olive at last.

May 3
Began reviewing in histology this morning. Practiced b.b. some this afternoon. Had my arm with me.

May 4
More histology and more chemistry. Jones grew enthusiastic on the subject of xanthene bases.

May 5
Went out to Maryland Oval to play St. Johns but got rained out. Got soaking wet and am not feeling any better for it. Saw Dr. Cole and got some iron carbonate from him.[38]

May 6
Miss Thomason taught our S.S. class this morning. Good lesson. Church service as usual. Went with Stewart to sacred concert for San Fran. sufferers at Druid Hill Park this afternoon.

May 7
Blue Monday. Same old thing.

---

[38] Rufus I. Cole, 1872–1966, was an associate in medicine and director of the biological laboratory. He developed the technique of direct blood cultures. Later he joined the staff of the Rockefeller Institute for Medical Research.

The Diary

May 8

Uncle Lee Denman has been in town for several days. Went down to the law offices of Marbury and Gosnell this afternoon and saw him. He volunteered to help me in case I needed it.

May 9

[No entry]

May 10

Sellards, Jeans, and I boiled bones today.[39] Went over to dispensary and saw Dr. Warfield about my throat. Postnasal catarrh. He gave me some salve for it. He looked at me and said, "You are from the South, are you not?" Quite a compliment.

May 11

More bone-boiling and more histology. Invitations from Ione and Mamie. We leave for Charlottesville, Va., in the morning.

May 12

Hopkins day. Baseball: Virginia 3, Hopkins 4. Lacrosse: Swarthmore 4, Hopkins 5. Had good time in Va. Saw Boyles, an old Bingham boy from Houston, Texas, also Dr. Lambeth.

May 13

Tired out from yesterday. Went to church this morning and slept this afternoon. Walked with Bush of Ga. tonight. He says a Negro is like a mule: "Pet him and he'll kick you."

May 14

Letters from Mama and Olive. Both anxious for me to come home.

May 15

Have begun our "please contribute" work. Pretz found out what was the matter with him by sucking a thermometer. Went to Bishop McDowell's Bible class in surgical building this afternoon: "Studies in John."

May 16

[No entry]

May 17

The laboratory was very odoriferous today. Drinkard's girl from

---

[39] Andrew Watson Sellards, of the class of 1909, became professor of tropical medicine at Harvard. Philip C. Jeans, also of the class of 1909, practiced pediatrics in Iowa City, Iowa.

Wallbrook came over to see him today. Think they are trying to capture him, as her mother has been inquiring as to what Drink is worth. She can play the piano if she can't do anything else. Letter from Olive tonight.

May 18
  [*No entry*]

May 19
  Feeling pretty tough today. Couldn't do much work. I went to meeting of American Pathologists and Bacteriologists.

May 20
  Good sermon today by a man from Detroit. Sellards and I rode sixteen miles this afternoon on wheels. I am pretty tired, otherwise I am feeling all right.

May 21
  Another blue Monday. My head feels thick. Saw Fletcher and Bush this afternoon. Bush's father has just been elected to the Georgia Senate. Letters from Mama and H. P. Burney.

May 22–23
  [*No entries*]

May 24
  Nurses' commencement today. Drink gets a letter from his Wallbrook girl to meet him on corner of Broadway and Baltimore. We saw him off with her. Letter from Olive—"Baby" sick.[40]

May 25
  Last lectures of the year. I got called on the last man in physiology.

May 26
  Helped revise list of Hopkins YMCA boarding houses. Feeling bum again today. Went to see Dr. Cole this noon. Letter from Olive.

May 27
  A rainy Sunday. Went to S.S. and church this morning and to church tonight.

---

[40] "Baby" was Cornelia Read Randolph, Olive's younger sister. Randolph Field in San Antonio was named in honor of her husband, Captain William Randolph.

May 28
Exam in circulation and respiration. I did mighty well, I think. Pretz's remark: "Oh yes! you are talking about the brain." Letters from Mama and Les.

May 29
Exam in secretion and digestion. Got another bull's-eye. Went across town to help elect Iglehart captain of b.b. team. I was awarded an *H*. More boarding house revision.

May 30
[*No entry*]

May 31
Have done nothing today but wait for the exam tomorrow. Did go to town and get a suit of clothes (the cost was $16). Saw Drs. Cole and Theobald.[41]

June 1
Exam in chemistry today. Did fine. If I can only do as well tomorrow! "Dr." White, the maker of the renowned love powders, is on trial downtown. They are having some great sport. Got my suit this evening. Letter from Mama and a little piece of blue paper.

June 2
Exam in histology: Dr. Harrison says, "Take any three sections and describe them. If you don't like the first three, bring them back and get others." Think I did well on it. Went to town and got me a hat and shoes. Packed my things tonight.

June 3
Went to S.S. this morning and took farewell of all of them. Couldn't go to church, because I had to go see Dr. Theobald about my eyes. Astigmatism. I will have to wear glasses. Stewart left this morning. Most of the fellows have gone. I go to New York in the morning. Took last walk up B'dway this afternoon with Watkins of Alabama.[42] Goodbye! Balto.

June 4
Had a time getting my ticket. Finally got off at 4 P.M. Got to New

[41] Samuel Theobald, 1846–1930, was professor of ophthalmology.
[42] Leon H. Watkins, of the class of 1909, practiced gynecology in Pasadena, California.

York at 8:30. Took the elevated 9th Avenue to 135th Street but couldn't get lodging there so after a long search I found a room at 126th Street.[43]

June 5

Got up early and came downtown. Saw Wall Street, Trinity Church, Battery, Aquarium, Liberty Statue. Took the Subway to Central Park and saw Metropolitan Art Museum and zoological gardens. Saw some of the residences on 5th Avenue. Took 6th Avenue "L" and came to 23rd Street where I saw the skyscrapers including the Flatiron Building. Went to Printing House Square and took the elevator and partly climbed to the top of the New York *World* Building. From this I got a beautiful view of New York and surrounding parts. Went to Pier #37 and bade goodbye to Fletcher, Bush, and Sprunt who are going to Charleston, South Carolina.[44] Went to Coney Island on the "L" and took in a few things: "Dreamland," "Baby Incubators," "Scenic Railway," etc. By night I was completely fagged out and ready to go to bed.

June 6

Couldn't sleep much last night on account of those infernal steamboat whistles and trucks. Got breakfast on Canal [*Street*] and a little later went to the pier to arrange my ticket and baggage. I had Mrs. Burlin mail my check to the pier, but I didn't get it. I thought I would have some trouble about it, but finally got it fixed up all right. At noon we sailed on the *S.P.S.S. Comms.* Rhea, Gundrum, and Haas of second-year class, all of California, are on board.[45] Coming out we passed the Battery, Coney Island, Statue of Liberty, Staten Island. It's fine on board. Got a little bit dizzy after we had been out about four hours. The sea is dotted here and there with sails. We passed *Captain Lawson,* one of the few seven-masted schooners. Also a French liner, *Barbarosa.* Pretty cold in the afternoon. No land in sight before dark.

[43] "It is very obvious that I didn't like New York. Aside from its bigness and its heartlessness, I don't think I would have liked it anyway, because some New Yorker charged me three cents for a two-cent stamp." Nixon Ms.

[44] Thomas Peck Sprunt, of the class of 1909, later taught at the University of Maryland and at Johns Hopkins.

[45] Sylvan Lewis Haas, of the class of 1908, practiced orthopedic surgery in San Francisco.

The Diary

June 7

We were skirting the Virginia coast when I got up this morning. No land in sight, only a few sails and a couple of steamships and one bark. Much warmer and more pleasant than yesterday. Diamond Shoal Light Ship passed and Hatteras sighted about 11 A.M. Saw lots of flying fish, a couple of sharks, and no ships. Sea is as blue as bluing and pretty rough. We've been in the Gulf Stream since noon. The English and the Dutch are sick, so they can't get up and reach all over the table for food. I have seen no land since yesterday at 4 P.M.

June 8

Nothing to break the monotony—no boats, no land, only a few sick people. I am reading Marvel's "Reveries of a Bachelor" and Howell's "Physiology" alternately—a good combination. The old Dago woman is able to be at the table—to our sorrow. My face is about blistered from sitting on deck in the wind.

June 9

We have been skirting the coasts of Florida. Passed Palm Beach this morning and Key West at 5 P.M. Saw an old Spanish tramp [steamer] grounded for fourteen months. It has been storming and raining all day long. Everybody sick. I took my turn at the rail this morning twice. Couldn't eat any dinner, but am feeling all right now. We are headed for New Orleans in a rather calm sea.

June 10

Have been crossing the Gulf. Worst sea we have had. Mighty rough. Couldn't keep the dishes on the table. I haven't been sick any more, thank goodness! No land and no ships seen at all. Saw all kinds of strange things: porpoises, dolphins, sea lions, Portuguese men o'war. The Englishman and his wife are in bed with the yellow box hanging on the bed handy. The old Dago has about lost his appetite, and that is saying a whole lot. He and his old lady have been sitting on the floor all day. Mr. Williams, a lightweight, has been very much alarmed lest he blow overboard. The Swedish sailor has been telling me a lot about the sea. The young man from Brooklyn and the sorry fellow from New Orleans know it all. They see men on the shore miles away. The Dutch steward has been telling us some wonderful tales of New Orleans. Says we pass Negroes singing "Way *Back* Yonder in the Cornfield."

June 11

Woke up at 3 A.M. and saw the jetties. A nice sail up the river; got to dock at 9:30. Came to S.P. ferry. Then took a turn on the Tulane Belt Line. Hot as blazes in New Orleans. Left at 11:55. Engine broke down at Sabine River. That put us one hour late. Had a few words with a third-class Englishman coming out of New Orleans about a seat. I simply told him that he was too insignificant to waste words on, that I would have nothing further to say to him, that I was above it. Came to hotel near I.&G.N. depot and went to bed about 1:30.

June 12

Couldn't sleep much: mosquitoes, crying kids, snorers, trains, alarm clocks, truckmen, and a few other things. Off to Mineola at 8 A.M. Arrived at 8 P.M. Went up to Reads' and saw all of them. Olive and I went out for a walk!

June 13

We went out to the Mill Pond this morning. We talked of "going to Quitman," but decided not to do so. Took dinner with Olive. Stayed at home this afternoon and tonight. Got in about 12.

June 14

We took a drive this morning. Went to Senator Stafford's and took dinner. We managed to stay too late to catch the 1:15 train, to our gladness. Had a long talk with the family and a longer one with Olive tonight. Told Mamie and all goodbye this afternoon. Left Olive about 12:30. Of course we took a very affectionate farewell.

June 15

Left Mineola at 7:45 A.M. Saw Tipton in Troupe. Had to wait there about three hours. Saw Brodie and Anderson on train and Paul and K. C. Miller in Austin.[46] Stayed in San Marcos tonight.

June 16

Left at 9:08. Saw Joe Hatchett and Flowers in Lockhart.[47] Got to Luling at 11:00 and will be here for quite a while. Went up town this afternoon and had to tell everyone when I came, how I was, how long they would have to put up with me, etc.

[46] These were friends he knew at college.
[47] These were other college friends.

That 1906 vacation at home is recalled as full of loneliness. I had been away so much and so long that I felt like a stranger. I was twenty-three years old and all my former friends had moved away or were at work, so I saw very little of them. It was during that lonely summer, however, when I made a snap diagnosis. Dr. M. W. Pitts asked me to go with him to see a man living west of town. This man had been sick several weeks. At the time we saw him, his main complaint was severe soreness in his muscles, more especially in his calf muscles. I elicited a history of diarrhea a few weeks before, which had followed the ingestion of pork. It so happened that I had seen trichinae in the dissecting room, so I suggested to Dr. Pitts that we take out a piece of muscle from the lower leg. He had no instruments with him, so we improvised by using a pocketknife and an ordinary needle and thread. In the excised fragment of muscle could be seen small grayish nodules which the microscope proved to be trichinae. This patient thought I was a real doctor until I told him that there was no treatment for trichinosis except to await the time until the parasites could become calcified and that was very indefinite. The lonely summer over, I was due back in Baltimore on October 1. The journal was resumed a few days earlier.

September 27
Got back to Baltimore this morning at four. Left home on 21st. Stayed three days in Mineola with Olive and had a fine time—two daily sessions of several hours each. Saw Kingsley this morning. Hear Miss Rhode is to be married. Went to see *Little Johnnie Jones* with Fletcher. Good play, medium company.

September 28
Only a few of the fellows are back. Went out to Electric Park this afternoon and saw the sights. Made some purchases downtown. Got letter from Olive. Wrote to Mama, Olive, and Sadie.

September 29
Studied bacteriology. Went to Alback's to vaudeville. Saw Brinda-mour, the jailbreaker. Rinde came in today. Mrs. Burlin lets the

window fall on her hand and does some yelling. Stewart came in tonight.

September 30
Went to S.S. and church. Wrote letters this afternoon.

October 1
Began making bacteriological media today.

October 2
Met Dr. Howell and Dr. Welch today. First physiological laboratory work—simple muscle contraction. More media.

October 3
More physiology and more media.

October 4
Some hard luck in media making.

October 5
[*No entry*]

October 6
Finished making media. Dr. Barker's clinic: typhoid and its complications. Three cases shown. One a laryngeal complication where the arytenoid cartilages were gone. Second where the middle ear was inflamed, otitis media. Third where there was a supposed perforation. An exploratory operation was done, but nothing was found. The patient began at once to get well after the operation. Early symptoms of perforation: sharp pain, rigidity of muscles of abdomen, fall in temperature, rise in leukocytes, distension of abdomen, vomiting, tenderness of abdomen. Perforations are most likely to occur in ileum because of Peyer's patches; and more often in men than in women.

October 7
Church and S.S. this morning. Good attendance at S.S.—fifty men. Went to oratorio, *The Vision of St. John,* tonight at Mt. Vernon Place.

October 8
Lecture by Ford.[48] Inoculated some tubes. The first of the Herter

[48] William Webber Ford, 1871–1941, was professor of hygiene and bacteriology. He also lectured on legal aspects of medicine.

Lectures[49] on "The Therapeutic Inoculation of Bacterial Vaccines and Its Application in Connection with Treatment of Bacterial Diseases" by Sir Almroth E. Wright of London. He is rather radical, says we need no more facts, but only to apply the facts already known.

October 9
Quizzed by Dr. Eyster.[50] Second Herter Lecture.

October 10
Tried all morning in vain to get frog stomach to contract. Third Herter Lecture. Went with Higgins to register as voter, but was not very successful.

October 11
Special Herter Lecture by Sir Almroth E. Wright on "Coagulation of Blood." Great ovation at close, great applause. Dr. Welch, in closing, said that he classed Dr. Wright with Pasteur and Behring. The inoculation against rabies by Pasteur, antidiphtherial sera by Behring and opsonic inoculation are the three triumphs of immunity. Spent another useless morning on involuntary muscle.

October 12
Finally got a contraction of that frog's stomach. It was very involuntary indeed. Saw Viola Allen tonight in *Cymbeline*. She was much better than her play.

October 13
Higgins brought my ring from the jewelers. Ate dinner with Mr. Thomason, the S.S. superintendent. "Good doings"—Ferenbaugh.[51] Talked S.S. afterwards. Went home with Miss Thomason out on West Fayette—a fine woman.

October 14
Church and S.S. this morning. Miss Thomason taught the lesson on the Virgin with Lamps. Fifty present. Dr. Miller gave the history

[49] Christian A. Herter, 1867–1910, taught at Columbia University and edited the *Journal of Biological Chemistry*. He was one of the organizers of the Rockefeller Institute, and he endowed a lectureship at Hopkins. His son became secretary of state.
[50] John A. Eyster was professor of physiology.
[51] Thomas Ludlow Ferenbaugh, of the class of 1909, served as a physician in the U.S. Army, attaining the rank of colonel.

of the YMCA. Wrote to Olive, Baby, and Dr. Nixon. Went to YMCA. Mr. Eugene Levering, donator of Levering Hall talked on "To him that hath shall be given."

October 15
Recitation and lecture by Dr. Welch. He called on me. Took walk with Gilcreest. Helped Higgins eat some cake his Columbus, Georgia, girl made him.

October 16
Stewart and I work on optics. Higgins has some excitement over the appearance of the clerk of the registry department. Stewart happened to be the clerk, however.

October 17
Work on astigmatism. Mr. Thomason of S.S. called on me.

October 18
Drizzly day. Color demonstrations by Dr. Howell. Saw Conner of first-year class, one of my S.S. lieutenants. Letters from Mama and Zeb.

October 19
Surgical clinic this morning by Dr. Finney: inguinal hernia and inner [intra] canalicular myxoma of mammary gland. Gilcreest called this afternoon full of questions.

October 20
Barker's clinic: Three cases of typhoid complications, one tuberculous pneumonia, six arthritides, and a boy with heart, spleen, and liver on the wrong side.

October 21
A rainy Sunday. Seventy at S.S. today. Wrote letters all afternoon.

October 22
A blue Monday. Rabbit autopsy: death caused by inoculation with staphylococcus aureus. Savoy Quartet made a little music tonight.

October 23
[*No entry*]

October 24
Used Maddox rod, Risley's prism, and phorometer today in getting

heterophoria—nice work. Also used ophthalmoscope and saw the fundus of the retina.

October 25

Lecture by Dr. Welch on water infection. Went to town this afternoon to get Moreland Stafford a wedding present.[52] Letter from Olive.

October 26

Stewart and I examined one another's eyes. His are slightly hyperopic, mine a little myopic. Saw Dr. Sowers take out a gallstone. Went to reception at church parlors: a pretty good crowd. Met Ledbetter, an ATO.

October 27

Dr. Barker's clinic: a typhoid puncture, neurofibroma, goiter, and acromegaly. The last man said he has never seen any man stronger than himself, says he can put six men on a table and lift the table. Saw the English Grand Opera *Madame Butterfly* this afternoon— very, very good.

October 28

Church and S.S. this morning. Ninety-three at S.S. Took dinner with Miss Helen Thomason. Miss Adelaide Porter and E. A. Deming were there also. Had a good time. We went to Vesper Service at St. Paul's at five.

October 29

Tried all morning to make nonpolarizable electrodes but in vain. Hart and Ferenbaugh could not get their experiment to work either,[53] so they took it out on one another. Hart to Ferenbaugh: "If you would wake up, we could do something." Letter from Alta.

October 30

[*No entry*]

October 31

Halloween. Worked demarcation and action currents today. Every kid in town has a cowbell, dragging it over the Balto. cobblestones and that makes a lot of noise. Maskers on the streets.

---

[52] The Staffords were friends.

[53] William Ernest Hart, of the class of 1909, practiced surgery in Pittsburgh, Pennsylvania.

November 1

Studied a little anatomy this morning. Had our first gross morbid demonstration this morning by Drs. MacCallum and Whipple.[54]

November 2

Anatomy this morning. Dr. Finney's clinic: sarcoma of nose. Excised whole nose. Another nose can be made from a finger and a flap of skin taken from the arm. Osteomyelitis of tibia. Chiseled the bone for half of its length. Widal's reaction in bacteriology.

November 3

Barker's clinic: a case of psychosis as the result of typhoid fever, a case of arthritis, two cases of lead palsy. Swarthmore 26, Hopkins 0. Saw *The Lion and the Mouse* tonight. Fine show.

November 4

One hundred and eight at S.S. this morning. Went over to Mr. Thomason's this afternoon. Wrote to Olive. Heard Dr. Emerson at the YMCA tonight. Good talk: two things are necessary for the success of the Christian physician, methodical Bible study, and methodical Christian work.

November 5

Heart work in physiology. Lecture by Dr. Welch on hog cholera. Medical meeting tonight: Dr. Cullen reported a case of a woman from whom an 89-pound tumor was removed, the woman weighing only 87 after the operation: the largest tumor on record.[55]

November 6

A strenuous day: worked all day in physiology trying to get through. Didn't want to waste the terrapin. Letter from Olive and paper containing the Stafford-Gibson wedding [*account*].

November 7

[*No entry*]

November 8

More terrapin heart work. Letters from Mama, Sadie, and Zeb.

---

[54] William G. MacCallum was a resident pathologist noted for his work on the parathyroids. George Hoyt Whipple, also a resident pathologist, received the Nobel Prize in medicine.

[55] This is in error. See Pat I. Nixon, *A History of the Texas Medical Association*, p. 214.

November 9

Finney's clinic: two hernial (femoral) operations; did them in thirty-five minutes; one appendicitis case. Went to reception tonight at home of Mr. Alcaeus Hooper at 2201 Maryland Avenue. Fine crowd. Good time. Met the two Miss Russells of 1613 Entaw Place. Munger of B.M.C.

November 10

Dr. Emerson's clinic: never diagnose with certainty a typhoid perforation case till you have seen the ulcer.

November 11

Rainy day. S.S. and church this morning. Slim attendance. Dr. Goodell of New York Calvary Methodist Church preached a fine sermon on the "Mystery of Godliness," 1 Timothy 3:16. He made a good talk at Ford's this afternoon also.

November 12

[*No entry*]

November 13

Motor-point experiment this morning. Got called on by Dr. Eyster. Mote in my eye this afternoon. Letter from Olive.

November 14

Kymograph experiment today. Worked on it till 5:30. Did pretty well. Stood up all day, no lunch, pains in my ankles, retired early.

November 15

[*No entry*]

November 16

Anatomy this morning. Finney's clinic: dislocation of hip joint: the head of the femur had gotten through the acetabulum. Second case: osteomyelitis of the hip joint. Went to church tonight at Mt. Vernon.

November 17

Felt this morning as though I was going to have some malaria, but feel better now. Dr. Barker's clinic: the little girl with typhoid psychosis was shown again and was much better. A case of Parinaud's conjunctivitis, the only case ever seen at Hopkins. Symptoms: nodular infection of conjunctiva with a little pus and but little lacrimation, enlarged preauricular lymph glands, also cervical and epitrochlear. Third case: phlebitis or thrombosis of femoral vein, a complication of typhoid, swollen and fevered leg. Fourth case: pyloric stenosis; treatment: gastroenterostomy or Finney's operation. Worked with Stewart all afternoon on physiological records. Big football scores: the western teams were shown up.

November 18
Another rainy Sunday of which we have had so many. Eighty-six at S.S. this morning. Heard Dr. Arthur T. Pierra of Brooklyn at YMCA on "Temptations and Opportunities of Medical Men." Dr. Sheridan preached the second of a series of sermons as to the hindrances to Christianity among Balto. men. Subject: "The Swirl of Self-Indulgence." Called on the Thomason household this afternoon at 2730 North Charles.

November 19
Dr. Foote's Bible class tonight.

November 20
[*No entry*]

November 21
A little hard luck today: worked all day doing tracheotomy, trephining skull, etc. of dog only to have the dog die before we got a record. A very misty day.

November 22
Mike breaks four out of six plates put in sterilizer. Letters from Mama and Olive. Note from Mr. and Mrs. M. R. Stafford—acknowledgment.

November 23
Finney's clinic: case one, tuberculous lymph glands of axilla. Case two, removed stone the size of ink bottle from kidney of woman seventy years old. Went to church tonight.

November 24
Worked till three on dog experiment, intracranial pressure. Good results. Pressure in femoral raised to the great height of 370 mm. with both vagi cut and intracranial pressure raised. Went with Drinkard to see his diabetic patient tonight. St. Johns 2, Hopkins 0.

November 25
Church and S.S. this morning. About one hundred at S.S. Miss

Thomason taught the lesson: the four *C*'s, conviction, choice, courage, and constancy. Heard Reverend Robert G. Freeman at Ford's this afternoon and also at the medical YMCA tonight, a pretty good talker. Heard Dr. Sheridan tonight on "Prevailing Business Methods Make Christianity Impracticable." From American Journal of Medical Association:[56] "It collects about the very sources of human existence, it pollutes the fountains of life, it befouls the sacred function of maternity, its defilement clings to the innocent infant ushered into the world." Letter from Jim Marley contained ticket to the Army-Navy game at Philadelphia.

Here in the diary an unusual thing happened: the writing pen changed from left hand to right. The only explanation for the change which I can now assign is found in the fact that our class had begun to see something of Harvey Cushing.[57] It was a delight to see him go up to the blackboard with a piece of chalk in each hand and draw the outline of the brain artistically and symmetrically, using both hands at the same time. So thought of ambidexterity must have prompted me to see what I could do with my right hand. The result could be called legible. The letters of the words are a little larger and a little less cramped than my left-handed effort. They could easily pass for the writing of another individual.

November 26
Learned the use of the sphygmograph this morning. Went to Dr. Foote's Bible class tonight. He continued his talk on Nathan.

November 27
[*No entry*]

November 28
Last day before Thanksgiving recess. Saw Lew Dockstader's Minstrels.

November 29
Thanksgiving Day and birthday. Studied this morning and saw the

[56] Apparently he means *Journal of the American Medical Association.*
[57] Harvey Cushing, 1869–1939, was associate in surgery. He later was Sterling Professor of Neurology at Yale and then went to Harvard and the Peter Bent Brigham Hospital.

Hopkins-Maryland football game this afternoon. We won 6–0. The score should have been much larger. Went to the dinner at five o'clock given at Central YMCA. A good spread and some good speeches. Thirty-one states and several foreign countries were represented. When I got home, I helped Stewart eat some of his Thanksgiving box. Texas played A&M College today at Austin.

November 30

Saw an operation (hernia) in private operating room this morning. Took supper with Dr. Sheridan in church parlors this evening. Good time.

December 1

Army-Navy football at Philadelphia today. Navy 10, Army 0. An open game full of sensational plays, lots of punting. Saw Jim Marley after the game. Met Gilcreest up there and also Dr. Barker and wife. Went around to the ATO house and met some of the fellows.

December 2

Ninety-seven at S.S. this morning. Frank McDaniel at Ford's this afternoon. Pretty good. Oratorio *The Daughter of Jairus* at Mt. Vernon tonight—fine.

December 3

Medical meeting tonight. Dr. Cushing showed several interesting cases of nerve removal and cerebral decompressions. Dr. Loevenhart read a paper on lipase. Dr. Thomas had a good paper on thrombosis of the posterior inferior cerebellar artery. Letter from Olive. Very cold tonight.

December 4

Did the "disrobing" experiment in physiology, anterior tibial and femoral pulse waves. Dr. Welch gave his first lecture on immunity today. Postcard from Mae at Spofford.

December 5

Stewart played the wild this morning by showing Dr. Hooker[58] an experiment after Dr. Eyster had refused to sign it off. Suppose I am implicated, though I am innocent. Ferenbaugh showed his knowledge of ancient languages by deriving the word *aerogenes*. Some sleet tonight.

---

[58] Donald R. Hooker, 1876–1946, was professor of physiology; he also edited the *American Journal of Physiology*. He was the inventor of the kidney pump.

The Diary

December 6
Tried the irrigation experiment this morning but had some hard luck and had to go without my dinner. Took walk with Johnson of Kansas tonight. Letters from Alta and Sadie.

December 7
Did the plethysmograph this morning. Went to the young men's meeting tonight—good meeting. Objection—"Too busy." References: Matthew 16, 26; 1 John 2:15–17. Ten degrees above zero tonight.

December 8
Did a little anatomy this morning. Gross morbid and an interesting autopsy: rupture of the uterus caused by presence of a dead fetus. Acute peritonitis. Dr. Barker's clinic at twelve noon. Case No. 1: ptosis sympathica due to pneumonia. No. 2: pneumonia. No. 3: chronic lymphatic edema. Heard Fritzi Scheff in *Madamoiselle Modiste* this afternoon—good.

December 9
[*No entry*]

December 10
One hundred sixteen at S.S. Had our picture taken by flashlight. Charles L. Mead at church and at Ford's this afternoon. A fine speaker. McCracken, the Penn. guard of '98–'02, a medical missionary in China spoke at YMCA tonight.

December 11
[*No entry*]

December 12
Went to meeting at surgical amphitheater of Southern Surgical & Gynecological Association—Kelly, Osler, Halsted, Welch, Williams, Young, Hunner, Cushing, Baer, Cole, etc. Last lecture by Dr. Ford in bacteriology.

December 13
[*No entry*]

December 14
Got our bugs today. I have two bacilli. Number fifty-six was my draw. One of the bugs looks like mouse septicemia.

December 15
Worked on bacteriology exam this morning. Bugs don't look like

they did yesterday. Think now I have proteus and Friedlander. Everybody has a different bug each time you see him.

December 16

Heard E. C. Mercer of the Jerry McCauly Mission three times yesterday: at Ford's, at YMCA, and at Westminister Presbyterian Church. He is an interesting character, a brilliant man. "The race horse and plow horse." "Alcohol will preserve a dead man and kill a live one." "A club is a place where a gentleman can go and get drunk and still be a gentleman"—Sol Smith Russell.

December 17

Up in the air on the big question. Proteus has overgrown everything, and I don't hope to see the second bug again. Worked all day and was not any the wiser.

December 18

Nothing doing for the bugs. Mine seems to be a hopeless case. That long-looked-for second bug just won't put in an appearance.

December 19

Another day gone to the bugs and nothing accomplished.

December 20

Had our oral quiz under Dr. Dawson. Did all right. "Well," says Percy, "I am tired of asking questions. Mr. Nixon, suppose you tell me all about it." Tomorrow comes the tug. Dr. Welch gave his last lecture today. Told us to forget all about amboceptors, complements, etc., for a couple of weeks.

December 21

It wasn't half bad; had our physiology exam today. It was very fair. Think I did all right. Turned in my bugs today. Proteus was right. I found only the one on my plates. My second bug, which was Flexner's, was overgrown by Proteus. Dr. Ford told me he didn't expect me to get it out. Washed test tubes all the afternoon. Went downtown and got presents for Olive and Mamie, also a picture of the S.S. class.

December 22

Went over to the Maryland University and Hospital this morning. The hospital is all right, but the medical school is n.g. [*no good?*]. Sat in Mrs. Little's parlor with Moss and Higgins tonight and talked for about three hours. Went down the street with Higgins to get his watch and saw what we thought was wonderful. It was a small windmill affair which was turned by heat from the neighboring lamps and would not turn in the cold.

December 23

Went to church and Sunday school this morning. Small class. Most of the fellows have gone home. Heard Dudley Buck's oratorio *The Coming of the King* at Mt. Vernon. Letter from Mama containing a Christmas present of five dollars.[59]

December 24

Went with Higgins to the dispensary and saw him take a history. The little silly girl didn't want to submit to an examination. "I must ask Mama first." Higgins and I saw Robert Loraine in *Man and Superman*. Good show, lots of laughs.

December 25

Xmas day, and it's not like spending it at home, either. Wesson came over with me from breakfast and chatted for a couple of hours.[60] We had a pretty good dinner today. Called on Gilcreest this afternoon. Stewart has been in New York for several days.

December 26

Borrowed Rickett's *Immunity* from Wiesender and read it today. Got a match case from Sadie today and a watch fob from Olive. Higgins and I read together tonight *A Midsummer Night's Dream*.

December 27

Studied osteology this morning. Read some articles in *The Outlook* on Robert E. Lee. Higgins and I saw Annie Russell as Puck in *A Midsummer Night's Dream*. The company and the play were good—a fortunate combination.

December 28

Have studied osteology all day. Read up "myelogenous leucaemia" in Osler this morning. Read a good story in *The Saturday Evening Post* tonight, "Cast Away in a Parlor Car." Got a letter from Olive.

---

[59] "Back home, times were hard, what with only twenty inches of rain in 1906. But Mama saved five dollars for me. She knew I could use it." Nixon Ms.

[60] Miley B. Wesson, of the class of 1910, was later a urologist in San Francisco.

December 29

Have been reading Longfellow's *Hiawatha* today and have enjoyed it. Higgins has gone to Dr. Thomas's reception tonight.

December 30

Church and S.S. this morning. Went up to Watkins's room this afternoon and made a big hole in his big box from home.

December 31

Last day of the old year. Went up to hospital with Sellards to see him take some opsonic indices. He took mine for TB. Went with him tonight to his room and looked over his dissected pig larynx. Then we went to see Grace George in *Clothes*. Pretty good show. Came home and saw everybody shooting their little .32's. I couldn't find a single cartridge for my .45.[61] Lots of noise at twelve. Mrs. Burlin brought us up some cake and cider after twelve.

As we come toward the end of the journal, we find that the entries are becoming irregular. Here is the final installment:

January 1, 1907

Spent the morning in the library. Higgins and I tried to get a bicycle but couldn't, so we took a long walk out Charles Street. Went by the YMCA reception and got a handout. Saw all kinds of people over about Mt. Royall Avenue.

January 2

Studied cross sections of the head awhile this morning. Began work in pathology this afternoon. Letter from Olive. Went to the physiological building tonight. Occasion was the acceptance of the Warrington Hospital Library. Dr. Remsen presided. Good talks were made by Drs. Osler and Welch.

January 3

Began work in toxicology today. Jones gave a short lecture. Went across town this afternoon. Higgins is in bed today. Slight fever and tonsillitis. Letters from Olive and Mama. Mama said, "I hope you

---

[61] "That big .45 of mine I had rather foolishly taken out, and I went from store to store in search of ammunition. It was more foolish still to have taken it to Baltimore in the first place. I recall the look of alarm shown by the hardware dealers when they looked at the big six-shooter. Well could they have marvelled at this weapon. It was the Smith & Wesson pistol which Papa had carried through the Civil War." Nixon Ms.

have gotten your box all right," when in reality I hadn't seen a sign of a box.

January 4
   [*No entry*]

January 5
   Dr. Abel gave his first lecture on medical jurisprudence. Pneumonia autopsy at ten. Barker's aneurysm clinic at twelve. Went up to Carsten's room tonight and ate a bunch of his cake.

January 6
   Heard Bishop Wilson this morning–Heb. 11:27. Dr. Stone at YMCA tonight and Dr. Guthrie at First Presbyterian Church. Walked over with Higgins, Webb, Sellards, and Rinde.[62]

January 7
   [*No entry*]

January 8
   Began Dr. Lewis' course in topographical anatomy this morning. Autopsy at eleven. Dr. Welch quizzed on immunity at twelve. Dr. Thayer showed a case of Hodgkin's disease at medical meeting tonight.

January 9
   Autopsy—TB at ten this morning. Stewart, Higgins, and Burns came down tonight, and we ate some of Higgins's fruit cake.

January 10
   [*No entry*]

January 11
   Pneumonia autopsy at ten today. Went to the Young Men's meeting tonight. Good letter from Olive.

January 12
   Dr. Abel ranted some for us this morning.[63] Dr. MacCallum gave a good gross morbid demonstration. Gave me a pneumonic lung to

---

[62] Charles Watkins Webb, of the class of 1909, later practiced surgery in Newark, New York.

[63] John Jacob Abel, 1857–1938, was professor of pharmacology. He did work with the pituitary gland and in the area of renal dialysis and was an early proponent of the artificial kidney.

diagnose and describe. I batted his eye out. Dr. Barker showed a case of Paget's disease, dementia, and two cases of pneumonia.

January 13
A dreary Sunday. Saw Monroe at church this morning. Heard Dr. [*Harry E.*] Fosdick at Ford's this afternoon. He made a good talk on "Justification by Faith." Mr. Morris spoke at the YMCA tonight. The Savoy Quartette is furnishing the music at Second Baptist tonight.

January 14–15
[*No entries*]

January 16
Snowed all day long. Working on cross sections of the thorax. Little success in pathology today. Sent J. H. [*Johns Hopkins*] calendars to Olive and to Mama.

January 17
More snow, slippery. Some sleighing. Mike Ferenbaugh of Kenyon College, Ohio, came down tonight and we learned all about the liver. Had a specimen before us. Letters from Mama and Olive.

January 18
[*No entry*]

January 19
Gross morbid demonstration this morning: aneurysm, aortic insufficiency, nutmeg liver, emphysema of lung. Barker's rheumatism clinic at twelve. Worked all afternoon on pathology.

January 20
Went to church and S.S. this morning. Bishop Wilson preached. Devotional meeting at YMCA tonight. Higgins and I went to Mt. Vernon tonight.

January 21
Accident autopsy today. I was one of the five to write it up. Eleven ribs, sternum, leg, shoulder, and spine broken. Dr. Foote's class tonight. Plaintive letter from Sadie.

January 22
Made our autopsy reports today. Dr. MacCallum said they were very good. Turned in our unknowns today and both were right. Took walk with Gilcreest this evening.

This photograph of the young Pat Nixon in his school uniform was taken in 1902, while he was a student at Bingham School in Asheville, North Carolina.

Fannie Andrews Nixon, Pat's mother, stands in front of the old Nixon home in Guadalupe County, Texas, where Pat was born.

This old schoolhouse on the Nixon family farm provided Pat Nixon's early education. Seated in front of it are Pat's mother, his sons Robert and Pat, Jr., a neighbor, and Pat's wife, Olive.

This photograph was taken on the old Nixon homeplace on Fannie Nixon's eighty-seventh birthday. Pictured with Fannie, who is seated, are (*left to right*): Myrtle Nixon Allen, Corinne Nixon Hyman, Zebulon Vance Nixon, Jason Andrews (*seated*), John Philip Nixon, Ella Nixon Champion, Sam Houston Nixon, Alta Nixon Fisher, Beula Nixon Wood, Viola Nixon Wilson, and Pat Ireland Nixon.

This house, constructed in 1895, became the Robert Nixons' home when they moved to Luling.

Pat Nixon's mother, Fannie Andrews Nixon (*left*), and his father, Robert Thomas Nixon (*right*), taught their son the importance of hard work and a good education.

Pat's younger brother, Zeb (*left*), was his boyhood companion. His eldest brother, Dr. James Wesley Nixon (*right*), helped support his medical studies.

This cap-and-gown photograph of Pat Nixon was taken upon his graduation from the University of Texas in 1905.

In 1905 an eager Pat Nixon left Texas to attend medical school at Johns Hopkins. This picture was taken shortly before he left Austin.

Pat Nixon kept this photograph of Olive Read, taken while she was a student at the University of Texas, on his desk throughout his student days at Hopkins.

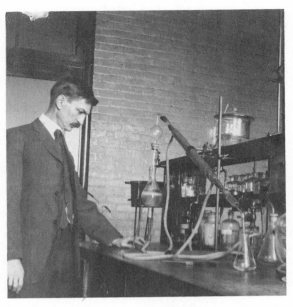

This student laboratory at Johns Hopkins School of Medicine is typical of those where Pat Nixon worked during his student days there.

In this picture of Pat Nixon's dormitory room at Johns Hopkins, note the photograph of Olive on Pat's desk.

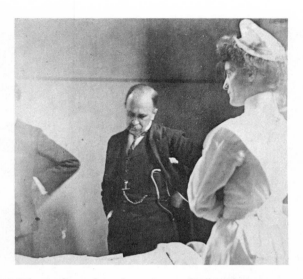

Sir William Osler is shown here lecturing medical students at a patient's bedside at Johns Hopkins Hospital during one of several visits to Baltimore he
made during Pat Nixon's stay there.

These Johns Hopkins medical students are pictured in a surgery amphitheater.
Pat Nixon is second from the left, top row.

A nurse is shown here pushing her cart through a ward typical of those at Johns Hopkins Hospital during Dr. Pat Nixon's residency there.

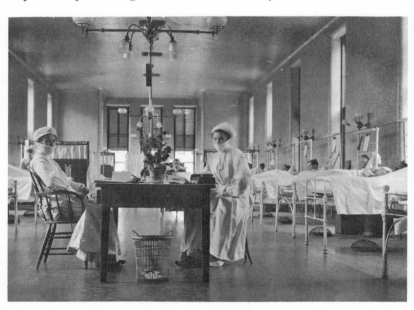

This is Johns Hopkins Hospital's Ward H, where Dr. Pat Nixon did his residency.

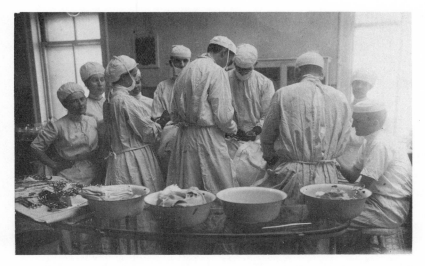

Here doctors perform surgery in an operating room at Johns Hopkins Hospital. Dr. Pat Nixon is fifth from the left, facing the camera.

The Johns Hopkins School of Medicine Class of 1909 poses here for a class picture. Faculty members, seated on the second row, include Lewellys F. Barker and Harvey Cushing, sixth and seventh from left, respectively. Class members, identified by number, include: *1*, J. L. Birdsong; *6*, P. I. Nixon; *21*, C. R. Austrian; *25*, W. L. Estes, Jr.; *27*, T. L. Ferenbaugh; *38*, G. R. Pretz; *42*, C. R. Essick; *47*, H. Q. Fletcher; *49*, T. P. Sprunt; and *51*, W. A. Baetjer. Photo courtesy of the Alan Mason Chesney Medical Archives of the Johns Hopkins Medical Institutions.

Olive Read Nixon smiles from the young couple's first automobile, a Hup-mobile 20.

Built in 1912, this house at 202 East Courtland Place, San Antonio, was the home of Pat and Olive Nixon and their children.

Dr. Pat rocks his first-born son, Pat, Jr., in San Antonio, 1912.

Dr. Pat sits at the desk where he did much of his writing, in his home in San Antonio.

Dr. Pat's four sons are pictured here in their military uniforms during World War II. *Left to right*: Ben, Pat, Jr., Thomas, and Robert.

Dr. Pat is shown with some of his family upon the publication of *The Early Nixons of Texas*, in 1957. *Left to right*: Dr. Pat; brother Zeb; sisters Beula Wood, Mollie Allen, and Alta Walker; and niece Ruth Allen.

Two of Dr. Pat's greatest sources of pride were his writing and his family. Here he receives the Summerfield Roberts Award for his book *The Early Nixons of Texas*, published in 1957.

Dr. Pat and Olive sit in front of their San Antonio home, surrounded by their children and grandchildren. Their sons, second row, left to right, are Pat, Jr., Thomas, Robert, and Ben. On the third row the daughters-in-law stand behind their husbands. This photograph was taken around 1960.

The Diary

January 23
[*No entry*]

January 24
Had some great sport today. Dr. Lewis took the topographical anatomy class up on the roof and there we sawed up a bunch of cadavers which had been frozen stiff by the weather. Had our little toxicology quiz this afternoon. Easy work. Went down to Mike Ferenbaugh's room tonight and studied the heart. Incidentally, collected a YMCA dollar from him.

January 25
More sawing today. Went to reception in church parlors. Good time. Met the three Miss Fullers of 1204 McCulloch Street—pretty fair.

January 26
Dr. Abel preached his weekly sermon in toxicology this morning. Autopsy at ten. MacCallum showed up the medical men on their diagnosis of carcinoma of stomach. Nothing found but pleurisy and nephritis. Barker's clinic: one typhoid case, lead colic, hysteria. Spent the afternoon on pathology.

January 27
Dr. Munhall of Philadelphia taught our S.S. class this morning. Heard him again at Ford's this afternoon. Heard Dr. Forbes of Philadelphia this morning, Mr. Robert Smith at YMCA tonight. Partridge, Webb, Cashman, and I went to Mt. Vernon. *Woman of Samaria* oratorio by Bennett—good.

January 28
[*No entry*]

January 29
Autopsy at ten. Aneurysm case in which Dr. Halsted had put aluminum band around aorta above and below the aneurysm. Operation not successful—aneurysm ruptured.

January 30, 31, and February 1
[*No entries*]

February 2
Reviewed the vagus nerve this morning. Recitation in gross morbid this morning. Went to Dr. Barker's clinic at twelve. Spent the evening

in pathology. Went with Higgins tonight to see Otis Skinner in *The Duel*—fairly good.

February 3
The regular Sunday routine—S.S., church, and YMCA. Dr. Hunner spoke at the last place.

February 4
[*No entry*]

February 5
Eight inches of snow today. Went down and studied bones with Mike Ferenbaugh. Letter from Olive.

February 6–7
[*No entries*]

February 8
Autopsy this morning—pneumonia—Dr. Fabyan. Went down to 21 East Mt. Vernon Place to a reception. Met two Miss Owens.

February 9
[*No entry*]

February 10
Historical meeting tonight. Paper on early medicine in Boston by Dr. Mumford of Harvard and one on "Haller" [*Albrecht von Haller*] by Dr. Hemmeter of University of Maryland.

February 11–14
[*No entries*]

February 15
Cerebrospinal meningitis autopsy today. Stick [64] diagnoses the case as enlarged prostate and later as carcinoma of rectum, which turned out to be cotton. Mike F. threatens to hypnotize Bill Estes and make him kiss Miss Stevenson. Letters from Mama and Olive.

February 16
TB meningitis autopsy this morning, child two-and-a-half years old. Quiz in toxicology, did pretty well. Went over to cage this afternoon and practiced a little baseball—twenty men out, good prospects.

[64] Edward Wentz Stick, of the class of 1909, practiced industrial surgery in San Francisco.

The Diary

February 17–18
[*No entries*]

February 19
First dog experiments in pharmacology today—great sport. Sellards the anesthetist, Cole the orderly, and Nixon the surgeon. The dog died at least four times, but each [*time*] with good hard puffing we brought him back. Loevenhart and Amberg would rave when anything out of the ordinary happened. Took walk with Sellards tonight. All the time plugging up for anatomy.

February 20
[*No entry*]

February 21
Showed some of the fellows and also Lewis a sclerotic coronary artery which was a bronchus. Heard Dr. Sabin lecture on the structure of the spinal cord. Practice this afternoon in the cage.

February 22
Washington's birthday. Went over to McCoy Hall to commemorative exercises. The honorable Hannis Taylor, formerly minister to Spain, was the orator of the day and spoke on "The Relation of the South to Pending Problems." Saw Maxine Elliott in *Her Great Match* tonight.

February 23–May 9
[*No entries*]

May 10
Pretz, Cashman,[65] and I went out to Evergreen, the home of Mrs. Buckler, the wife of one of the trustees, to a reception given to Hopkins students. Dandy place out there. Everything was turned over to us. The little girls would have us ride the pony. I got two lilies-of-the-valley as a prize for my horsemanship; Thompson and "Stovey" Brown got pitched off for theirs.

May 11–12
[*No entries*]

May 13
Essick learned this morning that his mother and brother were

---

[65] Bender Zelotes Cashman, of the class of 1909, practiced gynecology in Pittsburgh, Pennsylvania.

151

killed in a railroad wreck out in California.[66] The class has appointed a committee to express to him our sympathy. Went to the clinical-pathological conference this afternoon. Had some "strange contagion" up there. A graduate from Hopkins, who was once a medical missionary in Turkey, died with an obscure disease. At necropsy, nothing was found but a vast accumulation of fatty acid crystals in the abdominal lymph glands and in the mucosa of intestine. There was evidently some interference with fat metabolism.

May 14–29
   [*No entries*]

May 30
   Had my practical exam in pathology today. Began at 10 A.M., finished at 6:30 P.M. 'Twasn't very hard, but the strain was great. Lost my fountain pen tonight. Couldn't find it anywhere, though I knew it was in the room. Worried so about it that I couldn't study, so went to bed.

May 31
   To my great surprise, I found my pen right in the middle of the table. I couldn't believe my eyes. Think yesterday's exam was having its effect last night. Had my written exam in pathology this afternoon. Think I hit it pretty hard. Moss left this afternoon. He is stopping over in Washington tonight to see his girl; how I envy him! The "fusser's club" held forth tonight with Miss Asher as its nucleus: the last session for the year. The "gamblers" also adjourned for the year.

June 1–4
   [*No entries*]

June 5
   Have been working the surgical dispensary for three days, bandaging and taking histories. The members of the fusser's club sent Miss Casto a number of postcards tonight. It was Higgins's night. He leaves for home tomorrow, so we left him a clear field with the "nucleus" as its center. Have been reading *Counsels and Ideals from Writings of William Osler* by Camac. "The only real success comes when the man and the opportunity meet and match." "To study med-

   [66] Charles Rhein Essick, of the class of 1909, practiced in Reading, Pennsylvania.

icine without books is to sail an uncharted sea, while to study books without patients is not to go to sea at all." "Throw away, in the first place, all ambition beyond that of doing the day's work well."

June 6

Had a game of tennis with Gentry of Kansas this afternoon.[67] He was most too much for me without any practice. Higgins and Burns left this afternoon. I am all alone now, but so far have conquered that feeling of lonesomeness. Went room hunting this morning and to my great surprise found one at the first place I tried, 1720 Fairmont Avenue.

June 7–11
  [*No entries*]

June 12

Went over to see Dr. Warfield, 700 North Howard Street, and had him remove part of the middle turbinate bone on each side. I suffered some pain. It bled all day and night. Had to sleep with my mouth open.

June 13–17
  [*No entries*]

June 18

Have been working in the dispensary. An accident case came in this morning. The patient, a Negro man, died soon after his arrival. One-fifteenth gram of strychnine was given subcutaneously and salt infusion was done to no avail. Went out to the band concert at Patterson Park tonight with the "nucleus" (Miss Asher) and spent quite an enjoyable two hours.

This diary has been copied *in toto* because it sets out the many details of my life as a medical student. It should be borne in mind that I was only a second-year man at the end of the diary. Read after a lapse of [*many*] years, the comments and observations show evidences of serious purpose and mature thought.

---

[67] Ernest R. Gentry, of the class of 1909, served as a physician in the U.S. Army, retiring with the rank of colonel.

4

Internship, Residency, and Return to Texas

⤳๑๏๑⤳

My work as an intern began promisingly. [*I wrote*] to Olive on September 1, 1909:

> As I had planned, I arrived here [*Baltimore*] at 3:40 this morning. I came out to the hospital at 5:00, and by 8:30 I was in the operating room wearing my hospital togs.
>
> My journey was uneventful except for one or two happenings; at one time there was a woman with melancholia across the aisle from me and a young lady behind me who persisted in sticking her shoeless toes through my chair; I don't know whether she wanted me to tickle them or not. And last night a West Virginia funeral party tried to beat a fellow out of a cup from which he had sold them coffee.
>
> To say I am well pleased with my place and the outlook for the coming year is to put it lightly. I am domiciled in a large room on the east side of the administration building; it is fitted up with bed, two tables, lounge, dresser, washstand, bookcase, and a fireplace with a marble mantelpiece. It is a palace compared with the little economical box I have been in for the past two years. But my room is not the best of my possessions; my place on the staff here is a good one; I expect to learn a good bit about gynecology by September next. I'll tell you about my work later. [And this in a postscript] You will be pleased to know that I haven't had a real attack of lip biting since I left; I caught myself in the act a couple of times, once for instance, when the shoeless maid behind me said "have saw."[1]

[1] This was probably a habit Olive had called to his attention.

155

The Southern Baptist Convention met in Baltimore in May, 1910. The key figure of the convention, as in many others, was Dr. George W. Truitt of Dallas. I spoke of this to Olive and continued with the opera and theaters:

I heard Dr. Truitt yesterday morning. He preached a fine sermon to a packed house. Webb and I had a chair between us on the back row of the gallery, from where we could hear fairly well but could not see. Last night I heard a Mr. Shakespeare from London, England; he is a descendant of the bard of Avon, and for this reason, more than any other perhaps, everyone wanted to hear him. One man near me said he was going home as soon as the speaker began. He just wanted to be able to say he had heard Shakespeare! I had the pleasure of standing throughout the service but did not regret it as the sermon was a good one.

I have been out more this week than I have for a long time and, following on the heels of reunion week, it has gone pretty hard with me. I heard an English grand opera company in *Il Trovatore* Tuesday night and of course enjoyed it. It happened that two of Sheridan's old plays were presented here during the week by two different companies. *The School for Scandal* by the company from the New Theater in New York was especially enjoyable. *The Rivals* by the Ben Greet Players I enjoyed also but not so much as the first named. It was surprising to me how much humor there is stored away in those old plays written over a hundred years ago.

[*In a letter of January 23, 1910*]: For the first time in nearly a year I went to the theater last week. I saw Sothern and Marlowe twice, in *Romeo and Juliet* and in *The Merchant of Venice*. Of course a lovesick swain like myself was bound to be delighted with the balcony scene, for it suggested certain scenes I have had with my little girl, though I must say that Sothern made a better Shylock than Romeo, while Marlowe was equally fascinating as Juliet and as Portia.

My feeling toward the stage has changed, perhaps the style of popular play has changed. I have wasted so many nights at the theater in the past that I had rather sit down in my room and read a good book than listen to the suggestive stuff that the popular mind of this generation is clamoring for; I do not like this and never have; I have to hear enough of it, I'm sorry to say, from those round about me. I am not opposed to theatergoing altogether, though I have great sympathy with the man who is, but I don't ever expect to go to another musical comedy; I am too busy a man now and after I am married I expect to spend my idle evenings reading and talking with my darling little wife—something worthwhile and that brings satisfaction and peace and joy to an earnest soul.

But I continued to be a devotee of grand opera. The same month that I wrote the above, I had this to say to Olive: "I heard Ponchielli's *La Gioconda* Wednesday night, with Caruso and Emmy Destinn as the stellar attractions. I enjoyed the music ever so much, but have decided not to go again if I have to stand. I wouldn't have gotten in at all if I had not been lucky enough to find a street urchin who sold me his place in line for ten cents; as it was, I got in with the people who had been waiting since two o'clock for the ticket office to open. A little excitement was added by the arrival of President Taft just before the curtain rose."

Here are three theater items which I recorded far too casually:

> I heard with pleasure the Boston Symphony Orchestra with Melba as the soloist Tuesday night. . . . I heard the Boston Symphony Orchestra Wednesday night. Mischa Elman, violinist, was the soloist. I enjoyed this concert more than the one a few weeks ago, principally because the solos were more to my liking than those of Melba. . . . I saw Sarah Bernhardt in *La Femme X* last night. The play was in French so I didn't understand very much of it, but I was familiar with the story and was able to follow pretty well. One did not need to understand much; it was enough to see and hear "the divine Sarah," young at the age of sixty-seven. I had intended to see her in *Camille* but was unable to do so on account of the emergency case I mentioned.

I made two interesting trips to Washington in August and December, 1910. As I reread some of my old letters, the contents of which have long ago slipped my memory, I am pleased that so many of my diversions were educational or recreational or both. Here is the way I presented these two visits to Olive:

> My baseball enthusiasm took me to Washington yesterday to see a baseball game between Detroit and Washington, I having an idle half-day and accidentally having car fare. I got there a little late and, as a double header was scheduled, the best I could do was a seat on the ground in center field; but before the second

game began I had a dandy seat right at third base—a species of
Yankee nerve which I have acquired. It was a great pleasure to
me to see the best players in the business play, and especially Ty
Cobb, the king of them all. He is a small man and most unassum-
ing; one would never think that he had a million dollars, a wife,
and baby, in addition to his baseball reputation.

I went out to the aviation meet Thursday and saw some wonderful sights. I can't begin to tell you of all that I saw. You can get
a better idea from the newspaper that I sent you. The sight of a
man-built machine gracefully rising into the air for an indefinite
period of time and as gracefully alighting is surely the most wonderful thing I have ever seen in the way of human achievement;
it is no less wonderful than would be the sight of a giant bird
with wings thirty or forty feet long flying through the air.

The Christmas I spent at Johns Hopkins Hospital as an intern
was very enjoyable, and of course I had to give the details to
Olive:

I told you in my last letter that locally I had nothing to look
forward to, Christmas. A most unexpected invitation to dinner
today changed my outlook; it came from a nurse who lives here in
the city. It is against the rules of the hospital for the nurses to
have anything to do with the doctors socially, but as this particular
nurse invited trouble by inviting me, I could not be so ungrateful
as to refuse. And I'm mighty glad I did go, too, for I had a fine
time. The dinner, which was dandy, was not the greatest of the
attractions. I found a family of three sisters, all very attractive,
one a widow who does newspaper work, another more ancient
who insisted on negative answers as to whether I had read so and
so, and a third—young, good-looking, and engaged. The fiancé of
the last, a Mr. Adams who seemed to have his eye on the widow,
Miss Craigen (the nurse and sister to the trio), and I completed
the company. This is one of the few social engagements I have
enjoyed in Baltimore. I really felt at home, and that is very unusual since I am away from home and away from you. The too-
apparent happiness of the engaged couple brought to my mind
the thought of how happy I would be if my precious little girl
could be with me.

In the way of weather, Christmas could not have been more
ideal: cold, clear weather till early this morning when it began to
snow. Tonight the ground is covered with six inches of snow.

The nurses kept up the annual custom of singing Christmas

carols at five o'clock this morning. The doctors were invited to participate, but the hour was not altogether agreeable. A chorus of about fifty voices, accompanied by an organ on rollers went from ward to ward and sang carols. I heard them when they were near my room and didn't mind such a pleasant awakening, even at five in the morning.

All the wards were beautifully decorated and Ward H is just as pretty as any of them. All the dozens of electric lights were fitted with red shades, and holly and mistletoe and Christmas bells were used galore. A picture of the ward with its three chiefs, Miss Bampfield,[2] Dr. Schaefer, and me, was taken this morning; if it is good, I'll send you one.

Old Santa Claus has been good to me. Amongst other things, he left me a watch and *A Certain Rich Man* by William Allen White. The watch was without crystal and hands; it was accompanied by this verse:

> For Dr. Nixon here's a watch;
> With it please to keep the time.
> Take the pulse and put it down
> And after this *don't borrow* mine.

It came from the operating-room nurses, from whom I often borrowed a watch to get the pulse in giving ether.[3] Another nurse gave me a red, white, and blue rubber ball; I didn't know what significance to put on this gift.

Evidence of the strenuous work I had inherited as an intern was furnished in letters of September 12 and November 6, 1909:

> The work of the week just passed has been strenuous; twice we operated from 9 A.M. to 5 P.M.; after which time I had to go to the ward and attend to things there. Last Sunday I went to church, but today I dressed six patients, and it took till after church was over. I like it though. I like to do things as long as I am able physically.

[2] She was head nurse in Ward H.

[3] The following letter to Olive, dated August 7, 1910, explains why Pat was watchless at the time: "Jamie Nixon—that's one of Dr. Nixon's boys—wrote me a couple of days ago that he wanted his watch. I have been wearing his watch for five or six years, you know; now that he is going to the university, he needs his watch." Box 1 Folder 6, Dr. Pat I. Nixon Papers, Trinity University Archives, San Antonio.

At the end of a strenuous day I am tired and sleepy, but sleep will not satisfy nearly so much as a quiet talk with you. Dr. Cullen, one of the associate professors, operated today from 9:00 to 4:00 and kept things pretty lively, not stopping for lunch.[4] I was "on instruments," so I had to bear the brunt of the operator's dissatisfactions. From 4:00 to 5:45 I was busy on the ward, so that the fifteen minutes before dinner were the only ones that I could call my own.

The young doctor was presuming to play the dual role of moralist and martyr on October 3, 1909:

We had our first emergency at night one night last week. The patient was brought to the hospital at eleven o'clock with general peritonitis; by twelve she was on the operating table and by two o'clock, after eating a lunch, I was ready to retire. I think I have never seen such a depraved creature as was this patient, a girl of nineteen, married and separated from her husband, a victim of two loathsome diseases as a result of which she was brought to us, filthy, covered with vermin and their bites—a revolting creature fallen to the depths of degradation, which I hesitate to present to one so beautiful and good and pure as you. For her sake, five men risked much, and one of them much more still, for after we opened the abdomen some of the pus came within a fraction of an inch getting into my eye. From such an accident, one of the men on the gynecological staff here lost his eye a few years ago. This girl is my patient on the ward, and it falls to me to look after her and dress her incision. I have her on "special isolation," so that she is in a room to herself and none of the things she uses gets near the other patients. I have another patient, a girl away from home, who is paying for her transgressions; in her case I think I have succeeded in helping her, and that not alone in a physical way, but what can I do with my emergency case? Nothing; she has almost ceased to be human and has reverted to the plane of the beast.

The case described in a letter under date of October 10, 1909, was carefully studied and recorded. The notes were preserved and served as the basis of a paper on "Acute Dilatation of the Stomach Following Gynecological Operations," read before the

[4] Thomas Stephen Cullen, 1868–1953, was associate in gynecology. He developed the frozen-section method of tissue diagnosis.

Texas Medical Association and published in the *Texas State Journal of Medicine*.[5] This is the way I presented it to Olive:

> I had a woman last week with an ovarian cyst weighing sixty-five pounds. After the tumor was removed she weighed only one hundred pounds. The tumor was so large and heavy that when she lay down she had difficulty in getting up. Yet she walked a mile to catch the train a couple of days before. Her waist measure changed from fifty-two inches before operation to twenty-eight inches after operation. The tumor was perfectly benign, but it is hard to see why a woman in this day and time would let a thing like that keep growing. In connection with this case, I made a brag diagnosis on a rare postoperative complication (acute dilatation of the stomach). I'm really very proud of my diagnosis because only about two hundred cases have been reported in the literature, and of these only a small percent have been diagnosed correctly.

A little later, another medical item was added: "It is now after supper. I stopped my letter to see a transfusion. A physician who is a patient in the hospital had become so anemic that his life was in danger. The transfusion consisted in suturing an artery from the arm of a healthy brother into a vein of the patient and leaving them for forty minutes. It was real exciting, as both donor and donee were awake. This is the second transfusion I had seen; the first was done on Joe Brown [from La-Grange, Texas] when his spleen was removed."

A letter of November 21, 1909, contained these reports of medical experiences:

> Night calls have come too frequently lately to suit me. I was called to the ward at 3:30 the other morning to stop a postoperative hemorrhage. I packed the wound and then came back to my room. At 5:30 a second call came, and I repeated the process. It was 8:30 before the bleeding started again, so that by this time I did not have to be awakened.
>
> I had my first real struggle with the "Grim Monster" Friday night and he won. All of the advantages were in his favor, so I do not feel especially bad about my defeat. It was a case of general

---

[5] Pat also read this paper before the section on gynecology and obstetrics of the Southern Medical Association at Houston on April 23, 1920.

streptococcus peritonitis (the streptococcus is the most virulent bacterium). The case had been neglected and was admitted to the hospital in an almost moribund condition. We operated Thursday night and could foresee the outcome of the case as soon as we saw the condition of the abdominal cavity. She did fairly well until Friday night at 11:30 when she began to get rapidly worse until the end came at 1:45. We did all we could for her, but to no avail. I stayed with her constantly from 8:00 until 1:45. It was one of those cases where the medical man has to confess his utter inability to combat an infectious process.

The Journal Club is progressing nicely. At the last meeting I reviewed a thirty-two–page German article. Even this early I can see improvement in my reading of German.

A case of smallpox and a correct diagnosis is reported on December 12, 1909. I had seen a few cases of this disease, which was more than an occasional disease in Texas at the turn of the century.

Ward H was the scene of considerable excitement last week because a case of smallpox developed in the ward. The eruption was only slight, and this the woman had had three or four days before saying anything about it. Dr. Schaefer discovered the eruption first, it being in one of his patients, and thought it was chickenpox.[6] I suggested that it looked more like smallpox, so the resident physician was called in, and he confirmed my suspicion. The woman was isolated at once and soon taken to a detention camp. Everyone about the ward, patients, orderlies, maids, nurses, and doctors, was vaccinated immediately. Dr. Cullen and I vaccinated all of the patients and one another, so this, my first experience with vaccination, was an extensive one. Only eight days have passed since the woman left the ward; the incubation period is from nine to fifteen days, so that the danger of other cases developing is not yet over. [Two weeks later I added this sequel:] Before this woman was taken to the quarantine hospital, Miss Madelaine Moysey, my Canadian friend, was appointed to nurse the case. Five days ago she came down with a genuine case of smallpox. Of course she also had to be taken to the quarantine hospital; luckily for her, another nurse from here, who had had the disease and is hence immune, accompanied her. All of us on

[6] Solomon W. Schaefer, of the class of 1909, practiced as an internist in New York City.

the ward wrote her a letter last night, expressing our sympathy and wishing her well.

By January 23, 1910, I had been an intern for five months and was telling Olive how speedy I was in the operating room. A word, however, should be said in defense of expedition in the surgery of that day. No dependable antibiotics were to be had, and shock and loss of blood were not easily combatted. So speed, consistent with safety, was essential. After coming to San Antonio, Dr. R. Stuart Adams—the first and perhaps best of our local anesthetists—summed up the problem this way: "No lost motions, no lost moments."

"I did my first big operation some days ago and got along all right. I finished an operation in thirty-five minutes which it takes Dr. Richardson,[7] the resident gynecologist, thirty minutes to do, and got a good result."

In a letter to Olive under date of October 30, 1910, I had this to say: "Yesterday, it fell to my lot to take the place of one of the doctors in the cystoscopic clinic, and I must say I'm glad it was so, for I had some good work. Ordinarily there are only two or three patients in this clinic; yesterday there were six, two of which were good kidney cases which I succeeded in working out. I don't know why I tell you about this, unless it is because of the personal elation at having done a difficult thing easily and well."

After about eighteen months on the gynecological service, I transferred to the surgical department, where for six months I found the work active and interesting, as attested by these extracts:

> My new work is very satisfactory; it is quite different from the work on the gynecological side. I am seeing a lot of the little things in surgery which I shall be called on to look after. I shall feel better qualified to practice medicine after having had a few weeks of this work.

> The past week has gone so rapidly with me because of the

[7] Edward H. Richardson, 1877–1973, was also associate professor of gynecology.

activity of my new work. It is quite different from the work of the past year and at times very exciting. On Friday night we had an unusual case of traumatic rupture of the intestine, and no sooner had we finished the operation than we were called to one of the wards to see a patient on whom a tracheotomy had to be done. Of course the work is not that active all the time, but there is activity enough to make it interesting and to make me wish for a little more sleep at times.

We had a very interesting old Kentucky colonel on one of the private wards a short time ago. He was distinctly of the old-school type: during his convalescence he wanted to go downtown but had some trouble getting a permit; he gave vent to his indignation by saying, "Here am I, a man who has swayed thousands by the eloquence of my words, who has to telephone Dr. Arthur Fisher[8] for permission to go downtown." One night he said, "Doctor, there are 100,000 people anxious to know how I am tonight: 50,000 in Louisville and 50,000 scattered throughout our dear Southland." He stopped everybody he met in the halls or corridors and told them how well he was feeling.

I hadn't written a page last night before I was called to the operating room, where I helped Dr. Heuer do an appendix.[9] We hadn't finished this case before another, a liver abscess, was brought up to do. As a result I retired at 1:30 to get up at 7:30.

Today I started on my new duties as second-assistant surgeon, there being only two men on the staff above me; in the month that is to come I expect to get a great deal of useful experience. When asked to stay on in Dr. Gatch's absence,[10] I felt that I would be guilty of ingratitude if I refused. I believe it will be time well spent.

I am getting impatient for the time when I can go to work in earnest. I can hardly force myself to stay here the few remaining months. I know that I ought to stay, and that is what keeps me here. I am far more self-confident than I was a year ago; it is a great encouragement to see the success of those who have begun less well fitted than I am. I feel that if I can begin right, I shall

[8] Arthur O. Fisher, of the class of 1909, taught at Washington University in Saint Louis.
[9] George J. Heuer, 1882–1950, was a resident surgeon; his specialty was surgery of the thorax.
[10] Willis Dew Gatch, 1879–1962, was a resident surgeon; later he became professor of surgery at Indiana University.

not have much trouble. There's one thing sure: the sooner I have the encouragement of your presence with me, the sooner I shall be what I am to be. I have long been convinced that my success depends more on you than it does on me.

When I was an intern, an epidemic of diphtheria broke out among the nurses and hospital staff members. The authorities considered the situation serious enough to justify closing the medical school, the hospital, and the outpatient department. One of my classmates, Dr. Charles R. Austrian, had charge of the situation, especially the laboratory work.[11] He took cultures from the throats of everybody about the hospital, and those with positive findings were put in the isolation ward. Soon the ward was full of patients, including such prominent members of the faculty as Dr. William H. Welch, Dr. William H. Howell, and Dr. F. P. Mall. The situation thus became as amusing as it was serious. To lighten the tension, I decided to pose as a reporter for the *Baltimore Sun*. I called up Austrian and told him that as a reporter I had come out to investigate the epidemic. I quoted Dr. W. P. Morrill from the Sydenham Hospital across town as suggesting that the culture media used were contaminated and that the whole business had been bungled. Dr. Austrian became very excited and very outspoken in his denials. Of course, nothing went into the *Sun*, although Austrian spent some anxious hours. I learned that Dr. Welch and Dr. Howell laughed heartily about the hoax.

In a letter to Olive, I added this amusing footnote about the epidemic: "The dispensary resumed work on Thursday, and the hospital will open tomorrow, so we all are told. At the present time there are only seventy patients in the whole hospital. Fumigation is the order of the day. The thoroughness with which some of this has been carried out is illustrated by this incident: one of the laboratories in the physiological building was formaldehyded for twelve hours and left sealed till the next day. When the room was opened an old hen flew out of one of

[11] Charles Robert Austrian, of the class of 1909, returned to Hopkins as associate professor of medicine.

the shelves and joyfully announced that she had laid an egg."

Dr. Cullen and Dr. Richardson were my closest friends among the Hopkins faculty. They took a close personal interest in me and my welfare; especially true was this during my internship in gynecology. Dr. Cullen, like several other Hopkins professors—including Osler—was a Canadian. Judith Robinson's *Tom Cullen of Baltimore* does not do full justice to this important man. While I was on the hospital staff, I was flattered that he trusted me to do some of his research work in the library.

These three Cullen items were sent to Olive in July, 1910, and January, 1911. My days in Baltimore were about over. These associations with these great gynecologists remain as happy memories. Lest he should be criticized for operating on the old lady under unfavorable conditions, let it be said that we made a second trip to see her and she was doing well.

> Thursday afternoon I went with Dr. Cullen, one of the associate professors of gynecology, up to Frederick, from where we were taken in an automobile eight miles in the country to see a patient. We found an old lady of seventy-four with symptoms of appendicitis. We operated at midnight and found a ruptured appendix. As there were five doctors and two nurses in the house, everything went pretty well, but operating in a private home is quite a different proposition from operating in a hospital where you have everything you want. After getting something to eat we returned to Frederick and got to bed at 2 A.M. At 7 we caught a train for Baltimore.

> Friday afternoon Dr. E. K. Cullen and I went out canoeing. We were on a tributary of the Chesapeake Bay, and the water was pretty rough; we were right out amongst the whitecaps. It was a delightful afternoon's diversion; we had a light canoe which would jump with every stroke we made; and it was so pleasant in the cool sea breezes that we were sorry when night came.

> Three other members of the staff and I went to Washington yesterday as the guests of Dr. T. S. Cullen to see the surgeon general's library. Colonel W. D. McGaw, who is in charge of the library, very kindly conducted us through and explained everything to us. The library is a great institution; it is the biggest of its kind in the world. It is doing a great work for the medical

world, both here and abroad. Among many other things, it has between fifteen hundred and sixteen hundred medical periodicals which come weekly or monthly. This gives you an idea of how much time an up-to-date medical man has for things other than medicine.

Dr. Hunner was most patient with the shortcomings of his students. I learned many practical things in gynecology from him. He was very kind and very friendly. Naturally, I had to let a prospective doctor's wife know about him and his wife:

> Dr. Hunner is one of the visiting men on our staff that I have not mentioned to you before. He is the fourth member of the staff, being ranked by Drs. Kelly, Russell, and Cullen.[12] I ate dinner with Dr. Hunner on Tuesday night, and of course the change from hospital fare and hospital atmosphere was very agreeable. I am much encouraged by Dr. Hunner's history; he has been practicing eight years; he has a good practice, a fine home, a congenial wife, two daughters, and one son. My highest hope will be realized if, eight years from now, the same can be said of me. Mrs. Hunner, who was a trained nurse, is a fine woman and good-looking with it; she has learned typewriting and looks after all Dr. Hunner's correspondence and history taking. While Dr. Hunner was out, I asked her what she thought of the life of a physician's wife; she replied that she preferred it to all others, saying it was a pleasure to make a few sacrifices which she knew were for the good of her husband and his work. I then asked her opinion of long engagements. She answered, "I think they are the only thing; if they were more common, unhappy marriages would be less frequent. Dr. Hunner and I were engaged three years." I ventured in reply that that was not very long, that I knew a couple who had already been engaged six years and who could testify to the value of long engagements.

My opinion of Dr. Richardson was well summarized in a letter to Olive on January 29, 1911. His personality and his capabilities have projected themselves through the intervening years in increasing luster.

> If my letter to you is not finished this morning, it will be because of a very welcome invitation I received a few minutes ago.

---

[12] William W. Russell, 1866–1923, was associate in gynecology. He was a founder of the American College of Surgeons.

Dr. Richardson, who was resident gynecologist last year and who is without a doubt the best-liked man who has ever been about the hospital, invited Dr. Cullen and me to dinner with him today. I was not slow in accepting the invitation, which I knew could be recommended both from the gastronomic and the social aspects. You know Baltimore prides itself on being the gastronomic center of the world, and I am inclined to believe it since I first saw the interior of some of the crosstown dining rooms, though my boarding house and hospital experiences did not convince me of it.

[Later] Have just gotten back from Dr. Richardson's. Needless to say my two hours were very well spent. He has a dandy wife and a little girl about two years old. He showed me his office and his system of histories, bookkeeping, etc. I brought back with me a sample of his history paper, prescription blank, bill head, etc. His system is simple, and I like it very much.

Since my main experience [*during my internship*] was in gynecology, it was in that department that I learned to apply what I had absorbed in four years of medical education. Every opportunity was given to the interns by those in authority. As I look at a group picture of the hospital staff on my wall, memories of many happy days and loyal friendships come trooping back. In this picture are Dr. Edward H. Richardson, resident; Dr. Ernest K. Cullen and Dr. John A. Sperry, assistant residents; Dr. Solomon W. Schaefer and Dr. Pat Ireland Nixon, interns; and Dr. Julius R. Blackman, extern. The seed which Uncle Lee Russell, Miss Ida Hunter, Professor Schofield, Colonel Bingham, and Dr. H. W. Harper had sown found fertile soil in the scientific atmosphere of Johns Hopkins. The work I did there and the progress I made proved to be justification for the confidence of those who believed in me, most of all my mother.

But I had been in Johns Hopkins long enough. While the residency system had been developed there and had many virtues, I could see about the hospital certain evidences of the impoverishing effects of a too cloistered life. The security and independence supplied by hospital walls, if too prolonged, could easily sap initiative and stifle ambition, to say nothing of the loss of touch with the practical side of the practice of medicine. This danger was later demonstrated by the attitude toward socialized medicine which was taken by so many of the full-time professors.

On June 25 [1911], I was anticipating my departure:

> I expect to sever my connection with the hospital on next Friday. After that step is taken, it will take me several days to get ready to shake the Baltimore dust off my feet. I am buying my instruments and practically all the supplies that I'll need, and it is making a pauper of me; one has to pay his weight in gold for surgical instruments almost. I have even gone so far as to have a thousand [*medical*] history sheets printed with my name on them. Although I can little afford it, I am not economizing on the things I shall need; such, I think, would be false economy. I'm going to fit up my office well and believe my money will be well spent.

The following was written on July 2 [*1911*]: "I am no longer connected with the J. H. Hospital. I took off my operating suit last night to don it no more. From now to the latter part of the week, I shall enjoy Johns Hopkins hospitality without giving anything in return. I expect to leave for Philadelphia about a week from today. After two or three days there, New York will be my second stopping place. I probably won't go to Boston as I had intended. From New York I shall go via Niagara Falls to Chicago and Rochester [*Minnesota*] where I hope to spend a week or two."

And on July 7 [*1911*], the night before I left, I was writing Olive my final Baltimore letter: "I'm leaving early in the morning on the Sunshine Train for Philadelphia. I feel that I'm already on my way to you and to happiness. Yet, after tonight, having told all my friends goodbye, I am far from happy. I am experiencing both sadness and gladness. You know how it is."

So after six years at Johns Hopkins, I turned my face homeward. These had been years of soil preparation and seed planting. They had been formative and fruitful years. I had received the best medical education that was available. I should have been able to walk alone medically. If I failed, the fault would be all mine. On July 8, 1911, I left Baltimore. I carried with me pleasant and satisfying memories. I carried with me also more than a modicum of gratification over what I had accomplished and confidence in my future capacities.

Before I left Baltimore, Dr. T. S. Cullen gave me a handful of calling cards. Dr. Cullen, then forty-three years old, was one of the outstanding gynecologists of the world. These cards, without any inscription, were the open-sesame to all surgical clinics. I was received with the greatest courtesy from Philadelphia to Rochester [*Minnesota*].

Fortunately, I resumed my diary at this time, and it can tell more than I can. The abrupt judgments which I passed on surgeon or surgical technique are, I hope, forgivable. I was young, very young at the time, and perhaps provincial.

July 8, 1911

Philadelphia. Bade farewell to J. H. Hospital this morning after two years of hospital life. There were many regrets at leaving, but prospect of getting out and doing something outweighs them all. Came to the city of brotherly love and find that I am "orientirt"— contrary to former visits. Went to the ATO [*Alpha Tau Omega*] house and passed the time of day with a couple of fellows.

I spent the afternoon at the _____ Hospital and saw Dr. _____ work. Iodine cleaning. Only one assistant. Saw the following operations:

Appendectomies. No retractors used. Catgut nearly always doubled.

Tumor of parotid gland—good dissection.

Inguinal hernia—layers not well dissected out—bunched up together; cord transplanted.

Hysteromyomectomy—20 minutes. Mass ties.

Papilloma of bladder—stovaine anesthesia—failure.

Dilation and curettage.

Empyema—five inches of two ribs resected.

Hemorrhoids—clamp and cautery.

Impression: technique of clinic very bad. A rough but rapid surgeon—uses his tongue better than his hands.

Spent a pleasant hour with Mr. and Mrs. Taylor Stewart at 5119 Cedar Avenue. Their nest is well feathered. No birds yet!

July 9

Spent three hours in Atlantic City this morning. Nothing worthwhile except an hour in the surf. There is a superficiality—even vulgarity about the place that is disgusting.

Dined with Miss Madge Magee, a Hopkins exnurse, at Norristown tonight. She has grown rather tall and quite pretty and paints as skillfully as ever. Had a general review of Hopkins gossip.

July 10

Had a half-hour's talk with Dr. Allen J. Smith this morning. Saw Dr. _____ work again this afternoon. His list:

Appendectomies: three, six minutes.

Appendectomy: double salpingo-oophorectomy. Twenty-two minutes. Pus tube ruptured; no closure of raw areas; no drainage.

Anterior and posterior colporrhaphy—usual operation; levators not seen.

Dilation and curretage; amputation of cervix.

Gallstones.

Inguinal hernia. Very poorly done by first assistant. Second assistant scrubbed for forty seconds (I timed him), rinsed off in bichloride and alcohol, and then took his place without gloves or gown.

Man of seventy etherized and brought before the clinic. Catheter inserted into distended bladder without difficulty with aid of nurse. Dr. _____ worked with scissors and forceps in hand all the time; first assistant didn't clamp a vessel or cut a ligature. Former impression magnified. Why the latter part of the motto on the wall: *Noli loqui. Noli tangere?* What harm would it do?

Something must be said about my visit with Allen J. Smith. Back of that half-hour which I spent with him was a long family friendship. For many years he was professor of pathology at the medical department of the University of Texas. All this time he was a close personal friend of Dr. J. W. Nixon. His advancement to the University of Pennsylvania was a great loss to Texas medicine. At the end of my third year at Hopkins, I spent several weeks working in his laboratory, where I was permitted to do many autopsies. It is interesting to record what I wrote Olive at the time:

My work has been progressing nicely. Dr. Nixon has an exalted opinion of Dr. Smith, and I am beginning to think he is right. He is a fine man with most interesting ideas. I love to sit and watch him roll a cigarette and then, between puffs, explain one of his original theories or tell me what I am to look out for when I begin my work in Texas. He is a busy man, yet he doesn't object to talking to me for an hour or more on any subject that happens to present itself. He is always ready to stop in the midst of his work and explain something to me. If he were in Baltimore, I know in whose laboratory I would spend my spare hours. He has just about persuaded me to come up here next spring and take the Blockley Hospital exam for an internship.

I appreciated his friendship then. I cherish his memory now.

As I moved on to New York, then to Cleveland and Chicago, and finally to Rochester, my diary contains many observations on many subjects. They are put down here for the light they throw on the life of a recent medical graduate. It should be remembered that they are the observations of a most untraveled young man.

July 11

In New York again. I never feel at home in New York; it's so big and wicked and forgetful of the rest of the world. Went to the New York Academy of Medicine, 17 West 43rd Street, and read a little. Took a "rubber neck" wagon up 5th Avenue to 90th Street. Walked from this to Mt. Sinai Hospital where I saw Dr. Moschkowitz do:

Cholecystectomy for chronic empyema of gallbladder and stone in cystic duct. He does far more cholecystectomies than cystostomies. Seventy-six cases last year; one death.

He did an appendix for my special benefit to show me what he says Dr. Kelly has called "the crude Mt. Sinai method": ligated the stump, cauterized, and dropped it back without inverting. Simple but rather heterodox. Result said to be good. Aseptic technique good. Operative procedure fair. Nurses all wore high-heel shoes. Everybody except the nurses sported a moustache. Cordial reception. "God bless you" after each case.

Saw the Giants and Pirates play—poor game, 13–4 Pirates. Wagner got four hits. Quartered for the night at New Amsterdam Hotel, 4th Avenue and 21st.

July 12

Hot, dusty, sultry city where people are falling on all sides from the heat. Twenty-five deaths yesterday. Saw two of the house men at the _____ Hospital try to do a hernia this morning. Rotten performance: Poupart's ligament divided; ring and sac not seen—and he didn't have a wet hair on him! Went over to the New York Hospital and had lunch with Armstrong, Thompson, McClure, and Newcomb. Met Dr. Wiltner there, just over from Prague; he had never seen iced tea before; he expected it to have foam! Good hospital; well systematized.

Went to Presbyterian Hospital and was shown around by Devan. Everything fairly new and clean. Saw several heat cases—one with temperature of 110°. Saw Dr. Woolsey do a gastrotomy; old healed ulcer found. Deliberate and very slow; for speed—or rather lack of it—he excels "Daddy" Halsted.

Dined with Wenning and Potter at the Roosevelt Hospital. Paid short visit to Bellevue. Saw Hawkins, Cody, and Booth. Very old hospital—full of old, chronic cases. Was surprised to see tonight an undertaker's sign on a Catholic church on 4th Avenue.

July 13

[*No entry*]

July 14

Got to Niagara Falls at 6:30 yesterday after a hot and dusty all-day trip through a good country. Was in time to get a glimpse of the falls. Took a walk through Prospect Park and then crossed over to the Canadian side, where an excellent view of the falls is possible. The beauty of it all defies all description: one can only stand in awe and look and look and look. Saw the rays of the setting sun as they fell in a rainbow on the mist of Horseshoe Falls. Came out again at 11:00 P.M. and saw the scene by moonlight.

Up early this morning, took the belt line from Horseshoe Falls to Queenstown on the Canadian side. Crossed to American side to Lewiston and came back via the whirlpool and whirlpool rapids—a trip more than worthwhile. Falls 170 feet high. American Falls 1,100 feet wide; Horseshoe Falls 3,000 feet. Water 180 feet deep below. Took a car to St. Catherines, Ontario, where I greatly surprised Miss Jessie Graves with a call; found her on her vacation from Hopkins. Walked down to the Willard [*Welland*] Canal; had tea together and an altogether pleasant afternoon. Talked Hopkins of course. Dachshund—great dog. Came back to Buffalo and caught the nine o'clock boat for Cleveland. Promise of a storm outside. Promise of a sleepless night inside: no stateroom available.

July 15

No storm without or within last night. I got a stateroom after all and slept like a top. Arrived Cleveland 6:30 A.M. Went uptown and got breakfast. Car fare, 3¢. Looked up Norton and Ledbetter at Lakeside Hospital. Took lunch and dinner with them. Saw Dr. Weir do a transperitoneal nephrectomy: lumbar Pott's the reason. Dr. Sloane did excision of both breasts of a man and circumcision. Nurses in room. Tonsils by Dr. Abbott.

General system of hospital very similar to Hopkins: same arrangement of buildings; same system of histories and charts; same instruments, treatment, etc. Gas anesthesia; Teter method—given by nurses.

Cleveland is a city of cops; seventeen seen at once.

En route to Chicago 10:45 P.M.

July 16

Arrived Chicago 7:40 A.M. Located at Hotel Grace, Adams Street. Went to Fourth Presbyterian Church. Was disappointed to find that Dr. Stone was away. Took a walk in Lincoln Park this afternoon. Great place: large; full of trees; good driveways; well kept; on the western shore of Lake Michigan. Chicago, "the windy city," is quite different from New York: it is more beautiful and less in a hurry. Today (Sunday) everything is wide open: barbershops, saloons, theaters, etc.

July 17

Attended A. J. Ochsner's Clinic at Augustana Hospital 8–12. His list:

Complete breast. Closure without grafting.

Appendectomies, two acute, one chronic. Mesentery and appendix clamped and cut. Stump inverted. No ligation or cauterization.

Two hysterectomies and double salpingo-oophorectomy. Transplanted ovary under rectus fascia in one case. I was surprised to hear the man on my left say to me, "That's my wife." He was not a physician.

One right salpingo-oophorectomy.

One amputation of cervix, dilation and curretage, and tamponade of cervix with bismuth paste. Keys' sounds used as dilators.

Fistula in ano incised. Big Ochsner clamps used for everything. A rapid but not a finished surgeon.

Clinic reminds one of _____ [in Philadelphia]; technique not quite so bad. Operator rarely wore gloves and assistants did not change theirs after each case. Operator and first assistant wore no gowns. Clinics well conducted. Thirty-five visitors. Iodine cleaning.

Saw one of the house men suspend a uterus. He took a tuck in the round ligaments and called it Kelly's method! Appendix very poorly done. Profanity pervaded the operating room.

Went through Marshall Field and Company; huge establishment. Everything from a restaurant to a reading room.

Walked the grounds of the University of Chicago and the midway, which is the location of the original midway at the world's fair. Saw a little of South Park.

July 18

Saw the following men operate at Michael Reese Hospital: Dr. Andrews, a burly old Scotchman, slow, sure, deliberate. His list:

Indirect inguinal hernia, recurrent. Used rectus fascia for closure. Transplanted the cord—the rule. Drained—the exception. Used Kangaroo tendon. He did not do what Dr. Finney calls the Ferguson-Andrews operation. Returned sac without opening it.

Dr. Eisendrath, a chary and very conservative surgeon—pretty keen on diagnosis. His list:

Exploratory laparotomy. Retro sigmoidal mass and mass in cul-de-sac, probably tuberculous. Excised a bit for diagnosis but didn't explore further. Masses seemed to be abscesses; why not drain one above and the other below?

Excision of angioma of biceps muscle.

Appendectomy: subsiding. Usual operation, fairly well done. Catgut in skin.

Bottle operation for hydrocele. Dr. _____ apparently a cynical surgeon with a typical genitourinary temperament. No regard for nurses.

Removal of a sponge the size of a lemon which had been left in the scrotum at a former operation! Dr. Friend, a polite man.

Radical cure of femoral hernia. Chromic catgut purse string through pectineal fascia (?). Poupart's and Gimbernat's ligaments. Made rounds with Dr. Friend. Saw a good many postoperative cases, and one case of swelling to outer side of popliteal space, probably cold abscess.

Saw Dr. Ferguson work at St. Luke's this afternoon. A slow and finished surgeon. The methods of the man and his operating-room temperament remind one very strongly of Dr. Kelly. He is perhaps less irritable, but has a lot more special instruments! Not so rapid and not so skillful and not so finished as Dr. Kelly. His list:

Myomectomy followed by subtotal hysterectomy; smooth pelvis resulting.

Appendectomy: stump clamped with Ferguson clamp and cauterized; not ligated.

Multiple myomectomy in a patient about three months pregnant. Base of myomata ligated with interlocking sutures of catgut before excision. Knowing nothing of the history except that the operation was for metrorrhagia, it is difficult to see how the removal of three subperitoneal fibroids will produce any result other than a probable miscarriage.

Chicago seems to be literally alive with medical men: there are forty-two visiting surgeons to St. Luke's!

Spent a few minutes in the Board of Trade and saw a sight not soon to be forgotten: hundreds of men, young and old, crying like mad at the top of their voices; the air full of dust and smoke; the floor covered with paper and expectoration; the noise of the tickers just audible above the uproar; a few men seeming to have something that all the rest wanted very badly and were willing to do all that voice and fingers and money could do to get. To an unsophisticated onlooker the place looked like a veritable neurosis shop instead of a "board of trade for the mutual benefit of its members."

Am now at the C.&N.W. station, a beautiful place. Ran across Lindsay Baskett and talked with him for a half-hour. He was graduated from Ann Arbor in 1909 and stayed for a year's internship. Is finishing up in Minnesota at the present time. Expects to locate in El Paso.[13] Off for Rochester at 8 P.M.

It must have been that I had some preconceived ideas as to what I would see at various surgical clinics and as to how I would be impressed. For I seemed to have written with a critical pen in the first four cities, but in Rochester, I remained a long time to praise. The differing attitude was based on what I had heard, read, and seen. The doctors Mayo, Dr. Judd, Dr. Balfour, and Dr. MacCarthy were frequent visitors at Johns

---

[13] Lindsay Wilson Baskett did not settle in El Paso; he practiced medicine in Saint Peter, Minnesota.

Hopkins and were welcome ambassadors of good surgery.[14]
Likewise, Dr. Halsted, Dr. Finney, and Dr. Cullen were well
thought of at Rochester. So, while some preconceived prejudices may have existed, my impressions were based on more or
less solid ground.

July 19

At last I have reached Rochester, the surgical mecca of America.
Rochester is a beautiful little town of seven thousand people; surrounded on all sides by an amphitheater of low-lying hills, it is itself
situated on several small hills. The sidewalks and streets are good
and are lined by beautiful shade trees, mostly maple. St. Mary's Hospital and the excellent work emanating from it have made the place.
The Mayo brothers have donated a public park, a library, and a
YMCA building. The hospital itself is located in the edge of town
about a mile from the business section.

In order to escape the *hoi polloi* and perhaps to save a dollar or
two, I wasted a couple of hours today looking for a room in the residence section. Am domiciled at the Rochester Hotel. The hotel—
and in fact the whole town—is full of patients, pre- or postoperative.
And my how they do talk, especially the women. Each of them had
had or is to have a very serious operation. On inquiry, one woman
said her trouble was paralysis of the tongue, and all the time she was
talking a blue streak! It is interesting to figure out the diagnosis in
each case; there seems to be an especially good crop of goiters.

The following is the list of operations of the morning:

Dr. W. J. Mayo

Hysterectomies for fibroids.

Exploratory laparotomy.

Resection of cecum, or colon, and part of transverse colon for carcinoma. Lateral ileocolostomy. Time, one hour. No soiling. No drainage.

Nephrectomy for hypernephroma. Right-sided hematuria, pain,

---

[14] Charles Horace Mayo, 1865–1939, made a special study of goiter. William
James Mayo, 1861–1939, was a specialist in stomach surgery. Edward Starr
Judd was chief of the Mayo surgical staff. He served as president of the Ameri-
can Medical Association. David C. Balfour was a University of Toronto gradu-
ate. William Carpenter MacCarthy, the Mayo pathologist, graduated from
Johns Hopkins in 1904.

tumor. Right rectus incision, transperitoneal. Varicose veins, giving rise to profuse hemorrhage. Wound packed and clamps left on.

Resection of rectum for carcinoma. Permanent colostomy ten days before through middle of left rectus—the only sensible way. Patient in reversed Trendelenburg posture. Anus sutured. Long incision encircling rectum at its lower end. Coccyx (but no sacrum) removed. Dissection begun below and carried up beyond growth. Peritoneum opened. Bowel ligated, cut, and inverted. Practically no bleeding. Wound partly closed with silkworm gut and filled with vaseline. Time, one hour.

Dr. C. H. Mayo
Cyst of cornea.
Appendix.
Goiters.
Anastamosis of right recurrent laryngeal nerve—postoperative paralysis.
Appendectomy, Webster-Baldy suspension.
Suprapubic prostatectomy. Removal of stone.

Dr. Judd
Appendix.
Goiter.
Gallbladder.
Excision of tumor of navel.
Dilation and curretage.
Repair of old fracture of clavicle.
Excision of tumor of jaw.
Amputation of cervix, R. R. V. O.
Removal of nodule in breast.
Cleft palate and harelip.

I saw more of Dr. Will Mayo's work than of the others. He is certainly the most skillful, the most rapid, the neatest surgeon I have ever seen work. I can't describe the nicety and the ease with which he operates. He uses his hands and his head equally well. Too much cannot be said in commendation of his first assistant, Sister Josephine.[15] She adds no small part to the smoothness of the operations.

Attended the Surgeons' Club this afternoon at the YMCA building,

[15] Sister Joseph (not Josephine) was superintendent of St. Mary's Hospital and operating-room assistant to Dr. Will Mayo.

and three men reported on the operations of the day and there was general discussion. Mr. Stiles of Edinburgh is the star visitor at the clinic. About sixty visitors in all.

July 20

Had a real bath last night and slept like a top afterwards. Up at six this morning. Took a walk about the town. The climate of Rochester is delightful, the days are pleasant and the nights are delightfully cool. The sky is remarkably blue. Breakfast at seven. Operations at eight.

Dr. Will Mayo

Hysterectomy, double salpingo-oophorectomy for pelvic inflammatory disease and ovarian cyst; appendectomy.

The resection of colon and kidney cases of yesterday are both doing nicely. In connection with the latter case, he made these comments: Grawitz in 1883 first studied these tumors and concluded that as the kidney, which in fetal life is a pelvic organ, moves upward, it pushes the adrenal upward. In this process bits of adrenal tissue are ripped off and from these the hypernephroma arise. Pick, ten years later, studied Grawitz's material and his own and came to the same conclusion. Sturck (?) in about 1906 was the first to challenge this conclusion. He called attention to the fact that these tumors never arose from the adrenal itself and that they seldom arose from the kidney capsule where the adrenal anlage are most numerous. He considered these tumors as true kidney tumors. Wilson of the Mayo clinic studied the condition from a comparative anatomical standpoint and confirmed Sturck's conclusions. Some believe that they are mesoblastic in origin. They probably spring from the secreting tubules. They comprise 90 percent of kidney tumors; carcinoma next. They are often secondary in bone and prostate, and the metastases may be the first indication of trouble.

Gastroenterostomy, posterior; cure of postoperative ventral hernia. Found a duodenal ulcer just below the pylorus. This was inverted on a purse string. Then did a post-gastroenterostomy. Used three layers of sutures on posterior wall, one linen, two catgut. The bowel was incised down to the mucosa and the first catgut tier placed, lumen then opened and the second placed. Ninety percent of cases with stomach symptoms have nothing wrong with the stomach. One must think of the heart, lungs, liver, gallbladder, appendix, kidney, anemias, etc.

Dilation and curretage; appendix.

Pelviolithotomy. X ray showed stone. Stone found in pelvis. Stone steadied by Sister J.; the pelvis opened. Closed with catgut and flap of fat pulled over. Pyelotomy preferred to nephrotomy on account of less hemorrhage.

Resection of rectum for carcinoma; end-to-end anastomosis. Midline incision. Mesentery clamped and later tied. Bowel doubly clamped, above and below growth. Bowel divided and ends cauterized with hot irons. Lower end about four inches long. Three-quarters–inch stiff rubber tube passed through this. Upper end of tube fastened to proximal cut end of bowel and inserted into it. Cut ends then drawn together with interrupted Lembert's. Assistant pulled down on tube while Dr. Mayo picked up with clamps the distal loop about 1 inch from end; the result was an invagination of the upper into the lower loop. This result was maintained by interrupted Lembert's of linen and reinforced by Lembert's of catgut. Two cigarette drains, one on either side of rectum. These will be left in six to eight days, as leakage in these cases is late if at all. Sphincter ani dilated and tube anchored with linen. Operation not feasible if lower loop is not one and a half inches long. Has done the operation fifteen times with good results. I saw Dr. Finney do the same operation at J. H. Hospital.

Subacute appendix.

Dr. Charles Mayo

Right indirect inguinal hernia; appendix removed by extending division of exterior oblique upward and dividing fiber of interior oblique cord transplanted; main layer: catgut through exterior oblique, interior oblique, and Poupart's. Any opening of bowel leads to distention. Gunshot wounds of abdomen should always be operated on during first six hours; debatable from six to twelve; no one operates after twelve.

Goiter, adenoma. Seventy percent of goiters cured by operation. Thirty percent benefited. Three deaths this year; three died on train. When a one-sided nodule is removed, the isthmus should be divided to prevent pressure on trachea and for cosmetic reasons. Rogers and Beebee's serum is of use in soft exophthalmic goiters. No use in encapsulated cysts or tumors just as any serum is useless in ovarian cysts.

Cholecystectomy; few soft gallstones found. No pad under back. Packed gallbladder to explore ducts. Tube in three days.

Mayo operation for complete prolapse. Circular incision around cervix. Sponge dissection of anterior vaginal wall up to urethra. Bladder carried up. Peritoneum opened. Uterus drawn out and removed, with one suture, he ligated the uterines and drew together the two broad ligaments. This mass of tissue he fastened to anterior vaginal wall just back of urethra. Perineum repaired. Transverse incision. Muscles not dissected out. Pulled together en masse with five silkworm guts. No mucosa removed.

Dr. Judd
Appendix.
Goiter, colloid.
Goiter, cyst.
Goiter, exploratory.
Exploratory gallbladder and appendix.
Varicose veins.
Hemorrhoids.
Cancer of cheek.
Fibroma of breast.
Plastic on tendon of Achilles.
Tonsils and adenoids.
Freezing acne rosacea.
Alcohol injection of trifacial nerve.

July 21
The list of the day:

Dr. Will Mayo
Hysterectomy; double salpingo-oophorectomy for carcinoma of the body and ovarian cyst size of child's head; appendectomy. Cervix *not* removed. Myomata bear the same relation to carcinoma of the body as gallstones do to carcinoma of the gallbladder.

Same for large tube-ovarian abscess. Abscess ruptured—thought to be streptococcus; drained above. Gallstones present but not removed.

Posterior no-loop gastroenterostomy for duodenal ulcer the size of a fifty-cent piece; appendectomy. Ulcer covered with two Lembert's of linen. Usual gastroenterostomy. Used needle to mark out first line of suture. Used thimble but no forceps.

Exploratory laparotomy; appendectomy.

Exploratory laparotomy; inoperable carcinoma of stomach; nodules in pelvis.

Posterior pelviolithotomy for stone size of hazelnut. Second operative ventral posture, slight elevation of lumbar region. Difficult exposure; twelfth rib divided but not removed. Peritoneal cavity opened.

Dr. Charles Mayo

Right inguinal hernia.

Goiter, adenoma colloid. Typical operation: semilunar incision rather low, upper flap dissected well back; sternohyoid muscles separated and divided if necessary; superior vessels exposed and ligated; gland turned downward; capsule split, leaving posterior part behind (recurrent nerve often visible back of capsule); lower pole freed; isthmus divided; vessels tied; muscles approximated with catgut; platysma brought together with catgut, and skin closed with same catgut. One-third–inch perforated rubber tube inserted at midline. Tube out on second day. Patient up on third or fourth day.

All nodular goiters should be operated on, even in young people. Horseshoe goiter in the young should not; most of these will get well with (or without and in spite of treatment; nineteen out of twenty of these girls will get well without treatment). The muscles are divided in exophthalmic cases to avoid squeezing the gland.

Ligation of superior thyroid artery. Cocaine. Ligate low down after artery has branched so as to get veins and sympathetic nerves also.

Drainage of gallbladder for gallstones: suture of perforated duodenum.

Resection of jaw.

Goiter.

Mayo operation for prolapse: did not remove uterus.

Dr. Judd

Goiter, adenoma. Beautiful demonstration of recurrent nerve.

Goiter, cyst.

Goiter, adenoma.

Subacute appendix; 2½ months pregnant. High operative mortality in appendix abscesses during pregnancy. Diagnosis not easy to make. Give morphine one-eighth gram every four hours for twelve hours after operation.

Double salpingectomy; tuberculous peritonitis.

Epithelioma, lip; gland of neck.
Hemorrhoid; clamp and cautery.
Excision of specimen from lip for diagnosis.
Fistula in ano; incision.
Alcohol injection of infraorbital nerve.
Tumor of jaw.
Adenoids and tonsils.

July 22
(Dr. Will Mayo's day off)

Dr. Charles Mayo
Chronic appendix.
Goiter, adenoma.
Goiter, cyst.
Recurrent carcinomatous gland in axilla. Neat, rapid dissection.
Adhesions about gallbladder; Lane kink—easily seen. Used vaseline afterward—six hours of stasis after operation.
Gallstones; Lane kink. Cholecystectomy: release of kink. Morrison of England rarely drains gallbladder. Mixter of Boston thinks gallbladder is a rudimentary organ, hence always removes it. Dr. Mayo thinks it is an addition because certain lower animals, e. g., the deer, have no gallbladder; hence he prefers drainage to removal when possible.
Salpingectomy, right. Webster suspension.
Exploratory laparotomy. Appendectomy. Carcinoma lower down in rectum; to be removed next week.
Tuberculous peritonitis—man. Appendectomy.
Suprapubic drainage.

Dr. Judd
Goiter, adenoma.
Goiter.
Goiter, colloid.
Carcinoma of floor of mouth; cauterization.
Perineal prostatectomy. Midline incision—not a typical operation.
Needling, right eye.
Hydrocele of cord.
Dilation and curretage; Pozzi operation.
Hemorrhoids; clamp and cautery.
Manipulation of flatfoot.

Epithelioma of nose.
Resection of infraorbital nerve; insertion of screw.

July 23
Sunday, hence not a surgical day. Went to Baptist church this morning. Organ prelude sounded suspiciously like "Sing Me to Sleep." Wrote letters to Mama, Olive, and Jimmie. Read "Molly Make Believe."

July 24
Very cool last night and this morning. Wore my overcoat this morning. It is a little surprising to see the nurses walking around the street in uniform. They seem to think nothing of it.

The list: (Dr. Charles Mayo's day off)

Dr. Will Mayo
Appendix.
Appendix; drainage of gallbladder. Cholecystitis cases without stone usually have soreness pretty constantly without any acute exacerbations; slight temperature for months at a time; certain amount of weakness and sometimes chills. Three varieties: (1) strawberry gallbladder; (2) large, thin-walled gallbladder; (3) small, contracted and thickened gallbladder. There is usually enlargement of the glands along the common duct.

Gallstones removed and drainage; appendix; gastroenterostomy (posterior) for gastric and duodenal ulcers.

Anterior gastroenterostomy; had stomach resection about one month ago. Vomiting again.

Double dermoid cyst with ascites.

Exploratory laparotomy. Movable cancer of stomach about size of grapefruit; closure.

Resection of stomach for cancer.

Nephrotomy for stones in right kidney. Cystoscopy impossible. Left kidney explored first and found to be very atrophic, hence the right kidney was not removed. A good lesson to remember.

Dr. Judd
Goiter, cystic adenoma.
Appendix; Lane kink. Latter supposed by some to be due to a localized ptosis.
Epithelioma of lip; gland of both sides of the neck; beautiful dissection.

Suprapubic cystostomy; removal of stone.
Spina bifida; injection of iodine.
Chronic appendix.
Dilation and curretage; hemorrhoids.
Chronic cystic mastitis; local excision.
Ulcer, left cheek.
Freezing of birthmark.

I was elected reporter for Dr. Judd's room for today, as the appendage badges will testify. I dreaded the idea of reporting at first, but it was not so bad after I agreed with my backward self thusly: these fellows don't know but what you are a W. J. Bryan, so you go right ahead.

The Surgeon's Club developed into a farce this afternoon as evidenced by the fact that I was elected vice-president before I had become a member.

This is a good place to break into the diary with a remark about the overcoat which is here mentioned. So I did own an overcoat once upon a time. And that experience of being elected an officer of the Surgeon's Club was to be almost duplicated thirty-six years later when I was elected president of the Philosophical Society of Texas before I had attended a meeting. The reporters' badges were issued to certain designated doctors and were in the form of ribbons. I kept two of them, one for room number three and one for number four. The object of these badges was to permit the wearer to have a coign of vantage from which he could see all that went on and could then report intelligently to the Surgeon's Club.

The journal goes on page after page, listing operations with some comments by the surgeon and some by me. It would be repetitious to copy it all. One day Dr. Charles Mayo was excising a goiter under local anesthetic. I recorded the anesthetic as cocaine. I probably meant novocaine. I made this note: "Man very noisy. Dr. Mayo very sarcastic and almost cruel." This strange parenthetical remark by Dr. Will was set down on July 27, 1911: "Resection of sigmoid cancer. Tube method of end-to-end anastamosis. Patient explored elsewhere three weeks ago; very bad adhesions as a result. Tumor about ten inches from rectum. Very satisfactory operation. (Dr. Will remarked that he belonged to no secret organizations.)" And again, Dr. Will said, "The doctor who tells a patient that a sponge was left in by another doctor at a previous operation deserves to be ostracised."

On July 30, after noting that I had been elected secretary of the Surgeon's Club and that Heb Beall of Ft. Worth had gone home, I grew philosophical:

Didn't go to church today. Worshiped nature instead. Walked out south of town about two miles to a shady, secluded spot and read Thoreau's "Walden." I read and thought and dreamed of the days that were to come and was happy in the cool solitude of the morning. A man like Thoreau is to be envied in his simple, nature-loving optimism; gladly would I be one of his disciples. Away with Schopenhauer!

Had a good dinner. Couldn't enjoy it; glutton on my left licked his fingers and masticated audibly after the manner of swine.

Letter to Olive, and band concert at Mayo Park this afternoon. Presbyterian church tonight—the bell tolled—no funeral.

The next day, before putting down the list of operations, I had this to say: "A hot, sultry, rainy day; I'm tempted to retract all that I said about it being 'delightfully cool,' etc., here."

August 1 was an unusual day in several respects:

Went through the hospital wards with Drs. Judd and Steincke. Afterwards dined with Dr. Judd; a very agreeable and congenial man. Everything in hospital is very clean and neat. Only one patient seemed at all sick. Largest wards have ten beds; eight dollars a week. Some two or three beds; fourteen dollars. Some have one bed; twenty to forty dollars. Nurses looked fairly neat. Can't touch J. H. Hospital nurses. A startling discovery: I have had bedfellows for two weeks and didn't know it! I don't believe it is well to be too unsophisticated in such matters; it might not be bad to be able to live peaceably with all bugs, so far as you are able. For several days I have had hives and was wondering what I had eaten to cause it. Then, too, each morning I always wondered why my sleep was disturbed. I had about decided that it was because I was a nervous wreck. One of the doctors told me he left the hotel to get away from the bed bugs! That put me to thinking; I went to my room, looked around the bed, and there they were. I have decided that you can smell 'em better than you can see 'em and would recommend this method for their detection. Needless to say, I went to bed with fear and trembling.

Dr. Lynch of Nebraska came over and I demonstrated my gas machine to him; he seemed interested but I doubt whether he is the man to take up the work.

The gas machine was one designed by Dr. W. D. Gatch of the surgical staff at Hopkins. It was the first such machine in Texas and was widely used by Dr. B. F. Stout of San Antonio.

The last day at Rochester was Olive's birthday and began thus:

Had a horrible dream last night: I dreamed that I had lost a great deal of weight; my clothes fit me very loosely; my belt was built for someone else. I dreamed that, when I got to Texas, my friends and others were not glad to see me because I was so anemic. I waked and was glad that these things were not true, especially the last.

Then twenty-six operations are listed with some comments, and then the diary does some summarizing:

Dr. Will Mayo
Appendix.
Hysteromyomectomy.
Cholecystenterostomy for chronic pancreatitis. Technique like that of lateral anastamosis. No anastomotic clamps used. Linen used throughout. Protective drains.
Posterior no-loop gastroenterostomy for duodenal ulcer: duodenum directed to left.
Exploratory, stomach.
Resection of sigmoid colon for cancer. First stage. "Shotgun" operation.

Dr. Charles Mayo
Goiter.
Stone in common duct.
Ovarian cyst.
Appendix; Lane kink.

Dr. Judd

Inguinal hernia.

Exophthalmic goiter. Double ligation.

Goiter.

Acute appendix and intestinal obstruction. No fever and no vomiting. Second similar case in a week. Bowel very red and distended: ruptured in replacing. Glass tube drains.

Tuberculous glands.

Tendon transplantation for clubfoot. Took out wedge from astragalus; transplanted anterior tibial into insertion of peroneal muscle.

Closure of soft palate.

Adenoma of breast.

Entropion.

Plastic on scars of neck.

Dentigerous cyst.

Hemorrhoids.

Went to the post office and *that* letter didn't come, and I expected it. Left Rochester 3:50 P.M. Am now on a slow train through Minnesota. The country is beautiful with its alternating strips of green corn and bold pastures dotted with grazing cattle and brown wheat fields covered with the ripe grain in shocks. Best of all, I'm on my way to the dear old Lone Star State and to the things and to the people that await me there; this may account for this being "a slow train."

General observations on Mayo Clinic:

Iodine technique. Dry shave. Benzene followed in a few minutes by 3½ percent iodine in alcohol.

Much of the suturing is done with a double ligature; needle doesn't come unthreaded and strength is added. Needle holder used quite often.

Operators wash hands with plain soap and water; no brush except for nails; alcohol; Dr. Judd uses Harrington's solution. A gown is put on and kept on, usually all morning; a towel is pinned on the front of the gown between cases; gloves are changed between cases.

Usually each operator has only one assistant; there is a nurse or a sister on instruments and an intern to help with the instruments and to act as second assistant when necessary. Dr. Will Mayo has a very useful retractor for pelvic work: it fits between the patient's legs and retracts the lower angle of the wound.

Internship, Residency, and Return to Texas

All patients, rich and poor, walk into the operating room and get on the table. Ether is started, by a nurse, on the table; ether is given exclusively and, for the most part, is given well. All the dressings are arranged before the visitors are admitted. A short history of each case is given by the intern, and then the operation is begun. The operator always talks on some subject, related to or foreign to, the case on the table. The greatest freedom is allowed the visitors, all questions are gladly answered. Between cases the visitors return to the waiting room.

No stalk sponges are used. I didn't see a single pelvic drain inserted. French needles are not used.

All abdominal incisions of any length are closed with silkworm gut and horsehair; short appendix incisions are closed with subcutaneous catgut; also hernias. Thyroid incisions are closed with catgut, care being taken to approximate well the platysma first. A small tube drain (perforated) is inserted through the middle of the incision; comes out in twenty-four hours. Neatness and economy are prominent characteristics of the operating room.

Impression of the Mayo Clinic:

My impression is the same now that I am leaving as it was when I came. I think that St. Mary's Hospital, under the guidance of Drs. Will and Charles Mayo and Dr. Judd, is unequaled anywhere in the world—unequaled in excellence and amount of surgical work. The institution, thoroughly equipped in every respect, has sprung up in a medical desert; this makes the place unique and adds fascination to its traditions. The three men named in their individual fields (Dr. W. J. Mayo, the abdomen; Dr. C. H. Mayo, the thyroid; Dr. Judd, the face and neck) are masters. It is difficult to contrast them; they are all rapid, neat, and thorough. Dr. Will no doubt excels in head work; to the other two, and especially to Dr. Judd, I would give the palm for nicety of dissection and finish. None of them can compare with Dr. Cushing and Dr. Young in their respective fields, and I doubt whether Dr. Kelly would take a place second to them. My opinion, then, is on the whole quite good. However, there is a tendency to belittle and to ridicule the efforts of others which, to me, seemed reprehensible and unbecoming; their attitude toward gas anesthesia and phenalsulphonephthalein is an example. This, I believe, is not intentional altogether. The motto from Emerson on Dr. Charles Mayo's door to this effect is more characteristic: "Have something that the world wants and though your home be in the wilderness, the world will make its way to your door." There is a tradition concerning a poor widow woman who, when told that her bill was seventy-five dollars, said that she didn't have that amount but she would mortgage her two cows when she got home and send the money. Dr. Will Mayo receipted her bill and handed her a check for seventy-five dollars, telling her to buy her two more cows.

As to the doctors:

I am not a pessimist, nor have I lost faith in my fellow man. I must confess that I was not forcibly impressed by most of the visiting physicians. They did not come up to the standard, taken as a whole, of the ideal physician medically or otherwise. Many of them are uneducated; some of them can't speak English; some can't spell. Most of them are antiquated in their medical knowledge. Some of them talk too much, especially in the hearing of patients or patients' friends. Still, they are an honest, appreciative, well-meaning set of men. What I have said is not a criticism; rather a statement of the facts as I saw them.

Impressions of the trip:

The trip as a whole has been very pleasant. I was especially glad to see Niagara Falls. The cities *per se* were not out of the ordinary; to me there is a sameness about cities which soon grows monotonous. The medical and surgical work that I saw between Baltimore and Rochester was mediocre to say the least—most of it. Ferguson of Chicago did the best and cleanest work. Men like _____ and _____ impressed me as being men who knew they had a certain amount of work to turn out by a certain time and *must* turn it out by that time at all hazards; technique was sacrificed for speed. As a general rule, the surgery improved as I came westward; surgically, everything considered, I would place Baltimore between Chicago and Rochester, though in many respects it belongs far west of Rochester. I saw in all 212 operations by twenty-one different operators; most of these were in Rochester. The Mayo Clinic is especially good in surgery of the abdomen and thyroid; there were thirty-four goiters the first week I was there.

There can be no doubting that my time (twenty-seven days) and my money ($150) have been well spent. I have learned a lot of surgery and have unlearned a good deal that I thought was worth knowing; I have learned that the simplest method is usually the best method; the one point above all others that I got at Rochester is the great necessity of a thorough examination of the abdomen in every abdominal case. I'm sure my confidence in my surgical self has been heightened.

This is the last item in the diary:

August 4
My trip from Rochester to Mineola [*Olive's hometown in Texas*] was slow and uneventful. Now that I am in Mineola again, this is no time for diary writing—other things to do.

5
Medical Practice

〜୨ୣ〜

AFTER GRADUATION [*from medical school*] in 1909, I had had much to say about the time and place for me to [*begin my medical practice*]. Olive and I had talked about Austin and Dallas for a while, but only San Antonio had received serious consideration. The time was a more difficult question. We had agreed that we would marry when I was making one hundred dollars a month, as we felt we could live on that amount.

On October 10, 1909, I had sent Olive this word of encouragement:

> I had a long letter from George Pretz the other week. He has hung out his shingle as a general practitioner in Lebanon, Pennsylvania. He is one of the few members of my class who did not take hospital internships. He has done pretty well from the start. He tells me he got together a hundred dollars the first month and has done better each succeeding month. When I start out, if I can do that well for a few months, it won't be long before I reach the amount we set last summer. I'll tell you the truth, Olive, I'm getting tired of this single life. I've been single now for twenty-six years and I think it's time I'm getting me a wife. If I must spend the first thirty years of my life in single contentment, I want to spend the second thirty in married bliss and I want to spend them with you.

The matter of a license to practice medicine had been taken care of. I had taken the examinations of the State Board of Medical Examiners at Cleburne [*Texas*], in June, 1909. On June 24, I had written Olive when I finished the examinations. I used Chaney Hotel stationery:

It is 8:30 P.M.—just three hours since I handed in my last examination paper. It is needless to mention that I am tired in mind and body, and this faithful old left hand of mine refuses to write even to you; it has a right to be too, since it has pushed this pen at breakneck speed across a hundred pages or more of closely written legal-cap paper. Now that it is all over, I have allowed myself to give down; I was perhaps equally tired last night, but knew that I had to hold out against the strain for twenty-four hours longer.

As a result, I can't tell you much. I had no higher ambition at first than to make the required grade of seventy-five, but when I saw that I could do better than that I wanted to see how much better. I won't know for a couple of months what my grades are; the numbers getting one hundred in chemistry were put on the board yesterday and miraculously #158 was amongst them; it is most farcical that I, not having studied chemistry for four years, should make one hundred.

According to the *Texas State Journal of Medicine* of September, 1909, there were 183 doctors taking the examinations. Thirty failed or withdrew. Dr. F. H. Lundburg of Manor led the group; then came Drs. Samuel Schragenheim of Galveston and M. H. Boerner of Austin;[1] I was fourth with [*a grade of*] ninety-three.

With the coming of summer in 1910, we [*Olive and I*] had had some critical decisions to make. Our separation of five years had been difficult, and yet there loomed the possibility of extending our period of waiting very appreciably. In June I had gone into considerable detail:

You asked when I am coming home. To this question I can give no definite answer. Its answer is closely related to the answer to the question as to what I shall do next year. And this brings up a matter to which I have merely referred once before and about which I was very desirous of seeing you this summer. It concerns the desirability of my staying here next year. There will be a vacancy on the gynecological staff, and, although it has not been officially offered to me,

---

[1] Samuel Schragenheim was trained in Germany; he practiced medicine in Fredericksburg, Texas. Morris Hirshfeld Boerner was a 1908 graduate of the University of Texas; he was a U.S. Army physician.

I have good reason to believe I could get it if I want it. If I chose, I could stay on the staff and in about three years become resident gynecologist with the whole department in my care; such a course would mean, aside from a great deal of clinical experience, three or four hundred major operations, of which I shall have had only three or four by the end of this year. I want you to give this matter your careful consideration and let me know what you think of it; I want you to look at it from your viewpoint and not from mine. From my standpoint, it seems that the question can be narrowed down to your deciding whether you want a mediocre medical man for a husband three years from now or a superior one about five years hence. Think it over carefully and honestly, and let me know your conclusions. If I did not have you, I am quite sure what I should do, but since I have been so fortunate as to win your heart and to enjoy the inspiration of your love and sympathy, I most certainly will not disregard your opinion in a matter that concerns you and your happiness so closely.

And this brings up the question of your becoming a trained nurse, a question we have mentioned once before only to condemn. I must say I am not very enthusiastic about it, although it is to be considered. If we should think it best for me to stay here for a long hospital service and we should decide that we could not live apart any longer, then we might begin to think about your coming here to the training school. This is only a suggestion, and I shall have more to say about it later.

Very quickly had come Olive's reply; as was to be expected and as she has done ever since, she expressed her complete willingness to fit her life into mine, to subordinate her plans to mine. But fortunately it was not necessary. Dr. Kelly had entered the picture, and all our decisions were meaningless. So, on July 3, I had written her the news which we both accepted as good. The joy of both of us would have been heightened if we could have known that our wedding day was exactly two years off:

During the past week, something of importance has happened to me. I did not get the appointment to the vacancy on the staff here. At this moment it is hard for me to say whether I am sorry or glad; I am quite sure I am not sorry, although I can't say that I am glad.

195

Even before the appointment was made, I was debating in my mind whether I should accept it or not if it were offered to me. I applied for the place because I thought it was my duty to do so, knowing that if I followed it up my success would be assured, but to say the truth I was uneasy all the while for fear I would get it. Had the place been given me, in all probability I would have accepted it, and it would have been at least five years before I left here. That would mean that it would be at least seven years before we could begin to realize our plans in life, and by that time we would be old people, not caring for the things that unite our hearts so firmly now. So, Olive, I'm glad for our happiness' sake, and I know you are. Of course, I shall not have so rapid and so great a success as I would have had if I had taken the long hospital stay; although it may seem imprudent, I don't care to sacrifice my happiness for my success, especially because of my relation to you. Now I can see the day which heretofore has seemed so distant, when wedded happiness shall be ours.

With this decision definitely and wisely made, I had stayed on at Hopkins for another year and then visited several of the larger surgical clinics, as set forth earlier.

I arrived in Luling [*after stopping in Mineola to see Olive*] late in August, 1911. I took a month's vacation, but the practice of medicine was not pushed far into the background. On August 27, I was writing:

I returned from Gonzales Tuesday bringing with me $21.50 as my part of the spoils—medical spoils of the week. I feel very proud of myself that I made such a large sum of money by the sweat of my brow—rather than the skill of my hands. I have been around with the local physicians here and have done a couple of little operations for them. I have an idea that the town is full of hookworm disease. To prove this, my investigation, like charity, will begin at home; tomorrow has been set aside as the day for examining Walter Hyman's youngsters. He, as you possibly know, is one of my numerous brothers-in-law.[2] We found one case of hookworm yesterday in a child at the Orphans' Home.

I find that I have a large clientele of patients waiting for me here.

[2] Walter Raleigh Hyman, 1861–1943, married Pat's sister Corinne Pearl Nixon, 1875–1950. They had six children.

Every Negro on the farm has been nursing one or more complaints in anticipation of my homecoming. One man, when Mama told him I would be here only a short time, asked whether I wouldn't be here long enough to give them all a dose of medicine. Another boy, a playmate of my boyhood days, came around yesterday and put in his application for the position of chauffeur.

It was a happy day for Olive and me when on September 24 I could write her, using the stationery of Dr. S. J. Francis [*Luling physician*], that I would soon be on my way to San Antonio: "I leave here for our future home on Wednesday. I want to see about an office, a place to board, and a few other such necessities. I have put off going this long until Judge Denman returned from Alaska. Of course I hate to leave home because I realize that I shall not return again. Still, there is that intense desire to be up and doing. I want to make a start. I am anxious to see how well I shall succeed in putting into practice that which I have been storing up all these years. I am depending on you to stand by me through it all, and I know you will not fail me."

As I faced the responsibilities of the practice of medicine, I was thoroughly imbued with the ideals that cling so naturally to the medical profession. These I had absorbed from Comac's *Counsels and Ideals from the Writings of William Osler* and Sir Stephen Paget's *Confessio Medici*. As I thumb through these precious volumes, I find passage after passage marked and double marked. They gave needed nurture to the heart and soul of the man who was emerging from the timid and awkward boy as he left Guadalupe County 16 years before. But idealism was not enough. The grim fact was that patients were necessary and patients would be few. I arrived in San Antonio late on the afternoon of September 27, 1911. I carried in my pocket a letter from Olive in which she said, "I have every confidence in the world in you."

On October 6, this announcement was sent out: "Dr. P. Ireland Nixon announces that he has opened an office for the practice of medicine and surgery in the Moore Building, San Antonio, Texas."

A similar notice appeared in the local papers, giving my telephone numbers: office, 6837; home, 3704. I was proud of my office and had to tell Olive about it. I drew a diagram of my space, which was in reality a single room. The diagram showed a small reception room on the corridor, back of which were my consultation room and a small space for a laboratory. As I can now recall, the furnishings were most simple, but I was proud of it all: "I wish you could see my office; it is just as cozy as it can be. I thought I would be a little crowded for room, but I find that I'll be able to get along very nicely for a while. My reception room is a little small, but I won't need room for many waiting patients unless I am agreeably surprised again. Weathered oak bookcases, desk, table and chairs, a six-by-nine rug in the reception room and linoleum elsewhere, and a few pictures on the wall go to make my office a place that is attractive to me."

The matter of transportation was important and was easily settled except for the factor of cost. The era of the horse and buggy was passing, and the automobile was emerging. San Antonio was a city of 100,000. A good many of the streets had been covered with gravel, and soon a few paved streets would be showing up. The woes of the first cars were over. No longer was it necessary to back up the hill in the 1000 block of Main Avenue. Spare tires, doors, electric lights, and starters were unknown. The popular car was the two-cylinder Maxwell. I thought I was doing a little better by buying a four-cylinder Hupmobile 20. Woodward Carriage Company on St. Mary's Street was the dealer. The cost was about six hundred dollars. My license cost was five dollars and my license plate was number 1729. This number was issued by the city and was retained for several years until the state took over the licensing. The car was delivered on Saturday. Sunday night, after a long and tiresome journey, I was boasting to Olive: "I wish you were here to help me break in my machine. I went to New Braunfels this afternoon and had no trouble at all."

[*My office*] in the Moore Building was across the hall from

Dr. T. T. Jackson and his group and bore the number 605.[3] My door was timidly opened on October 1, 1911. No one seemed to know that it was opened for a purpose. On October 2, I treated my first patient. I went to Yancey in Medina County to see the wife of John Nixon.[4] For this trip of fifty miles over bad roads, I made a charge of fifteen dollars. The next day I made a house call on the same patient who had come into town; the charge was two dollars. The next day I saw her twice and no other patient. On October 5, I was called to Luling in consultation; for this I collected twenty-five dollars. This was my first collection. On October 6, however, I removed a toenail for Mrs. O—, and she paid me five dollars. My charge for an office call was one dollar; for a house call, two dollars. This was the usual charge, although it was reported that Dr. Adolph Herff and some of the older doctors were still making house calls for one dollar.[5] The moth-eaten daybook from which these figures were taken shows that on October 29 I operated on the father of S— K— of Luling. My ever-dependable letter to Olive contains the details:

Last night after I had begun to retire, I received a long-distance phone message from Dr. Nicholls at Luling to come down and do an operation.[6] I hastened to the station to find that the train had left before or about the time he telephoned, the time of its departure having been changed. I explained the situation to the chief dispatcher and after some difficulty prevailed on him to allow me to go on a freight train that was to leave in twenty minutes at 11:00 P.M. from the East Yards, a distance of about three miles from the station. A Katy train was on the track, and, on request of the dispatcher, the conductor stopped at East Yards and let me off. (This little incident with its two rather unusual courtesies is the only thing during the whole week that has caused me to feel that I was somebody.) I got to Luling at 2:00 A.M. and found an old fellow of

[3] Thomas T. Jackson was an 1893 graduate of the University of Texas.
[4] Dora Ann Wilson Nixon, 1870–1914.
[5] Adolph Herff, 1858–1952, a member of a famous family of San Antonio physicians, was an 1880 graduate of Jefferson Medical College in Pennsylvania.
[6] Clay Nicholls was an 1890 graduate of Tulane University.

eighty-one years with a strangulated hernia. Not a preparation had been made, so I had to begin and get everything ready. By 4:30 I was ready to start the operation, and by 5:00 the patient was back in bed. The old fellow stood the operation mighty well, and I hope for his recovery. The morning train which was due to leave Luling at 5:20 was three hours late; I was thus given a chance to eat breakfast with my people.

The old man later reported that "little Pat Nixon" operated on him. The fee of fifty dollars was most welcome. As a sequel to this operation, I removed S— K—'s gallbladder some years later under home conditions. It was here that I left in my first and only gauze sponge. After a few weeks, he walked into the office and stated, not strangely, that he felt like he had a lump in his side. Luckily, I found a few threads presenting at the old sinus tract and could remove the sponge without difficulty. S— appreciated my frank explanation and my honest facing of the facts, and so did I.

Mrs. D— T— was operated on the next day. Her uterus was removed, and I expected to collect $25. For the first month, I put $184 on the books and collected $57. This was a discouraging start. I still remember the time Mrs. Lillian Russell, with whom I boarded on Fourth Street, reminded me that one of my checks had been returned for lack of funds. I was obeying the injunction of Stephen Paget: I was beginning poor and was in urgent need of funds; so I had to accept the third phase of his advice: I borrowed of a friend. J. E. Fisher, Alta's husband, let me have $150, and this amount tided me over my greatest period of painful penury.[7]

It was rather natural that I should get some patients from Luling. Of great assistance was Dr. J. M. Watkins, who was my close friend till the day of his death.[8] The Luling *Signal* for July 8, 1915, carried this item: "Dr. Pat Nixon came over from San Antonio yesterday and with the assistance of local physicians made an amputation upon the leg of City Commissioner

[7] Joseph Edgar Fisher, 1851–1933, was a railroad man.
[8] John M. Watkins was an 1892 graduate of Georgia College of Medicine and Surgery.

A. Beversdorff, which has troubled him so much during the past several months. The member was cut off well above the knee. Mr. Beversdorff stood the trying ordeal fine."

Two important things happened to me in November, 1911. First and most significant, Dr. F. M. Hicks learned that I was in town.[9] He came close to worshiping anybody or anything that had even a remote connection with Johns Hopkins. Dr. J. M. T. Finney had taken out his appendix some years before. He thought that there were only two surgeons in the world, and Dr. Finney was both of them. I recalled at the time that Dr. Finney liked to show his Texas students a beautiful chair made of steer horns, given to him "by a G.P. [grateful patient] from San Antonio, Dr. F. M. Hicks." My introduction to Dr. Hicks was as sudden as it was welcome:

I went to a lunch at the St. Anthony given by the Bexar County Medical Society yesterday. As I was leaving the dining room, a tall gray-haired man caught me from the rear, and I thought he would shake my arm off before I could find out the cause of his over-enthusiastic greeting. My assailant was Dr. Hicks, one of the best-known physicians of the city. He had just returned from Hopkins and said he had heard there of the fine record I had made, etc., and wanted to talk to me. He took me around to his office, and we talked for about an hour. We had a lot of mutual friends and many other things in common. He said he would do all he could to help me and expressed a desire to have me help him with his operations.

My relations with Dr. Hicks were [to be] long, close, and rewarding. He was a medical father to me. I learned as much of the practical things of medicine from him as I did in medical school. Many, many times has his handsome gray head across the bed or operating table from me been a source of strength and confidence.

Sharing the waiting room with Dr. Hicks was Dr. B. F. Stout.[10] I helped Dr. Stout with some of his laboratory work as

[9] Francis Marion Hicks was an 1880 graduate of Bellevue Hospital Medical College in New York City.
[10] Beecher F. Stout, a 1900 graduate of Kansas City Medical College, was trained as a pathologist.

well as anesthesia. I had brought to San Antonio the first machine for administering nitrous oxide, one designed by Dr. W. D. Gatch, an associate of mine at Hopkins. When Dr. Stout was on his vacation, I did all his work, including tissue work and Wassermanns. Very soon I was giving anesthetics for several doctors. At times I acted as surgical assistant to these men, particularly Dr. Hicks and Dr. Paschal.[11]

The other important happening of November took place on November 14 [1911]. The daybook contains this simple record: "T. W. Labatt, visit, $2." This, plus a one-dollar office visit, was all for the day. Olive and Weir [Labatt] were then living on Olive Street, this perhaps for sentimental reasons. I wrote my Olive a few days later: "I was called to see my 'Olive' patient on Olive Street again today. I told her I had a very good friend named Olive. She and her husband have just started housekeeping in the nicest little place. Her husband is a brother-in-law of Dr. Heb Beall of Fort Worth.[12] It was through Dr. Beall that I was recommended to them." Mrs. Labatt, or Olive as she has been ever since, had a skin eruption that was distressing. Now, I didn't know much about skin diseases, but I saw quickly what was happening in this case. She had applied iodine, and then a doctor had prescribed an ointment of ammoniated mercury. Thus, mercuric iodide was formed, and this was setting the patient on fire. My advice was to withhold the salve and do nothing. With some misgivings, the advice was followed, and recovery was complete in a few days. The far-reaching effects of this negative action are beyond calculation. Medical attention to the Labatt family and [to] many [of their] friends resulted.

Mrs. J— B— was my first obstetrical patient. I delivered her on January 27, 1912, in a very modest cottage on Warren Street. My fee was sixteen dollars. I administered the first antimeningococcic serum in San Antonio to F— S—, who lived in what is

11 Frank Paschal, 1849–1925, an 1873 graduate of Louisville Medical College, returned to his native San Antonio in 1892 after nearly twenty years in Mexico. For five years he served as head of the San Antonio Board of Health.
12 Frank C. (Heb) Beall, a member of the class of 1906 at Hopkins, practiced surgery in Fort Worth.

now East Ashby Place. The serum was as new as was spinal puncture. There was a small epidemic of meningitis in the area, and I treated a good part of the patients. On March 1, the name of George Campbell appeared on my books for the first time. Henry Burney showed up two weeks later. These two, with their families, were close friends over a long period of time.

As I have said [*earlier*], I collected $57.00 in October, 1911. The next three months the amounts were $111.00, $62.00, and $149.60. After that, the problem of my professional existence was solved. From February on, my cash collections increased as follows: $285.50, $373.50, $384.00, $423.00, and $787.50. I put $2,910.50 on the books during these seven months and collected $2,403.50. When on June 1, I did a cholecystostomy on a Mr. R— and collected $200.00, I was over a very trying period.

As my professional prospects improved, hopes for an early marriage grew apace. [*Olive and I*] still didn't have opportunity for seeing each other very often. Olive was busy with her school duties, and I had scant funds for travel. I had visited Olive at Mineola on Sunday, January 21, 1912. Late in May, after her school had closed, she spent a few days with the Longs in Austin.[13] I, of course, saw her there; by that time my little car could negotiate the eighty tortuous miles in four hours. The date was May 26, and it was then that we set our wedding day for July 3.

Olive came to San Antonio on May 30 and 31. She was the guest of Dr. and Mrs. E. W. McCamish, who had formerly lived in Mineola.[14] It was on this visit that I gave her a diamond ring. Why this event had been postponed for seven years is not now clear. Perhaps it was lack of funds or ignorance of the proprieties.

During the month of June, Olive and I were unusually good customers of Uncle Sam; we each wrote daily letters. They were letters filled with impatience. For us clocks and watches

[13] W. R. Long was auditor of the University of Texas.
[14] Edward W. McCamish was a 1901 graduate of Rush Medical College in Illinois.

moved at a snail's pace. And yet there were many things of practical and immediate importance confronting us, especially Olive. My letter of June 7 was not of much help to her.

There are a lot of things I want to ask you. I have secretly consulted various books on "etiquette," "good behavior," "how to handle yourself during the Great Event," etc., but found nothing to help me. First of all, how many bridesmaids will you have, and how responsible will I be for them? If Nina should be able to come, were you counting on her?[15] Aside from Zeb and myself, how many men am I supposed to contribute? What do you want in the wedding ring besides the date? If you'll answer these questions, I'll get Zeb to tell me about the rest of it. This business of getting married is more complicated than I thought. I'm mighty glad that it doesn't have to be done but once.

For several days I have thought of writing that letter to your father,[16] but so far I have not succeeded in making a beginning. I have tried to get into the state of mind that I used to assume when I wrote to Dr. Nixon for money, but the charm would not work. I believe if I could see the old gentleman it would be a lot easier, for then my apparent complexity would appeal to his pity, and he would understand what I wanted. But it is so different now; I've got to put up a strong, logical argument in a clear, convincing style, or I won't get the girl. You've heard of the doctor's dilemma; here it is. What can I do, Olive? I'm hoping that the next day or two will afford me some triumphant moment which I can seize and write *that letter*.

Two days later I was relieved to write, "Congratulate me on my courage. I wrote to your father yesterday and asked him for 'one of his most prized possessions.' Do you think he will give her to me? I am all eagerness to know what he will have to say to me. I'll bet his letter will be full of frowns and questions."

On June 15, I rejoiced to announce: "The reply to that letter came today. Your father knew no reason why he should not give you into my care. He sent his blessing and that of all the family to you and to me."

[15] Nina Katherine Champion was the daughter of Pat's sister Elmira Isabelle and her husband Nicholas Champion, a Luling physician.
[16] Benjamin Franklin Read, 1840–1913, owned a mercantile firm in Mineola.

My letter of reply to Mr. Read assured him of my appreciation of the precious gift he had bestowed on me and of my determination to do all in my power to prevent him ever having cause for regret.

I received the [*wedding*] invitation on June 25, addressed by the left hand of Cornelia.[17] It read: "Mr. and Mrs. Benjamin F. Read request the honor of your presence at the marriage of their daughter Olive Gray to Dr. P. Ireland Nixon, Wednesday evening, July third, Nineteen hundred and twelve, eight fifteen o'clock, at their residence Mineola, Texas." An enclosed card stated: "At home after August first, San Antonio, Texas."

I cannot be expected to remember with any accuracy what happened on July 3. The experiences of seven years, the tedium that had been born of long waiting, the loneliness, the anxiety, the hope, the faith—all these had had a sobering influence on me. I do recall accurately that I was present on that day. The fact that I showed up at Olive's home with only half of my face shaved and she had to remind me of it after facial contact is in itself significant. This oversight would have made no particular difference, for all eyes were on the beautiful bride in her wedding dress of embroidered net over white taffeta. All of Olive's folks were on hand. I was represented by Mama, Zeb, Alta's Frances Walker, and Jamie.[18] On Olive's side it was an all-Read affair; Ione was maid of honor, and Irma and Cornelia (Baby) were bridesmaids, all dressed in pink taffeta. Hazel (Lady)[19] played the wedding march and the accompaniment for Madame Eugenie Munzesheimer as she sang "Oh Promise Me." Zeb was my best man. The groomsmen were Jamie and Ford Combs, one of Olive's many cousins. The preacher's name was Harmon. These few details were hazy in my memory and are here recorded at Olive's prompting.

But the passing of time and the flusteration and newness of the occasion could never cause me to forget the moment I an-

[17] Cornelia Read, Olive's sister.
[18] Frances Hamilton Walker was Pat's niece. James William Nixon, a son of Dr. J. W. Nixon, is himself a physician in San Antonio.
[19] Hazel Read, Olive's sister.

swered, "I will." Nothing could bedim the memory of those two words, nor could time blot from memory the plain wedding ring I placed on Olive's finger with its engraved assurance *Caritas Numquam Excidit*: "Love Never Faileth." Those two words, "I will," and the ring indicated that I had taken the wisest step of my life; at long last, Olive and I were married, and nothing else mattered.

A good deal was said about where we should go on our honeymoon. We considered New Orleans; but we gave that up because of the heat and the mosquitoes. Wisely we decided on Colorado. I argued that it "will be cool there and that physically it will be best for both of us. What we want is a quiet, cool place where we can spend our days near the heart of Nature, happy and undisturbed."

We thought the mountain country around Colorado Springs was most gorgeous and the Antlers Hotel most beautiful. Never had the grass been so green, the flowers so brilliant. Never had the stars and the moon been so awe inspiring. Never had cherry pie tasted so wonderful. And never did two lovesick and physically ailing people thrive so luxuriantly. Certainly the need was there; we were both run down in health, and both had lost weight. Olive weighed only 107 pounds, and I was down to 125. One day we were sitting on a park bench when an officious but observing woman asked me, "Brother, are you an invalid?" But a short month added ten pounds to both of us, along with a feeling of well-being which neither of us had enjoyed for many months.

These Colorado days were light and carefree. The thought of a sick patient or a cantankerous schoolboy was far from both of us. We spent many hours in North and South canyons; we walked or sat on the ground and drank in the beauty about us. Pike's Peak attracted us often. We went on wildflower excursions in the mountains by way of the railroad. We foolishly entered a rickety elevator and descended an abandoned mine shaft at Cripple Creek. But most of all, we just rested and ate plentifully of good food.

As we turned our faces toward San Antonio and Texas, we

could treasure many happy recollections. Although Olive and I had known each other for nearly eight years, this was practically the only time we had ever been together more than a day or two at a time. So most of all, we recalled our conversations about the long years of separation and the emphatic fact that they had come to an end. As we left Colorado, our thoughts turned to the future. We were both firm in the belief that our paths that had run parallel so long had now become one. The hope and the faith that had sustained us thus far were aglow with renewed intensity. We were eager to learn what the future had in store for us. We wanted to fit ourselves into the life of San Antonio as good citizens. We faced the future together and were unafraid. In quietness and confidence we looked ahead.

We arrived in San Antonio, our new home, on Sunday, July 28, 1912, and I was in my office the next day. Thus our long life together had begun. We had a room with Mr. and Mrs. E. Q. Lowery at 311 Richmond Avenue, the present location of the Nurse's Home of the Baptist Memorial Hospital. We took our meals with Mrs. Lillian Russell, 407 Fourth Street. In a month or so, we rented a cottage from Wallace Rogers at 216 W. Magnolia Avenue. Unfortunately, we had hardly gotten settled before the Rogers family needed the cottage for their own use, so we moved to 606 East Quincy Street, where Pat, Jr., was born. Here we lived until our permanent home was built at 202 East Courtland Place. We moved in on Courtland Christmas Week, 1913. Here Bob, Ben, and Thomas were born.[20]

This home, with a hundred-foot lot, cost $10,700, which was considerable at that time, but we knew we were building for the future. The lot, which cost $3,000, was from a tract of land formerly owned by Governor John Ireland, for whom I was named. Among the papers which came to me with the deed, is a copy of his will. We would not have built so early had it not been for the insistence of Uncle Lee Denman. I remember, as he and I ate watermelon together, how he argued that every

[20] Pat, Jr., was born in 1913; Robert Read, in 1914; and twins Benjamin Oliver and Thomas Andrews, in 1921.

professional man should own his own home. He offered to lend me the money through the San Antonio Loan & Trust Company, and this arrangement was made. The amount of the note was $4,000. It was at 8 percent and was to run for four years. The note, secured by a deed of trust on my farm in Gonzales County, was paid out in less than three years.

I did not get to spend our first Christmas Day at home. Dr. Paschal asked me to go to Brackettville and see J— C—. This trip of 130 miles in my little Hupmobile took five or six hours. I found the patient to have an appendix abscess. I brought him to the Physicians and Surgeons Hospital in San Antonio and operated on him the next day. Dr. Paschal insisted that I do the operation. He assisted me. I hated to be away from Olive on our first Christmas Day, but we were both glad to get that thousand-dollar fee. Mr. C— complained to Dr. Paschal about my charge. "You had better be satisfied," he was told, "I would have charged you twenty-five hundred dollars."

Figures in a ledger are poor indices of success, but they are important. These two figures should be mentioned for the sake of comparison: my first year's collections amounted to $3,326; from this point there was a gradual increase to $8,648 in 1916.

These notes on my early practice are given for what they are worth. For the rest of my long years of practice, my experiences have not been greatly different from those of the average physician. I have never desired or achieved a body- or mind-destroying practice. There are, however, certain incidents and experiences which may prove worthy of record. At least they are different and they happened to me.

During [Dr.] Sam Taylor's life, a woman and little girl were sitting in my waiting room.[21] I had seen this woman sometime before when she told me she thought she had "prostrate" trouble. This time, when I asked her into the office, she said, "No, I am waiting for Dr. Taylor down the hall. He thinks my child

21 Sam Harmon Taylor was a 1924 graduate of the University of Texas.

has whooping cough and doesn't want her to sit in his waiting room."

One night one of my most dignified patients ate a large Mexican meal, to which she was not accustomed. She developed violent nausea and retching, but was unable to vomit. I gave her two large glasses of warm soda water and sent her into the bathroom. Soon she began to empty her stomach, and then I heard her cry, "Oh! my teeth!" She had heaved her teeth into the commode and flushed it. When I returned the next morning, a plumber had dug a trench across the backyard and had found the teeth. "It took me twenty years to get a satisfactory set of teeth," the patient explained, "and I couldn't afford to lose them."

One day one of the Hartwell triplets—I think it was George—came into the office with warts on his hand. He was fourteen years old. Facetiously, I asked him, "Does your girl friend have warts on her hand?" He blushed and replied, "No, you took them off last week."

The story of the only bottle of whiskey in our home is a little unusual. Late one night during the days of prohibition, I was called to see a patient on Woodlawn Avenue. I found a prominent businessman of Dallas, who frankly stated that he had come to San Antonio to get on a prolonged drunk, that he had been here a week, that he had bought a case of quarts, and that the purpose of his visit had been accomplished. Now he wanted a hypodermic injection for rest, and also he wanted me to take away his last quart of whiskey. With all the conviction of a criminal and with full assurance that a prohibition agent was round the next corner, I got home with the whiskey. I put the bottle in the bathroom closet. It so happened that the closet had been painted recently, so the bottle became securely stuck. And there it stayed year after year. World War I was fought and won. The depression was on us before we noticed one day that the bottle was empty but still stuck to the shelf. We had no explanation until, by the process of elimination, we decided that Uncle George must have gotten it, since he cleaned the bathroom now and again. Uncle George was a fine old colored man of eighty. When faced with the accusation, he denied it vigorously. But when cornered, he admitted he got the whiskey, and it was good whiskey. When asked how he did it, he explained, "I took the tube off the fountain syringe and sucked it out!"

All my friends and patients know how I stand on the question of alcohol and tobacco. They know, too, that I am far ahead of the game of life because of my complete and continuous abstinence from both. However, I am thoroughly convinced that my influence has been more important in the direction of example rather than precept. Patients don't like to be preached at, even though they know they need it. Two illustrations will suffice.

A few years ago, I heard that C— was drinking too much liquor, neglecting his business, and generally making a mess of things. So I asked him to meet me at the Menger Hotel one day at noon, where we both ordered a good meal. C— was poorly dressed and was obviously hungry. As we ate, I talked to him about his accomplishments, how he had been a good newspaper man, how he had done a good job of writing, how he was respected in historical circles, etc. He listened attentively as he ate, but he continued to eat. When he had finished, he said to me, "Dr. Nixon, I am in the position of the old colored woman at the church. The preacher was talking about the Ten Commandments, and he was in favor of every one of them. As he took them up, one by one, the old woman violently cried out 'Amen, now you are preaching, brother.' This went on until he got down to where he read out, 'Thou shalt not kill.' Here, as usual, she was very outspoken in her approval. Then he read, 'Thou shalt not commit adultery.' The old woman shook her head and mumbled to herself, 'Ugh! ugh! He is done quit preachin' and gone to meddlin'.' "

The second illustration happened just a few days ago. P— A—'s promising youngster L— is a minister in the Episcopal Church. He has a small charge in a neighboring county. He came into the office complaining of a bad taste in his mouth. I noticed that he was smoking. This seemed like my chance. I have listened to preachers all my life, and a lot of them seemed to be pointing right at me. So I proceeded to explain how, if the human body is a temple, then tobacco might pollute it. He explained that his church preached moderation in all things, including liquor, tobacco, and food. It so happened that Pat, Jr., was to look at his ears, so he went into the waiting room and picked up the last issue of the *American Legion Magazine*. As I was leaving the office, he quietly said, "Dr. Nixon, I wish you would read this little thing." He then pointed me to an article which said that Louisiana's last Confederate veteran had just died at the age of 106. Prior to his death, he was asked for an explanation of his longevity. He explained that it was due to the "will of the Lord, three tablespoons of whiskey a day, and a pipeful of tobacco every thirty minutes."

Colonel George W. Brackenridge was one of my early patients, thanks to Dr. Mary Harper.[22] Dr. Harper had been the Colonel's private secretary for many years. Then he paid her way through medical school at Galveston, and she became one of the earliest and one of the best pediatricians in Texas. Colonel Brackenridge was one of the best-read men I ever knew. He knew a lot about everything. To test his knowledge, I asked him [*if he knew*] what a doodlebug is. "Yes," he said, "it is the larva of a snake doctor or ant lion." I had just read this in the *Book of Knowledge* and thought I had found something he didn't know.

I treated [*one patient*] for several ailments, the chiefest of which was prostatic hypertrophy. This condition gradually got worse, and he required frequent catherization. Rather than get up at night, I slept at his home for several weeks. One night about three o'clock, when he was particularly uncomfortable, he said to me, "Nixon, I hope old Methuselah didn't have this trouble."

About twenty years ago, certain glandular products were quite the rage for various ailments, one of these being sterility. One day, a woman came to the office stating that she had been married several years but had not conceived. She wanted chil-

---

[22] Mary Cleveland Harper was a 1910 graduate of the University of Texas.

dren, so I gave her a prescription for the preparation that was being used for that purpose. Two months later, she returned, all smiles, and announced that she was pregnant. I asked her to tell me about it. "Well," she said, "those pills were powerful. I put them in the bureau drawer and forgot about them. I have missed two periods."

I have made a special effort to be kind to the very young and the very old. One day, a little Mexican boy was in the office with his parents. I offered him a dime and he refused to accept it. He explained the situation to Mary Johnston.[23] This is what she recorded in her notes: "Little Pedro said Dr. Nixon offered him some money, but he wouldn't take it because his father had taught him not to take money from people who needed help." And to this I appended: "Little Pedro is ten—undernourished, poorly clothed—altogether woe-be-gone and one-eyed. But a veritable prophet!"

On one page of my scrapbook are two letters from two of my young friends. Little Clare Burney was five years old when she made a box of cookies for me. This note was in the box, "To Pat oh look in the box look in look in it it is something for you."

The second letter was from George Risien when he was about ten years: "I sure was glad to get my appendix. I am going to take them to school tomorrow to show everybody. I was afraid because I did not know what to expect. And was I surprised. Thanks a lot."

I have received a good many letters from my precious little friends. One day I went to see Annabelle Ansley. She was not too ill to chew bubble gum. And she tried to teach me the gentle art of bubble blowing. But I was a complete failure. When I reached the office, I wrote her this note:

Thanks very much for that piece of bubble gum. I enjoyed it all the way to town. Every block on the way I was trying very hard to blow a bubble. Just as I got to the garage, I blew a bubble the size of a marble. I consider this a success. I must admit that I was pretty well exhausted in the effort, however.

23 Mary Johnston was Dr. Pat's longtime secretary.

My main object in writing is to ask you what I was supposed to do with the gum after I quit blowing bubbles. I remember when I was a boy, it was customary to stick it behind the ear. Does your mother approve of this?

Her reply was well printed: "Dear Dr. Nixon I liked your letter very much. I want to tell you that you put the gum in water and you can keep it for two weeks. Love Annabelle."

An experience that came to [one] of my close friends should be recorded here. Dr. Tom Goodson had a friend and patient who was an excellent wing shot. A bird had very little chance in front of him. As Father Time caught up with him, his accuracy waned, and then finally he had to lay aside his gun. As a substitute, he propped open his screen door and seated himself in a comfortable chair nearby and swatted flies as they came in. He admitted, with some reluctance, that he enjoyed fly swatting about as much as he had bird shooting.

At least in one respect, I can say that I belong to the old school of medicine: rarely have I asked in advance whether or not a patient was able to pay for a house call. One night I was quite tired, so I retired early. At 2 A.M. the telephone rang, and I was asked to see a patient on Hays Street. To my inquiry, the man stated that he had the money to take care of the call. The place was hard to find. It was finally located underneath the viaduct, close to the railroad tracks. Here, using scrap lumber, tin cans, and anything else halfway usable, a crude room had been constructed. There was no bed, no stove, and no furniture. Here a sixteen-year-old boy was living with a girl of fourteen. The medical aspect was found in a resulting pregnancy, and I had been called to terminate it. I had hardly entered this dingy place when I found myself walking out. Manifestly, the fee was not mentioned.

Another experience was equally fruitless and equally instructive. It was early in the days of salvarsan. A man from New York, in the city for a few weeks, developed syphilis. I gave him several injections of salvarsan. His primary lesion healed quickly. The matter of payment was postponed time after time. One day, I was called to Luling in consultation, and on the train was my syphilitic patient. I knew he was on his way home. I asked him to pay his bill, which was quite considerable. He countered by saying my charge was excessive. I reduced it by half. He wrote out a check for the reduced amount. He might as well have made it for a million dollars. The check bounced.

While I have collected three one-thousand-dollar fees, my patients have for the most part considered my charges to be reasonable. Rarely has there been any complaint. Indeed, on a few occasions, my fees have been raised.

My contacts with organized medicine have been intimate and wholesome. It has been my desire to do my part. The Bexar County Medical Society was to some extent hampered by politics, in which I had interest only insofar as the welfare of the society was concerned. But for the most part, a clear and steady course has been followed, which was calculated to bring better medicine to the people and a certain degree of protection to the profession.

In 1911, the Bexar County Medical Society was in swaddling clothes, even though it had been in existence since 1853. The effects of reorganization in 1903 had not been fully felt. The minutes show that out of a membership of sixty, only five to ten attended the meetings. The society was a wandering outcast, unwanted and unclaimed, with no fixed place of meeting until 1915. In *A Century of Medicine in San Antonio*, I have set down the slow emergence of the society, and here can be found many items that are obviously autobiographical.

In my early years, I read several papers before the local and neighboring societies. A few were presented before the state association. My first paper before the Bexar County Medical Society was on November 12, 1912, the title being "Pyelitis as a Clinical Entity." During the next ten years, the following papers were read locally: "Chaparro Amargosa in the Treatment of Amebic Dysentery," "Nonbacterial Urethritis," "Can We Diagnose Appendicitis?" "Retroperitoneal Hernia into the Duodenal Fossae," "Inflammatory Tumors of the Abdomen," "Acute

Postoperative Dilation of the Stomach," and "Cervical Ribs, Their Significance and Management." As time went on I was inclined to read fewer papers. Of those titles mentioned above, the one with a question mark about appendicitis created widespread comment. It was published in the *Medical Record* in New York where the Associated Press got hold of it.[24] The idea was broadcast that here was a doctor honest enough to admit he could not diagnose some cases of appendicitis.

My greatest local contribution to organized medicine has been through the Bexar County Medical Library. As early as 1912, I was one of a small group of young men who created a nucleus for a library. Members of the group were Drs. B. F. Stout, H. H. Ogilvie, Homer T. Wilson, E. V. DePew, John B. Herff, William Wolf, C. E. Scull, and perhaps a few others.[25] An assessment of ten dollars a year provided several journals and our first furniture: two chairs and a journal stand. The growth of the library—how it moved to the Bedell Building in 1915, to Lexington Avenue in 1920, and to French Place in 1933—has been set down in *A Century of Medicine in San Antonio*. Dr. Frank Paschal was president of the Bexar County Library Association until the time of his death in 1925. He was succeeded by Dr. Homer T. Wilson until he became incapacitated. I became president and served until 1944. In that year, I became permanent director of the Old Book Department.

All along, I had been on the lookout for old books for the library. Some were donated and I bought some. But it was not until 1939 that this department began to grow. This growth came from funds which I solicited from some of my friends: Mr. and Mrs. John Bennett, Mr. and Mrs. George Parker, Mr. and Mrs. B. B. McGimsey, Mr. and Mrs. T. W. Labatt, Mr. and Mrs.

[24] Pat I. Nixon, "Can We Diagnose Appendicitis?" *Medical Record* 89 (March 11, 1916): 469–471.

[25] Evarts V. DePew, an internist, graduated from Rush Medical College in Illinois. John Bennett Herff, a surgeon, graduated from the University of Michigan in 1902. William M. Wolf, a surgeon, graduated from St. Louis University in 1932. Homer T. Wilson was a 1910 graduate of the University of Pennsylvania.

Sid Katz, Mr. and Mrs. Arthur Bird, Mrs. Ralph Jackson, Dr. William E. Howard, Dr. William E. Durbeck, and many others.

Through the generosity of these donors, the library has profited to the extent of about $75,000. Dozens of medical classics of other years and many modern medical histories and biographies have come to San Antonio. I must be frank enough to state that these benefactions have come as a result of the confidence in and friendship for me. It would be tedious to enumerate the priceless volumes that are ours. Just this word about Vesalius' *De fabrica humani corporis*. The provenance of this first edition, published in 1543, is interesting. A copy very rarely finds its way to the market. Harvey Cushing's census shows only sixteen copies in the United States. When Dr. Cushing died in 1939, his library went to Yale University. Included was a fine copy of the *Fabrica*. This put the Yale copy on the market, and we were fortunate in procuring it. I called up George Parker about it and told him it was available at $765. He wasn't particularly interested. However, he called me the next day. Now, lovable George Parker is an old ballplayer, and baseball is a frequent topic of conversation with us. "Say," he said on the telephone, "who is selling that book you were telling me about?" "Walter Johnson," I replied. "Say," he asked excitedly, "is that old Walter Johnson of the Washington Senators?" At this point I knew I was going to get the book, and even now I don't know what my reply was. I am very sure that I did not give him an absolute no for an answer.

My long and close association with the medical library has caused me to become familiar with some of the problems that beset librarians. One of these is the difficulty of getting books and journals returned. I signed out a book which I turned over to Al Hill after I had read it, and he gave it to Dave Keedy.[26] My many requests for the book came to naught. So, for the fun of it and with the librarian's permission, I assumed the role of

[26] Alfred Hill, a psychiatrist, was a 1938 graduate of Western Reserve. David M. Keedy, also a psychiatrist, was a 1937 graduate of the University of Rochester.

librarian and wrote myself the following letter, sending a copy to Al Hill:

I am writing you once more about the book you signed out from the library nearly two years ago. I am referring to Sperry's *The Ethical Basis of Medical Practice*. Never before has a book been out so long. It is a funny thing that you, who have been strutting around here claiming to be the daddy of this library, could do such an injustice to other doctors who have requested the book. More than once I have heard you boast of the generous portion of honesty and integrity which Sir William Osler instilled into your bosom. Is this a good sample of it?

I am not very smart, but why you, who claim to be so smart, would pull such a stunt as this is beyond me. You may boast of having so much superior knowledge, but around the library, I haven't seen any evidence of it. I think the word *mediocre* could be fitly used here.

You seem to be good at the art of subterfuge. You want me to believe that you lent the book to Dr. Alfred Hill, and he claims that a Dr. Keedy has the book. Knowing the high place in the medical profession these two claim to occupy, I don't take much stock in these claims. This bird Hill rushes into the library and gives a few orders in his hypermasculine voice, and away he goes.

As for this fellow Keedy, I wouldn't give him much. He lays claim to a lot of superiority too. He arrogates to himself certain high levels of intellectuality which most of us can't appreciate. Why is it that all psychiatrists have so little on the ball? You ought to be one yourself.

And now after two years, you claim that the said Dr. Hill returned the book and you lost it on the way home. And you expect me to believe that? It is a good thing you made the claim over the telephone. That old gag died years ago. Anybody who is as smart as you claim to be should be able to think up something better than that. I guess you thought I would fall for that one, didn't you?

Now, what are we going to do about it? I'll tell you what we are going to do. You might think you are going to get off by buying a new book, but that's not the answer. In flagrant cases such as this, we have another solution. The bylaws instruct the librarian to collect ten cents a day for each day a book is kept out. This figures up to $80.20. If Al Hill and that man Keedy actually had the book as you claim, why don't you call on them? And that gives me a chance to ask another question. Is it a fact that all psychiatrists have been just a little teched? I certainly have some evidence in that direction.

So be good enough to come across with a check, and I don't mean next year. I don't care whether it comes from H and K, who claim to be psychiatrists, or from you, who, like Harry C. McJohnson, claim to be a general specialist. Start the money in my direction. That's all I want.

I know what you are thinking. You'll get my job. No you won't. I'm quitting the job. I don't see how I have stood it this long, dealing with you three and a great raft of others just like you.

I still can't figure out why anybody who is as smart as you claim to be can be so stupid in this case. To me, you are a typical Johns Hopkins doctor: pompous, bombastic, and irresponsible.

Little did I think that anyone would take the letter seriously, but this reply came from Dr. Hill: "I am horribly mortified at having been the principal culprit in getting you into such a deal with Elizabeth, who is, I presume, the librarian. If any check writing is to be done or if I may help in any other way, including commitment, let me know."

Not to be forgotten as a source of funds for the library is the Saturday Roundtable. This group, started by Homer Wilson in 1918, has met every Saturday since that time. Each year, for many years, I have collected ten dollars from these Friends of the Library, and many treasured books have resulted. Some day a new library building will be erected. Even now (July, 1953) Bob and I are beginning to work on this project.

The two funds created by the publication of my first two books—the Century of Medicine Library Fund and the Mollie Bennett Lupe Memorial Fund—have been sources of revenue. The Harper Furnish Memorial Fund of one thousand dollars was set up by Mrs. John Furnish. This means twenty-five dollars to the library each year.

Some day the new library will be built. I hope our present efforts are fruitful. If the medical profession of San Antonio is to keep abreast, we must have an adequate, fireproof structure, which would symbolize the growth and the dignity of organized medicine in San Antonio. When the library is completed, I would be greatly honored if a plaque in the Old Book Room could bear this legend: "This library is the lengthening shadow of Dr. Pat Ireland Nixon, 1883–."

One indirect service to medicine was found in my membership on the Selective Service Appeal Board for District No. 2.[27] This district was made up of twenty-two counties of Southwest Texas. The other members were Chairman Henry P. Burney, Ernest J. Miller, Fred Nicholson of Lavernia, and M. M. Davis of Charlotte. The board was so set up as to have a representative from agriculture, labor, the legal profession, industry, and medicine. The San Antonio *Light* of November 30, 1940, carried a picture of this very conscientious and very capable board. Of the hundreds of appeals we handled over a period of six years, there was not one disagreement. That does not mean that we did not encounter some difficulties. Some parents tried to go over our heads, and that, so far as we were concerned, only made the plight of the appellant more difficult. Some few sent lawyers to Washington, but all in vain. We treated the poor and the rich with the same justice.

As I have grown older, there has been no feeling of envy or resentment at the success of young physicians. I have entertained a feeling of pride that Pat and Bob are gradually stepping into my shoes. It has been my desire to encourage and assist every worthy young doctor. To have traveled in midstream of medical practice for over forty years has been a thrilling and a satisfying experience. When, in the course of unremitting time, we older members of the profession find ourselves gradually but perceptibly drifting toward the quiet waters near the shore or circling in one of the stagnant eddies of the stream, we should accept our new relationships with calmness and equanimity. It is not so calamitous to be pushed aside. Indeed, that is inevitable. That is progress. That is real evolution. That's the way it must be.

Time has brought many changes. When I came to San Anto-

---

[27] See the San Antonio *Light*, November 30, 1940.

nio in 1911, it was a privilege and a duty to call on the older doctors. This happy custom of calling is no longer existent, and the medical profession is the loser thereby. As the new doctor comes in, he is lonesome and unnoticed. And the old doctor, too often, experiences the same isolation and loneliness as he goes out. Personally, I have always felt highly honored when a young doctor took time to stop to speak to me.

There have come a few heartaches, of course, as the years have piled up—heartaches that had to go unexpressed at the time. It is embarrassing to walk down a hospital corridor and evoke no sign of recognition, or to have a young nurse announce with some show of authority that visitors must leave the room until the patient is put to bed, or that only doctors were allowed to use the telephone. No discourtesy was intended in these instances. And there is no remedy. However swiftly and however well the race may have been run, there must come a time when brain cells flag and feet falter. When that time comes, recognition of the fact is essential, and adaptation must follow. Then it is that resentments are futile and ill humor is churlish.

Withal, the practice of medicine has been a glorious experience. It has been little short of a great adventure to have bridged the gap between calomel and penicillin. It has brought many satisfactions and many rewards. The ideals which had been planted in the heart of the twenty-eight-year-old doctor as he left Johns Hopkins were not too high. Indeed, the ideals of the medical profession have not changed and should not. I have tried to make my contribution toward increasing the goodwill and confidence of the people in doctors. The people believe in us. We must not fail them.

6

Politics and Public Health

〜♘〜

MY INTEREST in and knowledge of politics were slow to develop. It took me a long time to realize that politics and good citizenship are closely related, that, if good citizens don't take a hand, then government will be taken over by the base and corrupt elements.

I had brought with me a feeling of apathy toward political matters when I reached San Antonio in 1911. Among too many citizens there was a what's-the-use attitude, and there was much justification. [*For decades*] San Antonio had had the highest tuberculosis mortality rate of any city of the country, and the condition was accepted as normal. Indeed, every effort was made to conceal this ugly fact from the outside world; such publicity would be harmful to the business of the city. Most surprisingly, this willingness to sacrifice life and health for dollars lasted until comparatively recent years.

It is to the great credit of the medical profession of San Antonio that these deplorable conditions were exposed. The main problems lay in the trans–San Pedro Creek area where our Latin-American people were congregated in congested and inadequate quarters.

My part in San Antonio politics was based on the factors of bad sanitary conditions and the very obvious ignorance or indifference of the elected officials. My first official contact with the situation came in the form of a letter from Mayor C. M. Chambers under date of July 26, 1928: "This is to inform you that the city administration has appointed you a member of the city health board, in lieu of Dr. McCamish, deceased, and it is our sincere wish that you will favor us by accepting the appointment." From that date, over a period of twenty years, I was a member of this board, the county board, or the combined board. And for several years I was school physician.

So I saw the health problem from several angles, and it was ugly regardless of the view from which one observed it. Any part which I took in the local field of politics was grounded in the belief that I had learned the importance of public health from men as prominent as Dr. William H. Welch and that I could be of service in helping to correct conditions that had remained deplorable so many years. Men and women had been dying regularly and frequently from tuberculosis since 1846; that was just the natural thing. And children had been dying from diarrhea too; "summer complaint," they called it, and all due to hot weather. Sanitary gains had been pitifully small and slow. As seen from [a later] viewpoint, it seems that the distressing situation was due to these factors: failure to recognize the value of public health, public apathy, official indifference or incapacity, and rapacity and political influence of owners of Mexican corrals and other inadequate living quarters.[1]

The real and admitted fact was that the city health department was and had long been a political football, to be used for the payment of political debts, with its real purpose shoved into the background. It was the accustomed dumping ground for political hangers-on, regardless of their qualifications.

By 1938, I had waded into the political waters rather deeply—perhaps too deeply for one of my experience and my temper. Many others were aroused also. The people were at last

[1] "Most of the 'houses' are of one story or less. By 'less,' I refer to the fact that some of the roofs are not six feet high. Some of the shacks are 'singles' occupied by one, two, or three families; and others are one-story 'apartment' buildings. These are the worst of the lot. They are wooden boxes, slapped together with half- and quarter-inch boards and set up under one roof to string along half a block of street frontage. . . . Each 'apartment' is a single room about eight feet square. Some are smaller. Whole families live in these rooms. . . . Often these huts and sheds have no toilets, no running water, no drains or sewers." Ralph Maitland, "San Antonio: The Shame of Texas," *Forum and Century* 102 (August, 1939): 53.

beginning to emerge from their prolonged lethargy. I was on the city board of health at the time. The other members were Drs. J. H. Burleson, T. M. Dorbandt, L. L. Lee, and W. B. Russ— obviously a very strong and courageous board.[2] We were determined to do something about the health department. Among other things, we scheduled a program before the Conopus Club, the result of which was to get us fired by the mayor [C. K. Quin]. But it gave us a chance to parade the health situation before the people. The San Antonio *Light* of February 25, 1938, reported the meeting under headlines all the way across the front page: "Doctors Score S.A. Conditions."

The San Antonio health department is a refuge for ex–political office holders!

The West Side is a festering sore on the face of San Antonio!

Publicity accruing to the city in *Focus*, a national magazine, has more than nullified San Antonio's $60,000 advertising tax!

A charter amendment, placing the health department under an independent health commission, with employees on a civil-service merit basis, is the only solution to the problem!

These were highlights of addresses given Friday by two prominent San Antonio physicians, Dr. Patrick [*sic*] Ireland Nixon and Dr. Lee Rice.[3]

They discussed "The Health Situation in San Antonio," with Nixon outlining existing conditions and Rice providing the solution.

"Is it true what they say about San Antonio?" Dr. Nixon asked the Conopians, at the same time flourishing a copy of *Focus*, which charged that it was possible for a plus-4 syphilitic to obtain a health card from the health department, enabling her to find employment in a pecan-shelling factory.

Dr. Nixon answered his own question. He said, "Yes and no; mostly yes."

Dr. Nixon took occasion to point out that the local health problem is by no means new. He said: "The local health problem—San Antonio has the worst tuberculosis death rate in the country—is a very

---

[2] Thomas M. Dorbandt was an 1898 graduate of Missouri Medical College. Lavord L. Lee was a 1902 graduate of Birmingham (Alabama) Medical College; he was a pediatrician. Witten B. Russ was an 1898 graduate of the University of Pennsylvania; he was a surgeon.

[3] Lee Rice, a 1916 graduate of the University of Texas, was an internist.

old one. The conditions have been brought before city officials for at least twenty-six years."

The speaker pointed out that three independent health surveys have been made here in the past twelve years, two by the United States Public Health Service, and that all three have failed to bring any improvement.[4]

"The West Side is a festering sore on the face of San Antonio. Compound ignorance on the part of the people who live there, exploitation by the city politicians, low wages by employers, and lack of interest by common citizens are to blame," Dr. Nixon went on. "Something should be done about it."

Dr. Rice outlined his remedy for existing conditions, at the same time warning that even if it was a long-range program, that would take fifteen years. He said: "The only way the setup can be changed is through a charter amendment, placing the health department under a health commission headed by a trained health officer and with employees on a civil-service merit system basis."

The physician took occasion at this point to accuse city officials with blocking worthwhile amendments to the charter by putting up other amendments certain to pass. The charter can be amended but once in two years.

"However, every year the city puts up a charter amendment which is sure to pass, delaying other charter amendments for two years," Rice continued.

"The beautiful advertising tax amendment, which you voted, is completely nullified by *Focus*, and that type of story is going to continue."

"There is no real way to solve the health problem here in less than fifteen years, even with the setup I have suggested. It is a long-range problem."

Taxes were mounting and nothing was given in return. The Property Owners Defense League had been organized, and a large mass meeting was held at Tech High School on May 25, 1938. [*My address at the rally included these comments*]:[5]

---

[4] The U.S. Public Health Service made its surveys of public health in San Antonio in 1926 and 1935.

[5] For the full text of Dr. Pat's address see Box 3 Folder 2, Dr. Pat I. Nixon Papers, Trinity University Archives, San Antonio; hereinafter cited as Nixon Papers.

Politics and Public Health

The average individual has no conception of the department of our city government which is rather curiously called a health department. If it were really known how much absence of health there is in some parts of our city, directly attributable to this department, then perhaps the name of health department would not be such a misnomer.

The United States Public Health Service believes a well-ordered city health department should spend $1 per capita per year. San Antonio is practically doing this this year. The health department budget is $234,000, nearly ten times what it was in 1932. And just think of it, it is more than the entire budget of the health department of the State of Texas, which is only $219,000. And what do we get for it? So near nothing that it is pitiable. If you could go and see the roster of the personnel of our health department, you would not believe your own eyes: former baseball players, exgamblers, brokendown politicians, and loafers generally. And not a trained man in the whole outfit of inspectors. If the facts were known as to what the so-called inspectors really do, you would have a real surprise. There are about sixty of them, and ten trained high-school boys could do more than the whole sluggish outfit. There are a lot of stories about the capacities of these inspectors. I can't vouch for all of them. I really don't know whether there was a leper who was serving as a food inspector a year or so ago. You probably have heard of the dairy inspector who persistently urged the dairyman to dip his hydraulic ram. And there was a food inspector who heard a merchant speak of Oliver Twist, and he thought it was a kind of chewing tobacco.

But not all the employees of the health department are incapable. Dr. King knows a lot about public-health matters and could do something if he had the authority. The head of the nursing staff, Mrs. Gale, is very capable. And there are several young doctors over there who are doing good work.

This combination of rotten politics and bad health is not new to San Antonio. The city board of health in May, 1915, made a report to the City Council on health conditions and especially on corrals. Just notice how this problem has been bandied about, how it has been belittled, how it has been postponed, how it has been concealed all through the years. This report made twenty-three years ago depicts the unspeakable condition of filth, squalor, and disease that existed. What came of it? Exactly nothing.

In May, 1926, Dr. Drake of the American Public Health Association made a report in which he brought out that San Antonio led all the cities of America in the death rate from tuberculosis and intestinal disease in children. And incidentally, she still has this unsavory reputation. And don't be misled by inspired reports in the San Antonio *Express* or any other paper that most of these deaths are from people who came here for their health.[6] The figures show that 70 percent of them are Mexican. Thus 30 percent of our population furnishes 70 percent of our deaths from these causes. In other words, the death rate among Mexicans is about 300 percent higher than it is among whites.

Then in June, 1935, Dr. K. E. Miller, senior surgeon of the United States Public Health Service, made a survey. The same deplorable conditions were revealed. What came of it? Less than nothing.

So here we are in this good year of 1938, San Antonio, the laughingstock of all the municipalities of America. San Antonio, with its reputation blackened by *Focus, Collier's, Time,* and the *Journal of the American Medical Association.* San Antonio, the city of homes, the city beautiful, with a malignant cancer on her back.

Health conditions in San Antonio are compounded of ignorance and poverty on the part of our poorest citizens, greed on the part of their landlords, lower wages on the part of their employers, the prevalence of crime, the presence of poorly regulated prostitution, and the pitiful inefficiency and rank incapacity on the part of our public officials.

My most serious political efforts were expended in the direction of a city-manager form of government. The problem was difficult because a city ordinance provided that the charter could be amended at intervals of two years only. The politicians in control saw to it that the people never had a chance to vote on city-manager government by submitting some inconsequential amendment from time to time. They were afraid of a result that would send them into political oblivion. On March 2, 1939, a group of citizens met and began to plan for the election of May 9. Five outstanding young men were persuaded to make the race against C. K. Quin and his commissioners and Maury

---

[6] See, for example, the San Antonio *Evening News,* July 11, 1935.

Maverick and his followers. They agreed to submit to the people a city-manager amendment. They came, without justification, to be at times called "Dr. Nixon's ticket." This was because many of the early meetings of our group were held at my home.

A letter [*I wrote*] captioned "For a Better San Antonio," which was sent out early in May, told the whole story:[7]

Fellow Citizens and Voters:

This is a message of great importance to you. We know you are interested in the welfare of San Antonio and in the people who live here, so kindly read the entire letter carefully and deliberately.

For the first time in the history of San Antonio politics, we have a chance to vote for a group of men who offer themselves for public office with absolutely no selfish motive in view.

And why do we say this?

Because—

At the request of a large group of public-minded citizens, with no political axes to grind, these men left their jobs and positions to run for office. And at the same time, they pledge you that when elected they will, as soon as legally possible, submit to the voters and personally work for the adoption of a new city charter with a city-manager form of government. At that time, after thorough discussion, you can personally, through your vote, decide whether or not you favor such change. Such action, if adopted, will eliminate these men from the offices they hold. Can you ask for a more unselfish service by a group of men who are capable, public-spirited, and have families to support?

They are: Leroy Jeffers—Mayor, Francis C. Sullivan—Fire and Police Commissioner, Gibbs MacDaniel—Tax Commissioner, William V. Dielmann, Jr.—Street Commissioner, M. Abbe Strunk—Park Commissioner. *The Better Government Ticket.*

A city-manager form of city government is the sensible and efficient way to run a city of this size. About five-hundred other cities are doing so now with great success. An initial 15 percent reduction in your city tax rate is guaranteed by these men [*the candidates of the Better Government Ticket*]. The professional politician with his machine rule will be put out. Civil service based on the merit system will be installed in all departments. San Antonio will enjoy better

---

[7] For the full text of Dr. Pat's letter, see Box 3 Folder 2, Nixon Papers.

times, and the working man and woman will have a greater chance to prosper. The city will be run for the benefit of all its citizens and not for a selfish few.

For the welfare of San Antonio: first, retire Quin, his ticket, and other machine politicians; second, defeat Maverick, his ticket, and his selfishly ambitious political machine.

I was right in the middle of this two-month campaign. I neglected my work. I collected many hundreds of dollars. Every night I attended and spoke at one or more rallies. [*In a speech over WOAI on April 5, 1939, I had this to say*]: [8]

The health department as it has existed the past few years is a shabby, expensive farce. It has been headed and controlled by a layman who knows nothing about health and whose chief qualification for the position is that he knows how to control votes better than disease. The hollow mockery of the department is well exemplified by the report which is issued each year. It is a beautifully bound volume, well printed, and must have cost us a sizable sum. But what does it mean, with its charts and graphs and tables they have learned to make from some other city's report? As a matter of real fact, the report each year would be more valuable if the department would be content with the nice binding and just leave all the pages blank. Such an arrangement would reflect the activities of the health department in health matters and, in a subtle way, would represent the playful joke which the department plays on the citizens of San Antonio from year to year.

These reports will tell you of the vast number of inspections made, but they won't tell you how meaningless these numbers are, and how it is possible for the appearance of the report to be colored by the way the proprietors of the inspected premises vote.

These reports will tell you of the number of sewer connections made in a given year, but they won't tell you that up to a few years ago practically one-third of the area of San Antonio was unsewered, and they won't tell you how much of the city is still unsewered.

They will tell you of the number of corrals they have torn down, but they have waited twenty-five years to make a beginning. It is impossible to calculate how many cases of tuberculosis and how many deaths have resulted from this criminal negligence.

[8] See San Antonio *Evening News*, April 5, 1939.

They will tell you that, due to the outstanding efforts of the health department, only eight cases of syphilis occurred at Fort Sam Houston in 1937. This was so wonderful that the mayor congratulated the health department through the newspapers. Eight cases of syphilis among ten thousand soldiers! And they expect us to believe it! In that many civilians we would expect between five hundred and a thousand cases, and Uncle Sam's soldiers are not expected to have less.

If their figures for this disease are so grossly, so ridiculously, so impossibly wrong, what of their other claims in their annual reports?

[*My closing remarks were*]:

If Mr. Quin and Mr. Maverick accuse each other of being generally undesirable, what conclusions must the citizens of San Antonio draw? They must conclude that Mr. Quin and Mr. Maverick are both right. And that conclusion will relegate both these unwanted politicians to the political dumping ground, and thereby elect on May 8 Leroy Jeffers mayor of San Antonio.

The campaign was fought hard to the last night. There was much about which we were optimistic, but optimism was not enough. We had no ready-made machine. The election was close. Jeffers, for his group, received 11,172 votes; Quin, 15,441; and Maverick, 18,445. It was the chance of a generation, but there were not enough right-thinking people who were interested enough to vote. The result of this election postponed the coming of city-manager government for twelve years.

It was good to see Quin defeated, but it soon became evident that Mayor Maverick was not a very happy or complete remedy for the ailments of San Antonio. At least he was an improvement.

It should be said to the credit of Maury Maverick that he did permit the people to vote on the council-manager form of government. However, his support was halfhearted. Again on December 11, 1940, I was on WOAI, speaking on "Politicians and Our Health.":

As generations have come and gone, San Antonio has been continuously infested with more rapacious politicians than any city of comparable size. The result has been: inefficiency, ineptitude, and extravagance.

The story is told of an enterprising native of Mexico City who made a comfortable living by selling the skeleton of Juarez to American tourists eager to take home something with Mexican atmosphere. One day he sold the skeleton of *El Presidente* to an American. A few days later this American met the skeleton salesman and he had another skeleton which he was offering as having belonged to the president, this time a small one. The American remonstrated, saying, "I thought I bought Juarez's skeleton last week." "Very true, my friend," was the reply. "But this is the skeleton of *El Presidente* when he was a boy." The American accepted the explanation, bought the small skeleton, and went home ignorantly happy. In some such fashion as this, with the passing years, the politicians have sold their political skeletons to the citizens of San Antonio, and too many of us have been made to believe that we have been getting a bargain.

A recent example of politics at its ludicrous worst is this: one of our ring politicians was speaking on the purchase of voting machines. Of course he, like all politicians, was against it. Voting machines are too fair and too free of manipulation. With characteristic bombast and unconvincing logic, but with a delightful mixing of metaphors and anatomy, he reached his climax when he said, "We must take the bull by the tail and look him right in the eye!" Now, however difficult such a gymnastic feat should appear, it would be far easier than to reconcile the preelection promises and the postelection performances of the average officeholder in San Antonio.

Must the citizens of San Antonio continue to accept this political situation with supine complacence and indifferent disgust? The answer is emphatically no. On December 17, there will be given to us an opportunity to make good, businesslike government in San Antonio a permanent and progressive reality. On that day we will be given an opportunity to give to San Antonio a council-manager form of government. You have heard much of the merits of this form of government for American cities. Tonight, briefly, my desire is to present some of the advantages that will accrue to the health of our people.

That the need for health improvement in San Antonio is great, no one will deny. Year after year, decade after decade, San Antonio has stood out on the health map of the United States as a black spot. In

the minds of public-health authorities, San Antonio with its prevalence of disease and crime—the two usually go together—has become a reproach and a byword. As far back as the records go, this
city has had the unenviable reputation of having the highest death
rate from tuberculosis of all the cities in the country—three, four,
five, sometimes ten times as high. And a comparable situation has
existed with intestinal diseases of infants.

In Dallas, Fort Worth, Austin, and other Texas cities with council-
manager governments, conditions of health have greatly improved.
Qualified personnel has been assured by the presence of real civil
service. The health departments of these cities have been permitted
to perform their legitimate functions of promoting the public health
and are not maintained as disgusting departments of corrupt political
machines.

If San Antonio is to make progress in health matters, it must come
from the establishment of a program which is progressive and continuous—not disrupted and changed every two years. The politicians
have made a few forward steps, not of their own volition but under
compulsion. Mayor Quin made certain microscopic pretensions toward better health, but these were lost in an overweening desire to
stay in office. Mayor Maverick began his administration more hope-
fully, but it wasn't long before he was kicking the health department
around like a political football. That has been the difficulty all along;
it is so easy to put on as inspectors in the health department politicians who wouldn't know a germ from a cockroach. So the health
department of today is not greatly different from what it has been.

New living quarters built by the government are important, but
this is not a drop in the bucket. Likewise the erection of a tuberculosis hospital will care for only 150 to 200 patients and these few
will stay six months, a year, or longer. So there will be a very slow
turnover. What about the several thousand who infect their families
at home or who walk the streets and infect outsiders? Here is the
real problem: a case of tuberculosis west of San Pedro Creek is an
ever-present menace to the citizens north of Dewey Place and the
citizens south of Highland Boulevard and the citizens in between.
Whatever we may think of the health situation on the West Side,
these people are very distinctly our responsibility. They are here to
stay, and in the future they will be here in ever-increasing numbers.
For our own protection, this problem must be faced sanely and wisely. Politically-ridden health departments in the past have made no

impression on it, and for the future hold out no promise. We need a change. The council-manager form of government offers much hope. Those who are in doubt should realize that we have nothing to lose, that things could hardly become worse.

What San Antonio needs is a progressive, permanent plan for attacking the serious health menaces that beset her. A council-manager form of government, with the health department divorced from politics and in active cooperation with the State Health Department and the United States Public Health Service, will provide such a plan. It has worked elsewhere; it will work in San Antonio.

The people turned down the opportunity to improve their form of government. After such a succession of failures, one would think that I should have had enough. And, in reality, I had. But I got back into the fight under some combined pressures which I could not resist. It will be recalled that Mayor Quin had unceremoniously fired the board of health of which I was a member. A new board was appointed and it was a good board. In 1943, Gus Mauermann succeeded Quin [*who had returned to office at the end of Mayor Maverick's term*]. Late in the year, he and the board of health failed to see eye to eye, so the board resigned. There was a good deal of resentment on the part of the members of the medical profession, and they were refusing to serve on the board. The situation became so critical that the Chamber of Commerce felt obligated to step in. The city was without a board of health, and there was no prospect of forming one.

Mayor Mauermann requested the Chamber of Commerce to draw up an ordinance creating a board of health and insuring that the activities of the health department be freed from political interference. This ordinance provided that the board "shall be composed of seven members, who shall be nominated by the Chamber of Commerce and appointed by the Mayor, two of whom shall be practicing physicians and the others shall be laymen." The ordinance further provided that the director of public health, who must be qualified in public-health work, should be appointed by the board with the approval of the mayor. It charged the director with the responsibility of selecting his assistants, subject to the approval of the board, and of employing individuals thoroughly qualified for their respective positions and in conformity with "the standards of the merit system and any other regulations set up by the federal and state boards of health."

The chamber in turn, under the able leadership of B. B. Mc-Gimsey, asked certain groups in the city to suggest names for the several positions. The [*two*] medical members were left up to the Bexar County Medical Society, the Texas Medical Association, and three or four other organizations. I learned that I was the unanimous choice of all these groups. So the circumstances were such that I could not refuse. Some of my doctor friends felt that I was untrue to the medical profession when I accepted a position on this board. I assured them that I was not, but not until now have I set down all the facts. On October 12, 1943, the following notification was received from Mayor Mauermann: "This is to advise you that by action of the city commissioners today, you were appointed a member of the city health board. Having been advised by Mr. McGimsey that you agreed to serve, I want to commend you for your willingness to render this service for our city, and to say that it affords me great pleasure to send you this letter of notification of your appointment."

The other members of this board were Mrs. Leroy G. Denman, Dr. E. V. DePew, Nat Goldsmith, E. A. Baetz, Carl Krueger, and Reagan Houston, chairman. I consider this to be the most capable and the most conscientious group I was ever officially associated with in San Antonio. Mayor Mauermann gave the board complete control of the health department. He was present at practically every one of our meetings and showed not the least desire to interfere in any way. It was his energy and enthusiasm that gave the health program the impetus it so sorely needed.

The accomplishments of this board were too numerous and too far-reaching even to mention. If each member were asked what the major accomplishment of the board was, the unanimous reply, I believe, would be the fact that we persuaded

Lewis C. Robbins to become director of health. He was a young man, trained at Johns Hopkins, capable, honest, direct in his approach.

Dr. Robbins, in the uniform of captain in the United States Public Health Service, arrived in San Antonio in December, 1943. The way Dr. Robbins worked is difficult to set down. He used tact, diplomacy, and patience when the board might have been inclined toward frankness or even force. His sincerity and his ingenuousness made him the ideal man to head the department which had been the source of so much contention. Under his wise directing hand, the health department operated smoothly. The work of the board of health had become a routine pleasure. Progress in every direction was recorded. And then one day Dr. Robbins announced that he wanted to resign. World War II was at its greatest fury. The United States Public Health Service, to obtain needed personnel, had relaxed its requirements on height and weight for enrollment of permanent officers. Dr. Robbins, who was on a temporary basis, was just able to squeeze in. So we lost him—a young man whom we had all come to love.

After his departure, things went well until a severe epidemic of poliomyelitis developed early in 1946. I had become chairman of the board, and many medical decisions were left up to me. At the time, we had an acting director of health, but he was of little assistance. The epidemic started slowly but soon spread rapidly. We needed help badly. It came from a large group of interested doctors who met one night at the home of Dr. Walter Stuck.[9] After long discussion, it was decided that the situation demanded drastic action. [It was] recommended to the board of health that all schools, Sunday schools, and theaters be closed to children under fifteen. The board, after thorough consideration, adopted the recommendation, which was modified from time to time. Help also came from another direction, the Epidemiological Committee. This committee was the di-

[9] Walter G. Stuck, a graduate of Washington University in Saint Louis, was an orthopedic surgeon. He also served as associate editor of *Southwest Texas Medicine* and as president of the Southwestern Surgical Congress.

recting hand during the epidemic. It held daily meetings, reviewed developments, received reports of new cases, accepted suggestions, heard complaints, which were few but noisy, and made recommendations to the board. The course which the epidemic ran and the measures used to combat it can best be presented by quoting [*from*] a report I made to the board: "Summary of the Activities of the Board of Health During the Poliomyelitis Epidemic."

Mayor Mauermann and the city commissioners early recognized the potential hazards involved in this outbreak and made available $30,000 as an emergency fund. Without this fund and without the active assistance of the various departments of the city, the efforts of the health department would have been delayed, if not crippled.

The State Department of Health, under the guidance of Dr. George W. Cox, contributed personnel, equipment, and advice, when early action was essential. It was Dr. Cox who recommended chlorination of all drinking water, a recommendation which was carried out with dispatch by the city water board.

Disease is no respecter of boundary lines. The county, the City of San Antonio, Alamo Heights and other incorporated areas, and the neighboring army installations were all vitally involved in this epidemic. The county board of health, the local health officers, and the medical officers of the various army camps were anxious to make their restrictions and their efforts parallel those of the San Antonio Health Department. The polio wards at the Robert B. Green Memorial Hospital were in close touch with the city health department.

The work of the Chamber of Commerce cannot be overemphasized. Mr. C. J. Crampton gave up his work with the chamber and devoted all his time to the epidemic. He obtained priorities in garbage cans and wire screening and procured pressure sprays from Fort Sam Houston for the garbage dumps, which worked a near miracle in fly control. The assignment by the chamber of Mr. O. W. Thurston as a statistician was of much benefit to the epidemiological committee.

The cooperation of the Fort Sam Houston motor pool and Kelly Field motor pool was invaluable. These pools furnished trucks and drivers for the transportation of the field workers and for the TIFA fogger when no such equipment was otherwise available at the time.

The War Assets Corporation not only procured much-needed

equipment for the Department of Parks and Sanitation, but assisted the health department in procuring DDT products at two surplus sales at considerable saving in cost.

We are also indebted to the Slick Airways, San Antonio, Todd Shipyards Corporation, New York City, and DDT Products Manufacturing Company, Incorporated, of Houston, for the services and materials made available to San Antonio when they were most needed.

Throughout the epidemic, it was urgently necessary for the citizens of this area to be kept informed. Everyone was eager to know what was expected of him as an individual. Without the close and willing cooperation of all the newspapers and all the radio stations, this would have been impossible. The radio stations have given unlimited time to disseminating all types of information about the disease. The newspapers, by story and picture, paraded the many health hazards that beset San Antonio: deplorable garbage dumps, leaking and inadequate sewers, dirty alleys and vacant lots, open garbage cans, and squalid housing conditions. Without undue alarm, although given all the facts, the people were kept informed as well as instructed. Without depreciating the invaluable assistance from all the newspapers, a word should be said about the series of editorials on poliomyelitis which appeared in the San Antonio *Express*. Here were set forth in clear, simple language the known facts of the disease, the modes of transmission, the methods of control, the rationale of the restrictions imposed by the board of health, and the necessity for strict observance.

The board of health, at the onset of this epidemic, refused to accept the all-too-prevalent defeatist attitude that nothing can be done to control or modify an epidemic of poliomyelitis. It ignored the academic controversy as to whether the disease is contracted by direct contact or by contaminated food. Following the best available advice, it put into effect certain measures to counteract both modes of transmission. These measures were threefold: forbidding the congregation of children; widespread clean up, with emphasis on garbage handling and disposal; systematic and sustained use of DDT by individuals and by the fogger. Within two weeks after these control measures were instituted, there was a marked decrease in the number of cases. This decrease has continued, until now the disease has practically disappeared. Nonetheless, the toll has been heavy; ninety-eight cases, with much crippling, and twelve deaths.

There are two important by-products of the poliomyelitis campaign: the near absence of flies, mosquitoes, and other insects; and the marked reduction in the number of cases of all acute infectious diseases. These can logically be credited to the measures instituted by the board on May 11.

There were a few disagreeable episodes, which came from two divergent groups. The first was the ugly complaint of a few selfish owners of movie theaters and places of amusement, who had no qualms of conscience when the welfare of our children was at stake. These were easily dealt with. The other group was more difficult. They were a small handful of preachers who were sincere but misguided. Practically all church groups accepted the ban against the assembly of children at Sunday school as a necessary inconvenience. A group of Lutheran pastors protested the ban but added, "we believe civil authority must be obeyed. When the law is unjust we petition, as we have done." This word came from one of Archbishop Robert E. Lucey's assistants: "It is up to parents and the police. We have no objection if they stick a policeman at the door. In some parishes some children attend services. But our original instructions stick until the ban is lifted." It was only after a Methodist preacher accused the board of contributing to the delinquency of children that any serious notice was taken of these dissidents. This man was sincere when he defied the ban and opened his Sunday school. According to the papers, he said: "I derive my authority from the Lord, and I take orders from the Lord, not the city health board. . . . I have talked with the juvenile authorities, and they tell me that they expect dire results from the polio ban. They foresee a great increase in juvenile delinquency and feel that the full harmful effects may not become known for perhaps twenty to thirty years."

In a statement to the press, I replied:

It is sincerely to be hoped that the cause of religion in San Antonio has not been rendered a great disservice by him. Opposition of the clergy to scientific progress is not new. Religious fanatics burned Michael Servetus at the stake, and when chloroform was first used to relieve the pains of childbirth, no group protested more vigorously than the preachers. It was the invention of the devil, they maintained. What can the children of his church think when a minister advocates flouting the decisions of duly constituted authorities? Law observance by religious groups is more or less taken for granted. Certainly the Methodist Church, of which he and I are members, does not sanction or condone nonobservance of regulations set up by city ordinance and further strengthened by the sanitary code of Texas. What can our children think? In truth, juvenile delinquency is involved in this matter.

In the hope that he will reconsider, I would suggest that he do three things: 1. Make a visit to the poliomyelitis ward at the Robert B. Green Hospital. 2. Take a look at the ten black flags on the map at the city health department. 3. Read Nehemiah 9:17.

In 1947 Mayor Mauermann was defeated by Alfred Callaghan. Hardly had he [Callaghan] taken office before he began to tamper with the health department. This department had reached its highest peak of development, with the following as top personnel: Dr. Dudley A. Reekie, director of public health; Dr. W. V. Bradshaw, assistant director and chief of the bureau of medical services;[10] Chester Cohen, chief of the bureau of public health engineering; H. L. Crittenden, chief of the bureau of administrative services; and Dr. A. B. Rich, director of the laboratory. [The mayor] first set out to displace Mr. Crittenden with one of his political followers. Then he made untenable the position of Dr. Reekie, a man of the highest capacities.

The board held several meetings with the mayor in an effort to make him see the situation from a nonpolitical angle. I recall telling him that it was impossible for him to conceive of seven citizens neglecting their own business and trying to do something for the city without expecting some tangible reward in return.

Mayor Callaghan assured us that he was eager to retain the existing board, but we soon discovered he was trying to form a new board. The whole matter came to a head at a meeting of

10 Dudley Ainslie Reekie was a 1934 graduate of the College of Medical Evangelists in Los Angeles. Wilber Vinton Bradshaw was a 1934 graduate of the Medical College of Virginia.

the board on July 1 [*1947*]. Here are [*excerpts from*] the minutes of that meeting:

Dr. Nixon read a letter of resignation submitted by Dr. Dudley A. Reekie, city health officer: "The city attorney has determined that the ordinance of 1943 creating a board of health appointed by the Chamber of Commerce is in violation of the city charter. In view of this fact, conditions under which my services were employed do not now exist. For this reason my resignation as director of health, effective June 30, 1947, is herewith submitted."

"The resignation of Dr. Reekie, and its acceptance by the board," said Dr. Nixon, "makes it necessary for the board of health to name an acting city health officer." Dr. Nixon suggested the name of Dr. W. V. Bradshaw, Jr., assistant city health officer and chief of the division of communicable diseases. He revealed that he had discussed the matter with Mayor Callaghan and had secured his approval of Dr. Bradshaw. Mr. Krueger moved that Dr. Bradshaw be appointed to the position of acting city health officer. The motion was seconded by Mr. Goldsmith and carried.

Mr. Baetz informed the board that he had heard a great deal of discussion about the amount of money that has been spent by the health department and asked for a clarification of one point. "I understand," he said, "that the health department operates under the state and federal merit system and that observance of the standards set up by this system is required by the State Health Department in the employment of our personnel. Is my understanding correct, Mr. Chairman, or am I misinformed?" Mr. Goldsmith asked, "Are you inquiring about the fixing of salaries?" Mr. Baetz said that was what he had reference to. Dr. Nixon assured Mr. Baetz that he was correct in his assumption: "We are very definitely operating under the merit system. The ordinance creating this board of health is very clear in charging us with the responsibility for adopting the merit system."

Mr. Goldsmith said that, in addition to the ordinance requiring adoption of the merit system, it should also be remembered that if we refuse to adhere to this system, state and federal aid might be denied us. Dr. Nixon added: "That's right. Awarding of state and federal funds to any city health department is contingent upon adoption of the merit system."

Dr. Nixon then addressed the board in a most serious manner. "Public health in San Antonio," he said, "has reached a crucial point.

This board is faced with a critical problem. You will recall that Mayor Callaghan stated to members of the board at a luncheon meeting at the Menger Hotel on June 9 that he thought the ordinance creating this board of health was a good one and, with apparent pride, said that since taking office he had not sent anyone to the health department to be employed. We were encouraged by this statement, but this attitude on the part of Mayor Callaghan didn't last very long. Yesterday I received a letter from the mayor. That letter reads: 'This is to notify you and the board of health that I wish to replace Mr. H. L. Crittenden, who is carried on the payroll at present as chief of the bureau of administrative services, with Mr. Dillard Coy, effective July 1, 1947.'"

Mr. Krueger immediately protested: "The ordinance under which this board operates stipulates that all employees of the health department are to be nominated by the city health officer and approved by this board. We have no right to act on the suggestion contained in Mayor Callaghan's letter. I move that the letter be tabled."

It was decided that Dr. Nixon should reply to the mayor's letter as follows: "The City Health Board at its meeting today considered your letter of June 30 requesting the appointment of Mr. Dillard Coy as business manager of the department to replace Mr. Crittenden and, without considering the qualifications of Mr. Coy for the position, by unanimous vote declined to make the appointment. In order to explain the action of the board, it should be remembered that, when the members accepted their places on the board because of their interest in public health in San Antonio and because they felt it was their civic duty to serve, it was with the distinct understanding that the board would not be subject to political domination. It has so functioned up to the present time. Also by unanimous vote, the board adopted a resolution to the effect that the mayor be notified that, if it is his intention to dictate to the board as to the appointment of health department employees, the board suggests to the mayor that he either repeal the ordinance which places the hiring and firing with the board or that he ask for the resignation of the present members and appoint a board which will be more responsive to political influence. If, on the other hand, it is not his intention to insist upon the appointment of Mr. Coy or any other employee, then the board is willing to continue as in the past in what it considers the best interest of public health in San Antonio."

Referring to the letter received from the mayor and the above resolution, Dr. Nixon emphasized: "The subject of this resolution is the crux of the whole situation. It is the basis on which we operate. You can see how tragically serious the situation has become when the board is charged with the responsibility of hiring and firing and the mayor writes a letter such as I have just read to you. In its dealings with the mayor, this board has tried to exercise tolerance and dignity. We have tried reasoning, explanation, and compromise, but we have gotten exactly nowhere. We feel this matter has reached a climax, and the next move—perhaps the last move—is up to the mayor."

Addressing the fifty or more persons in attendance at the board meeting, Dr. Nixon said, "On behalf of the board of health, I should like to take this opportunity to thank the various individuals and civic organizations for the splendid support you have given us in our undertakings during the past several years. Without your confidence and cooperation, we couldn't have gotten anywhere. The board wants you to know that it deeply appreciates your interest and all of the effort you have put forth to further our public health program in San Antonio."

Then turning to fellow members of the board he continued, "I hardly know what to say to the board—hardly know how to thank you for the support you have given me as chairman, but I do know that no chairman of any board has ever received more confidence, support, and affection. You have given your time without stint. You have met with me night as well as day when it was necessary to solve some health problem with which we were confronted. This board has not failed. Your efforts have been rewarded with accomplishments. If this has been true for the past four years, perhaps some day this same record can be permanently established."

"I would like to give thanks," said Mr. Goldsmith, "to the chairman of this board for his untiring efforts at improving the public health of San Antonio at what we all know to be both a great personal and financial sacrifice. Those of us who are in business have been able to give our time without financial loss, but time is a financial element in the life of a physician."

At this point Dr. Nixon asked the audience if they had anything to say. Mrs. Sinkin, president of the League of Women Voters, asked for the floor. She said the mayor had raised two issues that she felt should be clarified by the board of health: "First, Mayor Callaghan is reported to have said that, inasmuch as he is responsible for the funds of the city, he feels that he should have an accounting of where the money goes and should also have a vote on the board of health in order to have a voice in deciding how money allotted to the health department is spent." Dr. Nixon replied: "The same system is being used now in accounting for money that is spent by the health department as has been used right along. It is the same system that was used when Mayor Callaghan was commissioner of taxation and had a voice in passing on expenditures. From recent published statements that are credited to him, one would think the health department has been spending money right and left without obtaining any results. The health department furnishes the mayor with a payroll accounting twice a month. Every item is listed. The board of health has no responsibility for his ability to understand the accounting figures, but they are itemized and placed before him. As to the second part of your question, the present ordinance was worked out among former Mayor Mauermann, the Chamber of Commerce, the Bexar County Medical Society, the State Medical Association, and the council for this Medical District. It was their recommendation that the board be composed of five laymen and two physicians. I don't know why they recommended that the mayor not have a vote, but I am sure this board has no objection to his being a voting member."

Mrs. Sinkin's second question was: "The mayor is reported to have said the health department is spending enough money to run a million-dollar concern. Is that true?" Dr. Nixon said that the health department is close to a half-million-dollar concern, a fact that San Antonio should be proud of, and he only wished the city did have a million-dollar health department. Mr. Baetz, a member of the finance committee of the board of health, commented on Mrs. Sinkin's question. "It should be understood," he said, "that the health department does not make purchases. All items to be purchased are secured through the city purchasing agent, by requisition. Charges have been made that the health department has more equipment than is necessary. I don't know that this is true. It is my understanding that we are not adequately equipped." Dr. Nixon then cited the scooters that have been purchased as an example of alleged extravagance. "But they save an automobile," he said. "Water samples and specimens can be collected just as easily with a scooter as with a car, and they cost much less to buy and to operate."

The board, thus faced by an impossible situation, resorted to resignation as the only decent way out. We had made every effort to placate the mayor and to make him see the folly of his ways. Resignation was preferable to dismissal.

It was a great disappointment to the board members. We had tried hard, and some success had come as the result of our efforts. We had removed the health department from the deadly snarl of politics where it had stagnated for fifty years and more. This was our particular pride, which we could share equally all the rest of our days. We could share, too, the mutual respect and trust that was ours. We had worked together for four years on problems that concerned the health and welfare of the people of San Antonio, never once questioning the sincerity of the other members, never once failing to come to a mutually satisfactory solution of the problem at hand, never once suggesting an individual for employment, or in any other way seeking to interfere with the health department which was operating so smoothly and so efficiently.

The San Antonio *Express* [*on July 12, 1947*] made this editorial comment:

This community is deeply indebted to the city health board that has just been virtually forced out of office, for almost four years of devoted, constructive service. Its professional and lay members alike were capable administrators, working in complete harmony with the department's personnel of executive direction, inspection, and nursing.

Facing the sweeping destruction of its efforts to carry on in the same efficient way, under the protection of an ordinance assuring it immunity from political interference, the board was left no choice but to resign in a body. Chairman Nixon and his colleagues were the victims of an attack of spoils politics at its worst.

As a postscript, it should be added that the calamitous results which were feared would come from the action of Mayor Callaghan did not materialize. He did not succeed in repealing the beneficent ordinance which took the health department out of politics. It was fortunate that an excellent director of public

health was found in the person of Dr. Austin E. Hill,[11] who
[was] supported by a good board of health headed by A. H.
Cadwallader, Jr., and also supported by the entire medical profession in San Antonio. Dr. Hill continued the good work set in
motion by Dr. Lewis C. Robbins and Dr. Dudley A. Reekie.

As a finale to my political experiences, it should be added
that I have come to see something new in San Antonio politics.
In 1951, the council-manager form of government was adopted,
with a good council and a good manager in C. A. Harrell. This
success was spearheaded by [Mayor] Jack White, who came to
be thought of as a symbol of good government and was instrumental in roundly defeating Alfred Callaghan. But he rather
quickly became a fallen idol in the eyes of the people. In 1953,
he was reelected along with a crew of [partisan] councilmen.
Relief came in 1955. The people of San Antonio rebelled and
expelled this group, and we again had a good council and a
good manager.

My last venture into the realm of public health was in 1949.
The San Antonio Chamber of Commerce had consistently supported all movements directed toward improved health and had
long had a committee on public health. For one reason or another, the work of this committee had stagnated. I was asked to
see if I could not revive interest in it. I summarized the progress
of the work in a report I made a year later:

"The day is short and the work is great. The reward is also great
and the Master praises. It is not incumbent on thee to complete the
work but thou must not therefore cease from it" [The Talmud].
Health is a people's most prized possession, too often properly appreciated only after it has been lost or undermined. Public health
has been too long taken for granted. There has been, and indeed still
is, a tendency to assume that poor health conditions in one section of
a city are no concern to those living in other sections. This assumption
is both fallacious and dangerous. A health hazard in one community
must become the business of the entire area.
San Antonio has long held the unenviable record of being a very

11 Austin E. Hill was a 1932 graduate of Baylor School of Medicine.

unhealthy city. In the death rate from tuberculosis and infant diarrhea, it stands at the top of the list of cities. During the past six years, great progress has been made. But much still remains to be done. Nothing short of a continuing, intensive program over a period of many years can give to San Antonio the needed improvements in public health.

San Antonio has been blessed by nature in many ways. The earliest travelers were struck by the mildness of the climate; they spoke of it as being "salubrious." We have no excessive extremes of heat or cold. Our water is cool and pure and plentiful. Our proximity to the Gulf assures adequate cooling breezes. Theoretically, therefore, San Antonio should be the most healthful city in the state. But such is far from the case. For this condition, political ineptness in the past is not the sole explanation. Apathy and indifference on the part of the general public must accept a good portion of the blame.

Certain local factors multiply the problems of public health in San Antonio. Chiefest of these is the large Latin-American population. Lack of sanitary facilities and ignorance of sanitary principles are of utmost significance. But looking more deeply into the problem, we see that the economic condition of these people is a big factor. This is manifest primarily in the housing situation, so that large numbers of people are closely crowded into small corrals. The result is inevitable: poverty, crime, and disease.

Other factors are the large unsewered areas and the river and several creeks which traverse the city. At times, especially after hard rains, these are little less than open sewers.

This committee has worked in close cooperation with the City Health Department. Under the guidance of Dr. Austin Hill, this department is on a firm footing. Its routine work is carried on in a satisfactory manner. However, because of lack of funds, certain essential activities have been curtailed or cancelled.

The public health committee has held twelve meetings, with attendance ranging from thirty to fifty. This has been an active committee, dealing with problems of the present and at the same time looking forward to the future and a more healthful San Antonio.

In connection with the polio epidemic, it should be said that it is little short of stupid to wait until April or May to begin a drive to clean up the city, perhaps after polio or some other disease has reached epidemic proportions. Every day should be cleanup day.

And it is very logical that spraying should be begun as early as February or March, with a view to preventing disease. The public health committee of the Chamber of Commerce has sufficient funds, which, it is to be hoped, will be used for early and regular spraying.

By way of giving emphasis to the fact that the solution of San Antonio's public health problems is to be found only in a prolonged and continuing program, a subcommittee has been appointed to arrange a long-range program for the future. This committee, under the leadership of Dr. Bonham Jones and Albert Biedenharn, has given a great deal of careful study to the problems involved, their report indicates.

[*According to the account in the* Express *of January 10, 1950,*] the Chamber of Commerce report [*based on the subcommittee's study*] included fifteen recommendations for a long-range health program for the city, embodying activities, many of which would normally be carried out by a city health department. These recommendations included:

Give the city health department more personnel for case finding.

Expansion of visiting nurses of public-health nursing service in the southeastern section of the city, which has more than its proportionate share of infant diarrhea.

Expand existing facilities for indigents to be immunized against diphtheria, whooping cough, tetanus, and smallpox.

Annual blood-test campaign against syphilis.

Control of insects, sewers, garbage, and water supply to reduce polio.

Public-health nurse visits to all babies not born in hospitals or attended by physicians.

Establishment of a mental hygiene clinic.

Enforcement of the corral ordinance; encouragement of private enterprise in low-cost housing, and "support efforts to keep public housing on a sound self-liquidating basis."

Extension and repair of sewer lines.

Improved garbage collection service.

Make approved water supply available to all homes in the city.

Insect elimination work by individuals and the city health department.

Increased public-health education.

Support all endeavors to make Robert B. Green a first-class hospital.

Expand facilities for handicapped children.[12]

[*My report on the Chamber of Commerce's public-health commit-tee concluded:*] Many of the situations that face San Antonio are peculiar to this city. Their ultimate solution lies in the distant future. This year and next year, we can make certain tangible gains, just as we have during the past several years. Patience and persistence must be our watchwords. Our citizens must be made to be continually health-conscious. Our public officials must constantly remind them-selves that the health of our people is paramount. Poor health is more of an evil than poor streets or poor law enforcement or poor gar-bage collection. "Until political greatness and wisdom meet in one, cities will never have rest from their evils, no, nor the human race" [*Socrates*].

[12] The Jones and Biedenharn Report is printed in full in the San Antonio *Express*, January 10, 1950.

7

The Family

~~⌒ゝဝℯ⌒~~

IT IS DIFFICULT for me to write about my family without an undue display of emotion. My feelings toward Olive have already been set down, or at least the attempt has been made. The love I bear toward her has been transmitted through her to our four boys. These boys have, each in his own chosen way, made lives for themselves. It has long been my contention that, if a son does not improve on the sire, it is the fault of the sire. Pat and Bob are better doctors than I ever hoped to be, and Thomas and Ben stand out in their work as dairy farmer and Air Force captain.

Pat's arrival on May 28, 1913, after a stormy journey for Olive, was a benediction to both of us, and we were doubly blessed when Bob showed up one year and one month later. Then there was an interval of seven years. This time we wanted and expected a girl. But, instead, on February 14, 1921, we got two boys—two very little boys; Ben came fifteen minutes ahead of Thomas. They were before their day. Just how little they were, we didn't know. They were so small that we didn't dare disturb them to get an exact weight. The first few months of life were most distressing. We tried all kinds of food, and nothing seemed to agree. We even kept two goats in the backyard. Gastrointestinal upsets were frequent and serious. Our copy of Holt's *Care and Feeding of Infants*, which we still have, was learned by heart, and the patience and sympathy of Dr. Mary Harper and Dr. George Cornick were a source of great comfort to Olive and me. But the burden of the battle was ours. It rended our hearts as, day after day and week after week, we looked into the thin, pleading faces of our little boys and felt so helpless. Truly we can say with Ambroise Paré that we treated them but God healed them.[1]

It was our harvesttime of happiness as we saw our boys through Travis Elementary School, Hawthorne Junior High School, and Main Avenue and Jefferson high schools. As they went through these happy and carefree years, our satisfactions were great to see them grow and develop and accept their obligations and responsibilities seriously. It was good to have Pat and Bob excel in their classroom work and other activities. Bob was president of about everything Jefferson had to offer. The twins did their schoolwork well, but it was on the tennis courts that they spread themselves. They won championship matches all the way from Texas to Manitoba.

Then came their college days; Pat, Bob, and Ben at the University [of Texas], and Thomas at Schreiner Institute. Bob seemed to have repeated my experience of uneasy progress at Austin. After his third year, I sensed his dissatisfaction and suggested the University of Virginia. His face beamed, for that was what he wanted to hear. He made the honor roll at Charlottesville; this meant he had made an average of 85 percent or more in his courses and was placed on the dean's list of distinguished students. Pat must have adapted himself better at Austin than his father and brother. He was on the honor roll the first year. He started out in engineering but switched to premedical work after two years and was easily ready for medical school after four years.

Pat's and Bob's sojourns in the medical department of Duke University were years of successful work. Pat's years in Baltimore, Walter Reed Hospital in Washington, and a long stay at West Point well fitted him to come into the office with me as soon as he was discharged from the Army in 1945. Bob interned at the University of Iowa and then spent three years as a surgi-

---

[1] Ambroise Paré, 1517–1590, a French surgeon, has been called the father of modern surgery.

cal fellow at the Mayo Clinic. His three years in the Air Force were fruitful from a surgical standpoint. When he came to San Antonio in 1947, he was one of the best surgeons of the area.

Ben and Thomas have been equally successful in what they have undertaken. Thomas, despite continuously hard work and five severely droughty years, has done well and bids fair to achieve a high degree of serenity.[2] The recognition of the dignity of hard work and the importance of grass stamp his character deeply. Ben's more than two thousand hours as a pilot in the Air Force have been taken in stride. He has experienced ineptness, dishonesty, and plain orneriness in his superiors; he has had the courage to speak out, but willing ears have been few. As he and his fellow fliers have passed over at the farm and elsewhere, I have found this prayer on my lips: "God bless them and keep them. May they fly with Thee and for Thee."

These factual generalities about our boys must suffice. If I should invade the field of feelings and pride and attitudes, my emotions would be unduly excited into use of superlatives.

Fairland Hills Farm has played a big part in the life of the Nixon family. It has been said that there are three ways to ruin a young professional man: to gamble, to support two family households, and to have a model farm. I could never aspire to the first two, but of the third, I may have been partially guilty. Purchased in 1920, the farm has meant much to every one of us. For Olive and me, it has been an outlet, a near place of retreat and rest. For the boys, it has been an undisguised blessing. It has kept them off the streets and has substituted a love of nature. They have had their donkeys, horses, and carts. They have spent many nights there, sleeping on the ground and later in the shack. They have had hayrides, parties, snipe hunts, and other enjoyments to which the out-of-doors lends itself.

The farm of 350 acres, eight miles from the city limits on the Bandera Road, had few improvements but was easily worth thirty-five dollars an acre. About one-third of it was in cultiva-

---

[2] Thomas took over the operation of Fairland Hills farm when he returned from service at the end of World War II.

tion. In true German tradition, Vincent Ehrler had built a small house and a good barn. At present, the improvements are adequate, and about half the place is in cultivation. Most of all, Thomas and Charlotte have a beautiful and comfortable home.

Anyone driving along the road or through the pasture will have noticed that much of the underbrush and many of the trees have been cleared out. Because of this, it has been frequently remarked that the farm is the most attractive place in the area. I can lay claim to this accomplishment. With the aid of axe, grubbing hoe, and tractor, I have improved about sixty acres. One beautiful spot, atop a hill, has been dubbed Persimmon Flat because of the large number of persimmon trees.

Until Thomas took over in 1947, no great amount of money was made on the place. Indeed, some was lost. But the many nonmonetary rewards outweighed any loss. Registered jersey cattle were used until Thomas added some holsteins. We have owned and developed many fine animals, among them Pogis 99th's Alcalde and Sophie's Fairland Tormentor. These two bulls were awarded gold medals by the American Jersey Cattle Club. The United States Department of Agriculture wanted to buy them, but we refused to sell. We have always had a high-producing herd, one of the best in the state. The first year Thomas took over, the Texas Jersey Cattle Club gave him a certificate for having the highest-producing herd of jerseys in Texas. What Thomas has accomplished has been done under difficulties, the greatest being four consecutive dry years. He has tried to encourage native and foreign grasses, but the drought has nullified his efforts. His main dependence has been found in the very brushy pasture where there is an abundance of oak bushes. But most of all, he loves the soil and appreciates the dignity of hard work.

The kids learned to be real horsemen. They, of course, had their spills but there were no serious injuries. I can't say as much for myself. I have been "throwed" by many horses. The boys like to recall the time I was pitched over a woodpile by a white mule. By accident, some years later, it was found that I had a healed fracture of a lumbar vertebra.

The Family

One of the first horses we had was Old Brownie. This fine saddle horse was loaned to us by Garrett Wilson, one of the best of men.[3] We kept him two or three years. A big bay horse was claimed by the twins. Old Brownie was enough for Pat and Bob, but the twins felt that they needed two horses, so we got a fiery horse named Little Brownie. These two boys and these two horses burned up the roads of the neighborhood; they even kept their horses part of the time in the backyard on Courtland Place. On New Year's Eve of 1939, Little Brownie was killed on the Bandera Highway.

While none of the boys sustained any serious injury at the farm, they did not escape elsewhere. There were definite hazards involved in horseback riding, driving mules, and tinkering with tractors. In town, it was different. Their regular play, their participation in games, swimming, taking their boats down the river, digging caves in the backyard, a toboggan-like contraption with flanged wheels which moved downhill across the yard at great speed—all these and many more helped to round out a full life for four healthy boys. These were the casualties: Pat, fractures of the clavicle and lower leg; Bob, fracture of a big toe; Ben, fracture of the nose; and Thomas, fractures of the forearm and upper arm.

The thing which our friends will remember best about the farm are the barbecues which we had over a period of twenty years or more. Each winter we would accumulate enough venison and wild turkey and have Loma barbecue it at the shack. Log seats in a circle about a huge bonfire furnished food and entertainment of unforgettable memories. The weatherman has furnished moonlight as well as snow and sleet, but never did we fail to go through with the barbecue; and always the guests came, sometimes as many as a hundred of them. Some of the log seats have survived; when I see them, I hear in memory the strumming of guitars and the voices of friends as they sang in the evening by the moonlight.

[3] Harrison Garrett Wilson, 1865–1942, was the husband of Pat's sister Viola Mae Nixon. He was a rancher and resided in Yancey in Medina County.

There is a seventh member of the Nixon family, and she is Loma Johnson Brown. We have had several maids through the years. Notable among these was Mary Harris, incapacitated in 1920. She lived many years after that, however, and it was a satisfaction to us to be of help to her medically and otherwise. But the one to whom we all opened up our hearts is "Lomie."

Lomie, also from the Gonzales country, came to us when Ben and Thomas were one year old.[4] She claims all our boys as much as we do. In their letters to us, the boys never thought of closing without sending their love to her. Sometimes there was more than a suggestion also, as this from Bob in Charlottesville in 1936: "You might tell Loma 'Hello' for me and that I still get hungry for those cookies of hers."

It is to her that they have turned for advice when some of their problems have seemed to be too weighty to be borne in solitude. And now, it is to her that their wives are turning for culinary, household, or personal help. To all of them and to us, Lomie has been counselor, confidante, consoler, and friend. By her good humor and common sense, she has saved many situations which might otherwise have been magnified into something serious.

Both young and old look upon Lomie as a member of the Nixon family. Little Bill, at the age of four, emphasized this fact.[5] "Loma," he asked, "how many grandchildren do you have?" "Let's see," she replied, 'there's Pat III, Peggy, John, Nancy, Barbara, Charlotte, Tom, Jr., and little Patricia and Ben." "That's not all," he hastened to add. "There's three more. There's me, Evelyn, and Bobbie."

Lomie has a nephew named Sam Mathis. Sam was always a regular churchgoer. One night at prayer meeting, his congregation was being more frank and direct than its white counterpart; members and friends were called out by name, and prayers were asked for their welfare. Little Sam, aged ten, rose to his feet, and all wondered whether he would name a colored friend

---

[4] In 1922.
[5] William Tabor Nixon, the son of Dr. Robert Nixon.

or a member of his family. It was neither; he asked the prayers
of the congregation for the safe return of the four boys of Dr.
and Mrs. Nixon who were in uniform. These boys did return
safely, and, when Sam in his turn lay cold and lonely in a Korean foxhole, we too prayed for his safe return. He did return,
though wounded. The Nixon family cannot find it in its heart
to think unkindly of a family or a race that can produce Lomie
and Sam. Lomie is truly the seventh member of our family.

Our Hupmobile 20 in 1912 was as much of a pioneer as we
were. We did much visiting and had many experiences. Once
on the way to the Rhinehart Ranch in Medina County, which
Dr. J. W. Nixon had recently purchased, we got stuck in the
bed of Seco Creek. I waded ashore and deposited little Pat,
aged six months, in what I thought was a safe spot. Then, as I
was pushing and Olive was guiding the car, she called out,
"Look yonder!" Our firstborn had rolled off into the water.

And again, we were caught in Seals Creek in a flash flood
west of Luling. Hardly had we waded out with Pat and Bob
before the car was covered with water. A nearby farmer took
us in for the night and gave us supper and breakfast. He would
accept no compensation but, as an afterthought, he said, "You
might pay me four bits for the rope I broke pulling out your
car."

Many times, even to this day, Olive and I have felt that some
protecting arm has been about us when danger came near. Several times, on the highways and in the streets, we have had our
car turn completely around and no harm came to us. Never will
we forget another experience on the way to Luling. It was many
years ago when there were practically no roads. It was late in
the afternoon when we entered the shadows of the lowlands.
The road, new to us, made a sharp turn and sloped steeply
downward. There, where the ferryboat should have been, the
deep and dark waters of the Guadalupe River yawned ominous-
ly. Our little car came to a stop on the very brink. The passing
of fifty years has not lessened our gratitude to God for deliver-
ance.

The Big Bend, the Carlsbad Caverns, and the Gila River

country were to us and the boys *terra cognita* long before good roads and civilization had left their defacing scars. Canyon exploration, cactus hunting, horseback riding, and other such activities early developed in our four boys a love for those wild areas. Thirty years after our first trip to the western country, Olive and I visited this area again. Some of our recollections were recalled in a letter [*to G. W. "Dub" Evans, Magdalena, New Mexico, May 20, 1952*]:

I have come to know something about the Evans family through eating their beef at Skillman's Grove, through the admirable work of Mr. Joe in establishing camp meetings over the Southwest, through reading Mr. Will's *Big-Time on the Old Ranches*, and now through following your delightful *Slash Ranch Hounds*. This country needs more such families of sturdy dignity, where worthy ideals and ambitions pass so easily and so logically from generation to generation. I will never forget a classic remark made by Mr. Joe. The conversation had to do with leadership—or the lack of it—in Washington. Mr. Joe spoke for many of us when he said, "I have always felt that, in order to clean out a creek bed below, you have to kick the hogs out of the springs above."

In 1928 I had the happy experience of making a horseback trip up the Gila River from the little town of Gila. In the party were J. M. Bassett and my two older sons. We stayed a week or two at a large run-down house near a hot spring on the bank of the river. This must be fairly near to Slash Ranch. The two things that stand out are scenery beyond description and fishing on horseback.

I have not said enough about your fine book. It is solid and substantial and will stand the test of time. It rings true. It springs from the heart of the area that has made America great. It depicts a heritage which no one should be permitted to forget. It reminds me of other days when my Walker hounds were my closest friends, and it prompts me to reread Agnes Morley Cleaveland's *No Life for a Lady*.

Nearer to home, Olive and I spent many unforgettable hours together. Easily recalled is a day on horseback at the Rhinehart Ranch. It was during the hunting season. This ranch was a hunter's paradise. Deer and turkey were on all sides of us, but we had no desire to kill. A bunch of Mearns quail or crazy quail, the only ones we have ever seen, appeared out of nowhere under our horses' feet. We watched them, beautiful and fascinating as they were, as they awkwardly tumbled and stumbled into a nearby thicket.

Another time we went to this ranch and took our camping outfit along. It was bitter cold. Olive sat huddled in the car while I set up camp. The first thing, of course, was a good fire. As I was clearing away some brush, Olive cried excitedly, "Look at your coat." I had worn my only suit with the expectation of putting on hunting togs in camp. The fire had spread through dry grass to the bush where I had hung my one coat. Olive experienced both surprise and satisfaction as she heard me use—the only time in our lifetime—the word "damn." But we soon forgot the coat with the tail burnt off. Our problem was to keep warm with inadequate covers. We used our woodcraft to contrive the solution. We placed cedar boughs under our first quilt and then put large stones, very hot and wrapped in paper, at the foot of the bed. When bedtime came, we had a warm bed.

Another hunting trip to the Rhinehart Ranch was full of adventure, this time shared by Weir and Olive Labatt. We carried lots of camping gear in a Collins Company truck and two automobiles. It was raining when we left San Antonio, and it was raining when we reached Hondo. Good judgment should have sent us home, but good judgment can easily be nullified by a hunter's enthusiasm. We struck out on unpaved roads about four o'clock in the afternoon. The first few miles of third-class roads gave us no great trouble. When the little-used pasture roads were reached, our problems began. The rain was incessant; the mud was black and bottomless. Nightfall came early. Hour after hour we plodded along, most of the time being spent in going from car to car with pick and shovel in hand. A few hundred feet would be made, and then mud would be caked solid between tires and fenders. Finally, all wheels ground to a stop at 3:00 A.M., five miles from the ranch house. Our two Olives and the children were wet and cold. Help had to be obtained. So I set out on foot. It was difficult to follow the road. When the Seco Creek was reached, I found it in flood stage. I could hear it roaring before I realized it was near. Poor swimmer that

I was, I heedlessly plunged in. With difficulty, I made my way from one clump of trees to another, sometimes on a small island, sometimes in water up to my armpits. I don't know how I made it across those several hundred yards of water. I am honest enough to admit that I believe Providence led me by the hand. For did not Isaiah record, "When thou passeth through the waters, I will be with thee."

Back in the pasture, the folks were having a miserable time. Everybody was wet and cold. Weir spent his last ounce of energy in digging mud from the wheels of my car, so he crawled into the front seat and, all hunkered up, tried to sleep. But there was little sleep that night. Pat and Bob, in the back seat with Olive, were constantly calling out, "Mama, make that man shut up." They were referring to his snoring, alternating with his shivering and complaining about the cold. It was very cold, and Weir had no cover. He made the mistake of removing his shoes from his swollen feet and couldn't get them on again. But the irony was that he found a heavy blanket under his feet the next morning. Olive [*Labatt*], Weir, Jr., and Blair fared no better in the other car. I reached the ranch house just as day was breaking, cold and exhausted but thankful that I had made it. Leroy had a good fire in the fireplace and I was soon warm and in dry clothes. Well do I remember how eager Mildred was to prepare my breakfast: venison, eggs, honey, and biscuits! Leroy hooked up a team of mules to a wagon, and we were soon on our way to bring in the women and children.

We set up camp in an unused rock house. The next morning, Weir was up well before day cooking Aunt Jemima pancakes and twirling them through the air with great abandon. On this trip, the Negro driver John asked me to take him turkey hunting. We found a big bunch before daylight. There was gobbling all around us. Very quickly, we got our limit of three each. We started to camp, with him carrying four gobblers and me two. On the way back, we killed a tremendous rattlesnake that had swallowed a half-grown rabbit; he had dislocated his jaws in the process. I said to John, "You give me your gun and take the snake to show to the folks." "No suh, doctor," he replied, "You give me them other two turkeys." So we continued, he with six turkeys and one gun, I with one snake and one gun. A picture of the hunters and the snake, still extant, shows his swollen mid-section. It was on this trip that our Olives showed their early boldness in dress; they put on trousers and walked right out in front of their menfolk![6]

We did a good deal of quail hunting, mostly on the ranches of Garrett Wilson, a brother-in-law, and Buford Nixon, a close first cousin.[7] Especially plentiful were the quail on Buford's place near Charlotte, both bobwhites and blue quail. This phase of our hunting is brought in so that I can remark that all our boys are mechanically inclined, especially Pat and Thomas. One cold December morning, we were on our way to Buford's. It was very foggy. As I was driving along beyond Harlandale, our Studebaker touring car (we had graduated from the Hup 20) plunged ahead at full speed without my cooperation. Something had gone wrong with the accelerator. I didn't know what to do except to try to hold the car on the road. It seemed that we were headed for oblivion or eternity. But not so. Pat, Jr., aged seven, sitting in the front seat with me, calmly reached over and turned off the ignition switch, and the car coasted to an easy stop.

Our expeditions, however, were not all to the west. Our fishing was done on the Texas coast. Long before tourist cabins appeared on the scene, we were each year stretching our tents near Fulton or on Lamar Peninsula. Here, too, conditions were crude and primitive. There were no surfaced roads, and many have been the times when we would get stuck in the deep sand. We would get out only by utilizing every device, including partial deflation of the tires. The brush of the area was almost impenetrable and the heat away from the shoreline almost unbearable. With the land breezes, there came swarms of mosquitoes

[6] In 1907, Pat had written to Olive: "I think you had better not ride with divided skirts. It's all right, I suppose, but I don't want you to do it. It might cause comment, and it's always best to stay on the safe side. However, this is only a suggestion, not a command." Dr. Nixon's unpaginated manuscript in the possession of Dr. Pat I. Nixon, Jr., San Antonio.

[7] Buford King Nixon was a rancher; he served as mayor of Pearsall, Texas.

from the stagnant ponds of the inland areas. Mosquito bars and smudge fires provided only a partial solution. But what fishing!

The place was ideal for our boys. They could play in the sand, paddle or swim in the water, fish off the pier, tinker with their sailboats, toy or real, spear crabs or flounders. These varying activities served to whet their appetites and tire their bodies so that they could ignore the nocturnal onslaughts of the mosquitoes.

Our fishing vacations were not restful vacations, just as our hunting vacations were not. We were active fishermen, out early every morning and back again every afternoon. The best fishing was near the pebbly reefs in Rockport Bay. The usual plan was to pile on Captain Head's boat, which could accommodate uncomfortably fifteen or twenty fishermen. He would pull out into the bay, often as far as St. Joseph's Island, and leave a few of us on each reef. Our technique was to wade out into waist-deep water and keep the surface agitated by use of the cork and the pole, which was usually a heavy cane pole with heavy line and hook. In a few hours, we would have plenty of fish: trout, redfish, flounder, sailcats, and occasionally some unusual variety. The captain rarely fished, but he liked to cook the fish as we caught them, and rarely did fish taste better than that he fried in a crowded corner of his boat.

Dr. F. M. Hicks was a great fisherman. Tarpon fishing was his favorite sport. On one occasion he was playing a five-foot tarpon when a much larger shark attacked and swallowed the tarpon. As he and his boatmen, both completely exhausted, pulled up to the pier with their shark in tow, the spectators were incredulous, until Dr. Joe Wooten of Austin,[8] who happened to be present, performed an autopsy on the marauder. So it was at Dr. Hicks's insistence that we made several trips to Port Aransas for tarpon and mackerel fishing. Of the latter, we caught plenty. But one tarpon experience stands out. Olive hooked and, after quite a struggle, landed the first fish. Within a few minutes, she hooked another and larger one. I, sitting right be-

[8] Joe S. Wooten was an 1895 graduate of Columbia University.

side her, hadn't had a nibble. With the second tarpon on her line, she offered me her pole, and I sheepishly accepted it. We had our two tarpon mounted, this being one of our few real personal extravagances. As visitors notice these fish on the walls of our shack at the farm, they often remark that mine is much larger. But they don't know why, and Olive is too ladylike and too well mannered to tell them.

Incidentally, Olive killed her finest turkey at 202 E. Courtland Place, San Antonio, Texas. It was a few days before Christmas. Ed and Beula Wood had sent us a fine gobbler.[9] One morning Olive went out to the coop to feed him. He was not there. Looking around, she found him high up in one of our neighbor's trees. We were very young then, and our turkeys were few. Olive was determined that we should not lose this one. So she went into the house and got her twenty-gauge shotgun. She shot him through the head. Including the lead that Olive put into him, he weighed twenty pounds.

From our earliest days we—all six of us—have been interested in all forms of nature study: birds, flowers, trees, cacti, grasses, animals, minerals—all of them. We have always had a cheerful backyard, thanks to Olive's green thumb. The showplace is a gorgeous elm tree with its limb spread of one hundred feet. The tree was set out by Walter Whall in 1913. It is difficult to drive into the yard without being reminded that here is a haven, a place where love is.

Shortly after we moved into our home, John Bennett gave Olive two *Nandina domestica* plants. John brought them from California, where he had been attracted by their beautiful red berries. For several years, Olive waited in vain for the berries, and then one year they appeared in profusion. One day—it was Christmas—she and I were sitting on the back steps when the little boy next door came around the house with his new red wagon filled with Olive's much-cherished red berries. Olive didn't wait long to cry out, "You little brat, you, what did you

---

[9] Edmund Franklin Wood, 1867–1946, married Pat's sister Beula Viene Nixon. He was a farmer and resided at Luling.

do that for?" Disappointed, the little fellow said meekly, "Well, all right, if you don't want them, I'll put them back on the bush."

Olive and I had our greatest trouble in the vegetable garden. We had learned from our elders that we should plant enough to give the birds one-third, the bugs one-third, and us one-third. Our portion was usually the least.

We were especially interested in birds. The usual run of birds visited us in town. We have had as many as fifty Inca doves at one time, usually ten to twenty. It was easy to see that they all were pigeon-toed. These very friendly birds roosted in nearby trees and shrubs. A small group roosted at the back door. On cold nights, they all wanted the inside perch. They would get on top of each other and then scrounge in between the nearest neighbors. This maneuvering for the warm spots would go on till darkness came. The most amazing situation would develop on those rare nights when only two doves came to roost. Each made every effort to get inside. It was something like leapfrog. These antics would go on till dark. Then each bird hunkered up to a small ball, resigned to the worst the night had in store.

For a good many years, we had something of a curiosity in our backyard. We noticed that a good many of the pecans had small holes drilled in them, never larger than one-fourth of an inch across. When the nuts were cracked, they were practically empty. We realized that this could not be the work of rats or squirrels. And then one day the mystery was solved. I saw a yellow-shafted flicker pull a pecan from its outer shell with his bill, fly with it to a nearby crotch of the tree, hold the nut with one claw, steady himself with the other, and then get busy with his bill. Since then, I have seen this performance twice.

There seems to be some discussion as to whether grackles dip their food in water to soften it. I have observed this at least a dozen times, and Olive and Loma have seen it three or four times. And I have seen these birds on three occasions fly in with the bread, always from the west. It may be that they patronize the Rainbo Bakery several blocks to the west.

Regardless of whether dunking of bread by boat-tailed

grackles is a well-established habit or an occasional observation, I have recently (May, 1963) observed a modification of this technique. We heard a loud and raucous yelping in the backyard, comparable to that of a bunch of half-grown wild turkeys. A pair of grackles were escorting three youngsters to the birdbath. The mother had about one-fourth of a slice of bread in her mouth. She held it under water for a few moments and then flew to the back of a chair where a noisy baby was waiting. The transfer was made without incident and then all the birds flew away.

There are other friendly minor patterns of our back and side yards; the imposing attitudes of our small doves, the courage and success of one of these little doves with one leg off, the unfailing refusal of all birds to fly down to the feeding ground until the two bellwethers have started to eat. But there is one experience that must be emphasized: I go up to the medical library once or twice a week, a distance of six or eight blocks. Some weeks ago, as I was returning from the library, I noticed that I was being shadowed; in the branches of some cottonwood and elm trees, a flock of English sparrows were flying excitedly back and forth and calling the stragglers to "come and get it." When I stopped, they stopped. When I stopped very long, they, in seeming disgust, flew on to the backyard, where they were waiting for me. This experience was observed on three different occasions.

At the farm we studied many birds, such as the vermilion flycatcher, slate-colored junco, garden oriole, Bullock's oriole, summer tanager, spotted towhee, white-throated sparrow, wood duck, and many others. I have repeatedly seen a prairie-runner snake wrap his body around the base of the birdbath and curve his head and neck to the water. I have seen an awkward woodpecker finally get in position to drink. On two occasions, I gently rubbed the back of a rusty lizard and had him fall to the ground hypnotized, asleep, or something else. Olive saw one of these.

The most beautiful bird to be seen at the farm is the vermilion flycatcher. We have usually had about a dozen pairs each year. So far as I know, Dr. Robert Nixon was the first to see and identify this bird in this area. The date was about 1942. There are two observations which are not mentioned in the books: As this bird hovers in the air, there is a continuous popping the bills together. And, as he descends, he nose-dives like an attacking airplane, only to flatten out gracefully a few feet from his perch.

As a supplement to what has been recorded above, I want to go into some detail, principally in regard to birds. Our deepest communion with nature was found in the Big Bend country. By good fortune, we found the Prude Ranch near Fort Davis.

Our many visits to the Prude Ranch have left indelible memories—memories of the fine Prude family, of many congenial friends and many experiences on foot and on horseback. Here we saw birds in profusion, most of which were within two or three hundred yards of the home. Year after year, we could count on seeing a Say's phoebe nesting on the front gallery, a barn swallow a few feet above the manger, and a curve-billed thrasher in a cholla cactus near the windmill. Each late afternoon we watched the flight of the band-tailed pigeons. They roosted in a canyon south of the ranch and used as a feeding ground a large, wooded area about two miles north. We had many fine chances to study these majestic birds at close range. It was easy to see the dark tip on the yellow bill.

One morning Olive and I witnessed a thrilling sight; twenty-four red-shouldered hawks were resting on the posts of a fence. They all faced westward and all had their wings outstretched. We watched them for quite a while, only about fifty yards away.

It was the Big Bend itself, however, where we found and cherished the greatest beauty in mountains and birds.

Our next-to-the-last trip was made in 1954. We made a twenty-mile horseback ride to the South Rim and reveled in the glorious view into the mountains of Mexico. At the nearby Boot Springs we used an Audubon birdcall and called up several different species of birds at one time: western tanager, canyon wren, house finch, tufted titmouse, scrub jay, white-necked raven, and golden eagle.

Enough has been said to show that congeniality played a big part in our life out-of-doors. By this is not meant an awkward familiarity, for awkwardness never entered into our relations. Here and in all of our many common spheres of interests, our desire has been to nurture and expand our personal affection.

For the family, our library has been as much of a gathering place as the dining room. We tried to make easily accessible to our boys many of the standard books of reference as well as many of the classics. We realized that they would partake sparingly, but they did get a taste and found it good. We are glad that their rate of absorption was not so great as to approach the predicament of an intensely neurotic family of our acquaintance. There were four old maids and one bachelor. One day, one of the women said to me: "Dr. Nixon, you don't know what is wrong with this family. It is too much religion, too much music, and too much books."

[*During student days at Johns Hopkins*] I did a great deal of reading outside of medicine. Many hours did I spend in the library of the hospital and university. That early, I must have realized how many good books were available and how few were the hours and the years. Most people don't read beyond the daily paper and an occasional magazine; but to a thoughtful reader, it is discouraging to be reminded that, if one book is read each week, only about two thousand books will be covered in a reading life of forty years.

As for Olive and me in later years, we have lived in our library. Few have been the nights or days when we were not reading or looking up something on some subject.

Before our marriage, we each had bought a few books which became a part of our joint library. [*Back in March, 1910, I had written to Olive*]: "The two hours after dinner I spent on the campus reading Kipling's stories. I must confess with you to being 'book-mad.' I have bought and read more books in the past six months than I have in any other six years of my illiterate

PAT NIXON OF TEXAS

existence. If we continue this, we shall have a good beginning for a library when the time comes for us to put our books on the same shelves. I warn you against adding Emerson, Stevenson, or Kipling to our collection, for they are to be my donations."

In connection with this joint library, which has grown and overflowed to adjacent rooms with the passing years—especially in the field of Texana—I enumerated certain relative values which Osler had prescribed: "Osler says every young doctor should have a library, a laboratory, and a wife and advises us to acquire them in the order named. I prefer to reverse the order, for, if I have you for a wife, I know I can get the other two."

I mention this single example to illustrate the reading habits which I learned from Dr. William Osler. His "Bedside Library for Medical Students" was presented in the following words:

A liberal education may be had at a very slight cost of time and money. Well filled though the day be with appointed tasks, to make the best possible use of your one or of your ten talents, rest not satisfied with this professional training, but try to get the education, if not of a scholar, at least of a gentleman. Before going to sleep read for half an hour, and in the morning have a book on your dressing table. You will be surprised to find how much can be accomplished in the course of a year. I have put down a list of ten books which you may make close friends. There are many others; studied carefully in your student days these will help in the inner education of which I speak:

    I. Old and New Testament.
    II. Shakespeare.
    III. Montaigne.
    IV. Plutarch's *Lives.*
    V. Marcus Aurelius.
    VI. Epictetus.
    VII. *Religio Medici.*
    VIII. *Don Quixote.*
    IX. Emerson.
    X. Oliver Wendell Holmes—Breakfast-Table Series.

It is not a little strange that Robert Burton's *Anatomy of Melancholy* was not included in this list, for this, the most erudite of books, was one of his prime favorites. He may have considered it too heavy a mental diet for a student. I reckon I am one of the few men in San Antonio or Texas who have really read this great book. As I thumb through my old and much-marked copy, it is satisfying to recall that Dr. Samuel Johnson said that this was the only book that ever got him out of bed two hours sooner than he wished to rise.

If I were in a position to recommend a list of books for young doctors—which I am not—my advice would be about as follows: "Read carefully Ian Maclaren's *A Doctor of the Old School* once a year; read carefully Harvey Cushing's *The Life of Sir William Osler* once every five years; read carefully Robert Burton's *The Anatomy of Melancholy* once in a lifetime; read the *Bible* carefully every day."

Olive early became a lover of poetry. Even now, she can recite many verses which Professor B. A. Stafford required her to memorize in the Mineola High School. My general reading has been quite varied. Biography, religion, history, historical novels, geography—all these were welcome.

However much our books on general subjects may have meant to us, our deep and abiding and continuing interest lay and still lies in the field of Texas history, with emphasis on the medical aspects. Here, Olive was the leader. The story of how our inquiring minds were first interested, then absorbed, and finally fascinated has been told. It was presented first at one of the early meetings of the San Antonio Historical Association, held at our home, and was later published as "The Genesis of a Collector of Texana" in the *Southwestern Historical Quarterly* in 1942.

The amenities of life have been innate with Olive and me. We haven't taken them for granted; they have just been a constant ingredient of our life together. Mutual courtesy and mutual consideration have existed from the very first. It was just as natural and normal for me to seat Olive at breakfast this morning as it was in 1912, when we faced each other across our first breakfast table. Outward and expressed evidences of gratitude or appreciation were never necessary or expected. We each had the capacity for sensing that which went unexpressed. On certain occasions, when for instance I would present her with a sample box of Whitman's with five stingy pieces of candy or a flower which someone had given me, it would in mockery be accompanied by my prefabricated speech of presentation: "In appreciation of what you have been, what you are now, and what you promise yet to be."

Our areas of kindred taste are so many and so widespread that our differences are hardly worthy of mention. She does belong to the Christian Church, while I am a Methodist. She still clings to a certain hankering for highbrow music; I am a rank apostate. She, far ahead of me, saw what a tremendous political and moral imposter a man by the name of Roosevelt was. And that's about all of our disagreements.

On the other hand, our areas of agreement are many: love of literature, love of Texas history and medical history, devotion to home and family, distaste for social prominence, distaste for individual or family publicity, love of the great out-of-doors, and personal loyalty.

In summary, it can be said that our associations have been happy and intimate. Our satisfactions have been many, our problems few and not serious. As we look back over our long life together, we can say, with the pious, that we have never spoken a harsh word to each other. But having said that, we hasten to add that we have endured some eloquent silences, which could well have been replaced by something more vocal.

Without effort and even without intention, Olive has fitted her life into mine and that of the family, always willing to play a minor role when necessary. This is not to assume that she has not been a major factor in the affairs of the Nixon family, for she certainly has. Hers has not been a life of self-denial; rather, her desire has been to make her life complementary to mine, and in this direction she has been eminently successful. Typical of her complete adaptation is the fact that, year after year, she has quietly listened to my small collection of yarns, and on occasion she has reminded me of one I hadn't told. I like to accuse her of composing this apt verse:

> If you can recall so many yarns
> With all the detail that mold them,
> Why can't you recall with equal ease
> How many times you've told them?

Time has taken its physical toll, but our love is still young. In retrospect, I am thinking of a beautiful girl in a blue dress.[10] Her grandchildren delight in the snowiness of her hair and the bigness of her heart. We face the west together, hand in hand, just as we had pictured so many years ago. Our love has never failed.

❧

The inexorable logic of facts and years is inescapable. Full recognition of this fact is essential. In a retrospective mood, it is seen that all the early years were in preparation for the later days.

There is a story about a literate man who had the confidence of his neighbors. On occasion, he assayed the role of prophet and, more often than not, his prophecies missed the mark. As he grew older, he became more cautious. One day a friend asked him for an opinion on the outcome of certain world trends. He replied that now he was sure of only two things: it was getting colder, and ten o'clock at night was pretty late. I appreciate his attitude.

As the evening shadows lengthen, it is rewarding to look back over the course of my life, which has comprised the most eventful period in all history and, at the same time, the most distressing. While great progress—intellectual, material, and even spiritual—has been made, yet we have not learned to live together, and wars and rumors of wars continue to plague the human family.

---

[10] Through the years, Pat had held in his mind a vivid picture of the way Olive looked in the blue dress she had worn when he first met her back in 1904.

In a backward look, it is heartening to recall how much has been accomplished since that timid boy emerged from Guadalupe County in the long ago. These accomplishments are not too closely associated with any inherent capabilities but rather with the many opportunities which presented themselves and with the many people who had confidence in me. Most of these were both friends and patients. Many of these were new and unknown to me, and yet they accepted my opinion and my judgment under serious conditions.

My experiences have been many and varied. I have tried to meet my problems without compromising conscience or courage.

And at the very end, I am willing to accept the philosophy of Sir William Osler:

I have had three personal ideals. One, to do the day's work well and not to bother about tomorrow. It has been urged that this is not a satisfactory ideal. It is. And there is not one which the student can carry with him into practice with greater effect. To it, more than to anything else, I owe whatever success I have had—to this power of settling down to the day's work and trying to do it well to the best of one's ability and letting the future take care of itself.

The second ideal has been to act the Golden Rule, as far as in me lay, toward my professional brethren and towards the patients committed to my care.

And the third has been to cultivate such a measure of equanimity as would enable me to bear success with humility, the affection of my friends without pride, and to be ready when the day of sorrow and grief came to meet it with the courage befitting a man.

Whatever I may have accomplished in any direction—medical, historical, civic, literary, religious—these are secondary to the glory of my family. There are twenty-four of us and every one is very precious to me. I know of no man in all the world with whom I would exchange places.

Chronology

1827 Robert Thomas Nixon, father of Dr. Pat Nixon, was born on April 13, in Randolph County, North Carolina.

1832 Laura Ann Wood, first wife of Robert Thomas Nixon, was born on February 18, in Randolph County, North Carolina.

1843 Frances (Fannie) Amanda Andrews, second wife of Robert Thomas Nixon and mother of Dr. Pat Nixon, was born on November 5, in Randolph County, North Carolina.

1852 Robert Nixon and Laura Wood were married on August 31. They moved to Texas and settled in Guadalupe County.

1872 Laura Nixon died on July 4. Robert Nixon and Frances Andrews were married on December 19.

1883 Pat Ireland Nixon was born on November 29, at Old Nixon, Guadalupe County.

1886 Olive Gray Read, wife of Dr. Pat Nixon, was born on August 2, in Mineola, Texas.

1895 The Nixon family moved to Luling, Texas.

1897 Robert Thomas Nixon died on March 27.

1900 Pat Nixon graduated from Luling High School on April 24, salutatorian of his class.

1902 Pat Nixon graduated from Bingham School, Asheville, North Carolina, on June 13, *maxima cum laude*.

1905 Pat Nixon graduated from the University of Texas on June 14. He entered Johns Hopkins Medical School in the fall.

1909 After graduating from medical school on June 8, Pat Nixon passed the Texas State Medical Board Examinations and was licensed to practice medicine in Texas. He began his internship at Johns Hopkins.

1911 On October 1, Dr. Pat began his medical practice in San Antonio.
1912 Wedding of Pat Nixon and Olive Read took place on July 3, at Mineola.
1913 Pat I. Nixon, Jr., was born on May 28.
1914 Robert Read Nixon was born on June 26.
1920 The Nixons purchased Fairland Hills Farm.
1921 Benjamin Oliver and Thomas Andrews Nixon, twins, were born on February 14.
1926 Dr. Pat Nixon was elected president of the Bexar County Medical Association.
1928 Dr. Pat Nixon was appointed to the San Antonio Board of Health.
1936 *A Century of Medicine in San Antonio*, Dr. Pat's first book, was published.
1939 Fannie Nixon died at Luling on December 7.
1941 Dr. Pat was elected president of the San Antonio Historical Society.
1946 *The Medical Story of Early Texas, 1528–1853*, Dr. Pat's second book, was published. Dr. Pat was elected president of the Philosophical Society of Texas. He became president of the Texas State Historical Association.
1952 Dr. Pat received the annual award of the San Antonio Conservation Society.
1953 *A History of the Texas Medical Association, 1853–1953*, Dr. Pat's third book, was published.
1956 *The Early Nixons of Texas*, Dr. Pat's history of his family, was published. Dr. Pat was elected president of the Texas Surgical Society.
1957 Dr. Pat received the Summerfield G. Roberts Award for *The Early Nixons of Texas* and the Clement E. Trout Award for "Surgery: A Cultural Factor in Early Texas."
1961 Major Ben Nixon died on January 22.
1963 Dr. Pat received an honorary doctorate from Trinity University, San Antonio.
1964 Olive Nixon died on October 29.
1965 Dr. Pat Nixon died on November 18.

Bibliography: Pat Ireland Nixon

⌒◞◟⌒

BOOKS

A Century of Medicine in San Antonio. Lancaster, Pennsylvania: Lancaster Press, 1936.

A Crowning Decade, 1949–1959: Laurel Heights Methodist Church, 50th Anniversary, with C. Stanley Banks. San Antonio: privately printed, 1959.

The Early Nixons of Texas: With Genealogies by Dr. and Mrs. Pat Ireland Nixon, Jr. El Paso: Carl Hertzog, 1956.

A History of the Texas Medical Association, 1853–1953. Austin: The University of Texas Press, 1953.

In Memoriam, Olive Read Nixon, 1886–1964: With a Tribute to Olive by Sterling Fisher Wheeler. San Antonio: privately printed, 1965.

Laurel Heights Methodist Church, 1909–1949, with C. Stanley Banks. Austin: The Steck Company, 1949.

The Medical Story of Early Texas, 1528–1853. Lancaster, Pennsylvania: Lancaster Press, 1946.

The Texas Surgical Society: The First Fifty Years, with Robert S. Sparkman, R. Wilson Crosthwait, Walter B. King, Jr., and R. J. White. Dallas: privately printed, 1965. Dr. Nixon's contribution to the book was primarily of an advisory nature; the book contains his presidential address before the society, October 1, 1956, "Surgery: A Cultural Factor in Early Texas." The address had previously appeared in the *Texas State Journal of Medicine* 53 (March, 1957): 159–164.

FOREWORDS TO BOOKS

Harry C. Oberholser, *The Bird Life of Texas.* Austin: The University of Texas Press, 1974. This foreword is dated 1961.

W. B. Russ, *A Doctor Looks at Life*. San Antonio: Naylor Company, 1952.

ARTICLES

"Acute Dilation of the Stomach Following Gynecological Operations," *Texas State Journal of Medicine* 16 (March, 1921): 481–486. This paper was read before the Section on Gynecology and Obstetrics of the Southern Medical Association, Houston, April 23, 1920.

"Alcoholic Injections for Relief of Pain," *Medical Record and Annals* 26 (September, 1932): 212–215. This paper was read before the Bexar County Medical Society, San Antonio, March 17, 1932.

"The Bexar County Medical Society and Medical Library Association," *Southwest Texas Medicine* 1 (May, 1934): 16–17, 21–22.

"Can We Diagnose Appendicitis?" *Bulletin of the Bexar County Medical Society* 5 (January, 1916): 36–38. This article also appeared under the same title in the *Medical Record* 89 (March 11, 1916): 469–471. This paper was read before the Caldwell County Medical Society.

"Cenizo in the Treatment of Catarrhal Jaundice," *Texas State Journal of Medicine* 29 (May, 1933): 39.

"Chaparro Amargosa in the Treatment of Amoebic Dysentery," *Bulletin of the Bexar County Medical Society* 3 (January, 1914): 89–98. This article also appeared under the same title in the *Journal of the American Medical Association* 62 (May 16, 1914): 1530–1533, and in the *American Journal of Tropical Diseases* 2 (March, 1915): 572–584.

"Chaparro Amargosa in the Treatment of Amoebic Dysentery," *Journal of the American Medical Association* 66 (March 25, 1916): 946. Although this article bears the same title as the previous item, the contents are different.

"Congenital Hypertrophic Pyloric Stenosis in Infants," *Medical Record* 99 (March 12, 1921): 433–435.

"Dr. Benjamin Harrison, Temporary Texan," *Journal of the History of Medicine and the Allied Sciences* 1 (January, 1946): 108–114.

"Fannie Andrews Nixon," *Frontier Times* 17 (March, 1940): 265–267.

"The Genesis of a Collector of Texana," *Southwestern Historical Quarterly* 46 (October, 1942): 177–181. This paper was read at

the summer, 1942, meeting of the San Antonio Historical Society.
"Gonococcal Infections of the Kidney: Report of Two Cases," *Surgery, Gynecology, and Obstetrics* 12 (April, 1911): 331–341.
The Handbook of Texas, edited by Walter Prescott Webb and H. Bailey Carroll. Austin: The Texas State Historical Association, 1952. In volume 1, entries for "Dowell, Greenville S.," p. 517; "Field, Joseph E.," p. 596; "Hadra, Berthold E.," p. 753; "Harrison, Benjamin," p. 779; "Herff, Ferdinand," p. 801; "Jalot, Medar," p. 903; and in volume 2, entries for "Liotot," p. 61; "Medical History of Texas," pp. 166–168; "Paschal, Frank," p. 343; and "Zerván, Federico," p. 952.
"History of the Bexar County Medical Library Association," *Texas State Journal of Medicine* 29 (September, 1933): 343–346. This paper was read at the dedication of the library on June 8, 1933.
"The History of the Bexar County Medical Society," *Health and Happiness* 5 (March, 1938): 6–8, 21.
"How I Kill Red Ants," *Farm and Ranch* 64 (November, 1945): 41.
"Hugh Hampton Young, 1870–1945," *Proceedings of the Philosophical Society of Texas* 10 (1945): 60–61.
"Inflammatory Tumors of the Abdomen," *Medical Annals of Southwest Texas* 6 (October, 1917): 217–219. This article also appeared under the same title in the *Annals of Surgery* 67 (March, 1918): 306–311.
"The Intravenous Use of Mercuric Chloride: A Note on a New Method of Administration, with Special Reference to Prevention of Vein Obliteration," *Journal of the American Medical Association* 66 (May 20, 1916): 1622.
"Judge Alfred W. Arrington, Judge William H. Rhodes, and the Case of Summerfield," *Southwestern Historical Quarterly* 55 (January, 1952): 341–357. This paper was read at the annual meeting of the Texas State Historical Association on April 28, 1951.
"Liotot and Jalot, Two French Surgeons of Early Texas," *Southwestern Historical Quarterly* 43 (July, 1939): 42–52. This article also appeared under the same title in the *Bulletin of the History of Medicine* 7 (November, 1939): 1049–1060. This paper was read at the annual meeting of the Texas State Historical Association on April 29, 1939.
"Lutein Cell Carcinoma of the Ovary," with Henry Hartman, *Southern Medical Journal* 28 (February, 1935): 161–166. This paper was read before the obstetrical and gynecological section of the

annual meeting of the Southern Medical Association, San Antonio, November 13, 1934.

"Multiple Consecutive Perforated Gastrojejunal Ulcers," with S. T. Lowry, *Medical Journal and Record* 128 (December 5, 1928): 584–586.

"Nonbacterial Urethritis," *Bulletin of the Bexar County Medical Society* 4 (February, 1915): 101–102. This article also appeared under the same title in the *Medical Record* 87 (April 10, 1915): 607–608.

"Notes and Queries: A Letter by Hyrtl," *Journal of the History of Medicine and Allied Sciences* 11 (January, 1956): 104–105.

"Organized Medicine in San Antonio," *Southern Medical Journal* 27 (September 1, 1934): 819–821.

"A Pioneer Texas Emasculator: Chapter from the Life of Dr. Gideon Lincecum," *Texas State Journal of Medicine* 36 (May, 1940): 34–38. This paper was read before the Texas Surgical Society at Fort Worth on April 3, 1939.

"Pyelitis as a Clinical Entity," *Bulletin of the Bexar County Medical Society* 2 (December, 1912): 14–25. This article also appeared under the same title in the *Southern Medical Journal* 6 (July, 1913): 462–467.

"The Relation of the Old to the New in Medicine," *Southwest Texas Medicine* 1 (June, 1934): 9–10. This paper was read before the Bexar County Medical Society in San Antonio on October 26, 1933.

"Retroperitoneal Hernia into the Duodenal Fossae," *Annals of Surgery* 65 (April, 1917): 457–462.

"Robert Koch," *Medical Record and Annals* 26 (May, 1932): 164–165. This paper was read before the Bexar County Medical Society in San Antonio on March 24, 1932.

"San Antonio's Health," *Health and Happiness* 5 (May, 1938): 6–7. This paper was delivered over San Antonio radio station WOAI on June 14, 1946.

"A Short Account of the Bexar County Medical Library" in Henry Schuman, comp. *Sixty-five Notable Milestones in the History of Medicine in the Bexar County Medical Library*. San Antonio: privately printed, 1961. This was originally read at the dedication of the Bexar County Medical Library Building, San Antonio, September 17, 1961.

Bibliography: Pat Ireland Nixon

"Spontaneous Rupture of the Normal Spleen," *Journal of the American Medical Association* 96 (May 23, 1931): 1767.

"Surgery: A Cultural Factor in Early Texas," *Texas State Journal of Medicine* 53 (March, 1957): 159–164. This article was incorporated into *The Texas Surgical Society: The First Fifty Years.* This was Dr. Nixon's presidential address delivered before the Texas Surgical Society on October 1, 1956.

"The Texas Medical Association, 1853–1953," *Texas State Journal of Medicine* 49 (May, 1953): 274–278. This paper was read at the annual meeting of the Texas Medical Association, Houston, April 28, 1953.

"Walter Goodloe Stuck, M.D.," *Southern Medical Journal* 44 (September, 1951): 869–870. This commemorative address was delivered at Laurel Heights Methodist Church in San Antonio on March 25, 1950, and repeated before the Texas Surgical Society and the Southwestern Surgical Congress.

EDITORIALS

"The Budget Plan of the Bexar County Medical Society," *Southwest Texas Medicine* 2 (August, 1935): 3–4.

"The General Practitioner, Must He Pass?" *Southwest Texas Medicine* 2 (May, 1935): 7–8.

"Health Insurance," *Southwest Texas Medicine* 2 (June, 1935): 7.

"Hematology—Pernicious Anemia," *Medical Annals of Southwest Texas* 6 (April, 1917): 91.

"Medical Boat Rockers," *Medical Record and Annals* 33 (August, 1939): 193–194.

"Medicine at the Crossroads," *Southwest Texas Medicine* 2 (March, 1935): 7–8.

"Minimum Standards for Physicians," *Texas State Journal of Medicine* 45 (August, 1945): 550–551.

"Must America, Like Rome, Reach a Paretic Period?" *Southwest Texas Medicine* 2 (July, 1935): 3–4.

"The Origin of Syphilis," *Southwest Texas Medicine* 2 (September, 1935): 3.

"Prevention of Diphtheria," *Health and Happiness* 1 (April, 1933): 11.

"Some Plan Must be Found," *Southwest Texas Medicine* 2 (April, 1935): 7–8.
"They Wrought Well," *Junior Historian* 9 (September, 1948): 1.

BOOK REVIEWS

Barrett, Monte. *Sun in Their Eyes*. In *Southwestern Historical Quarterly* 48 (October, 1944): 304–307.
Duffy, John, ed. *The Rudolph Matas History of Medicine in Louisiana*, Vol. 1. In *Journal of Southern History* 25 (February, 1959): 115–116.
Duffy, John, ed. *The Rudolph Matas History of Medicine in Louisiana*, Vol. 2. In *Journal of Southern History* 28 (November, 1962): 504–506.
Frank Howard Lahey Birthday Volume. In *Texas State Journal of Medicine* 36 (October, 1940): 458–459.
Gambrell, Herbert. *Anson Jones: The Last President of Texas*. In *Southwestern Historical Quarterly* 51 (April, 1948): 371–373.
Haagensen, C. D., and Wyndham E. B. Lloyd. *A Hundred Years of Medicine*. In *Texas State Journal of Medicine* 40 (June, 1944): 304–307.
Huson, Hobart. *Dr. J. H. Barnard's Journal*. In *Southwestern Historical Quarterly* 54 (January, 1951): 370–371.
Merritt, Webster. *A Century of Medicine in Jacksonville and Duval County*. In *Texas State Journal of Medicine* 46 (October, 1950): 788–789.
Moorman, Lewis J. *Pioneer Doctor*. In *Texas State Journal of Medicine* 47 (July, 1951): 485.
Reagan, R. G. *P. Reagan, Country Doctor*. In *Southwestern Historical Quarterly* 67 (October, 1963): 313–314.
Rosen, George, and Beate Caspari-Rosen. *400 Years of a Doctor's Life*. In *Texas State Journal of Medicine* 43 (March, 1948): 734–735.
Young, Hugh. *A Surgeon's Autobiography*. In *Southwestern Historical Quarterly* 44 (January, 1941): 392–394.

Index

~᥯᥯~

Index

Juarez, Benito, 230
Judd, Edward Starr, 177–178, 181–185, 186, 188–189
Junior Historian movement, 28

Katz, Sid, 216
Keedy, David M., 216–218
Kelly, Howard A., 42, 87n, 175, 195; in Hopkins "Big Four," 14, 86; as member of Hopkins faculty, 87–90; Nixon's opinion of, 15, 87–90, 175–176, 189; at YMCA, 88, 115
Kelly Field, 235
Keyser, R. Brent, 110
Kingsley, Charles R., Jr., 114n; as friend of Nixon, 114, 117, 119, 121, 122, 133; as Hopkins student, 108, 112
Kirby, Helen, 82
Klebs, Arnold C., 99
Koch, Robert, 99
Korean War, 255
Krueger, Carl, 233, 239, 240

Labatt, Olive, 202, 257, 258
Labatt, T. Weir, 202, 215, 257, 258
Lakeside Hospital, 174
Lamar Peninsula, Tex., 259
Lee, Lavord L., 223 and n
Levering, Eugene, 136
Lewis, Warren Harmon, 118 and n, 119, 121, 149, 151
libraries, medical, 23–25, 146, 166, 215, 218–219
Light (San Antonio), 219, 233
Lipscomb, Willoughby, 61–62
Little's boarding house, 101, 144
Loevenhart, Arthur, 121 and n, 142, 151
Long, W. R., 82, 203 and n
Lowery, E. Q., 207
Lucey, Robert E., 237
Luling, Tex., 8, 60–61, 66, 196, 255
Lundburg, F. H., 194

McAllister, Walter, 42
MacCallum, William C., 90, 138 and n, 147, 148, 149
McCamish, Edward W., 203 and n, 222
MacCarthy, William Carpenter, 177 and n
McCrae, Thomas, 114
MacDaniel, Gibbs, 227

McGaw, W. D., 166
McGimsey, Brooks B., 215, 233
McGimsey, Mrs. Brooks B., 40n
McKinney, Dannie, 53–54
McKinney, Wesley, 53
McMillan, Bob, 79
Magee, Madge, 171
malaria, 117
Mall, Franklin Paine, 90, 113 and n, 115, 165
Marburg, William A., 14
Marley, Jim, 124 and n, 141, 142
Marshall Field and Company, 175
Matas, Rudolph, 66
Mathis, Sam, 254–255
Mauermann, Gus, 232–233, 238, 242
Maverick, Maury, 226–227, 228–229, 231, 232
Mayo, Charles Horace, 177–178, 180–183, 185–190
Mayo, William James, 177–179, 181–182, 184–185, 187–190
Mayo Clinic, 21, 251
Meader, Fred Marlin, 116 and n
measles, 62
medical equipment, 136–137, 141, 202
medical history, 29–34
medical journals, 23, 36, 88–89, 161
Medical Record and Annals, 37–38, 215
medical schools: evaluated, 13, 144; expenses in, 92–93, 101. See also individual schools
Medical Story of Early Texas, 24, 31–33
medical students: courses for, 91, 108; demands upon, 90; female, 115–116, 119, 120; health of, 16; living conditions of, 15; recreations of, 16, 93, 95, 96, 109, 114–153 passim
medicine: advances in, 12; professionalization of, 12–13, 27–28, 31, 47, 214
Menger Hotel, 210
Mexican Americans, in San Antonio, 38, 43, 221
Meyer, Julius, 65
Michael Reese Hospital, 175
Miller, Ernest J., 219
Miller, K. E., 226
Mineola, Tex., 23, 133, 191, 196, 203, 205

Index

23–28, 63, 131, 145, 146, 152, 197, 215–218, 256, 265–267; boyhood of, 6–7, 51–57, 59–60, 61–65, 67, 68; character of, 10–12, 18–19, 21, 29, 43, 45–46, 48, 67, 76, 106, 111–112, 270; and council-manager government, 39, 226, 227–228, 230, 231, 244; death of, 48; diagnostic skill of, 17–18, 102, 110; early education of, 7–8, 58–59, 62–64, 69; as family man, 43–45; finances of, 92–93, 183, 208, 213–214; health of, 8, 16, 62–63, 69, 99, 117, 129, 252; historical interests of, 28–29; home of, 207–208; influences on, 5, 10–12, 23, 63, 64, 74, 76, 87, 90, 169, 197, 266; as intern, 155, 159–168; letters from, described, 14–15, 17; marriage of, 203–206; medical career of, 5, 22–23, 45–46, 85, 109, 160, 193–194, 197–199, 208–214; at medical school reunion, 110–112; as medical student, 86–87, 88–90, 91–92, 95, 101–107, 110, 113–129, 133–153; musical performances attended by, 120, 134, 137, 142, 143, 145, 149, 157; papers written by, 78, 214–215; plays attended by, 93–94, 115, 116, 124, 135, 138, 145, 146, 150, 151, 156; political activities of, 38–40, 221–247; political affiliations of, 41, 224, 227; on public health boards, 39, 221–226, 232–244; recreation of, 16, 44, 93–94, 96–101, 156–157, 251–253, 256–261; relations of, with patients, 202, 203, 208–209, 210–214; and religion, 46–47, 115–129 passim, 134–150 passim, 156, 174, 268; as school physician, 222; social life of, 95–96, 107, 139, 149, 150, 151, 158–159; at University of Texas, 77–79, 80–82, 83; and YMCA, 11, 97–98, 107, 114, 117, 128, 136, 138, 140, 144, 146, 147, 148, 149, 150. *See also* individual family members
Nixon, Pat Ireland, Jr., 43–44; birth of, 207 and n, 249; childhood of, 250, 251, 253, 255, 256, 258, 259; genealogy by, 36; medical career of, 48, 219, 249, 250

Nixon, Pat Ireland, III (grandson), 254
Nixon, Patricia Ann (granddaughter), 254
Nixon, Robert Lee (brother), 51n
Nixon, Robert Read (son), 218, 254, 264; birth of, 207 and n, 249; childhood of, 250, 253, 256, 258; medical career of, 219, 249, 250–251
Nixon, Robert Read, Jr. (grandson), 254
Nixon, Robert Thomas (father), 4–5, 6, 8, 35–36, 51 and n, 52, 62n
Nixon, Sam Houston (brother), 5, 51 and n
Nixon, Thomas Andrews (son), 27, 44, 207 and n, 249–251, 252, 259
Nixon, Thomas Andrews, Jr. (grandson), 254
Nixon, Viola Mae (Mrs. Harrison Garrett Wilson), 51 and n, 253 and n
Nixon, William Tabor (grandson), 254 and n
Nixon, Zachariah, Jr. (ancestor), 36
Nixon, Zebulon Vance, 51n, 52n, 204, 205; and baseball, 7, 66; childhood of, 7, 52, 53, 64, 66, 68; and Denman farm, 81, 92n; letters from, 113, 116, 119, 136, 138
Nixon family: chores of, 52–53, 68; fishing trips by, 259–261; and gardening, 261–262; nature study by, 261; Pat's attitudes toward, 43, 250, 251, 265, 267–269, 270; relations among, 43–44, 249, 251, 265, 267–269; vacations of, 255–261
Noguchi, H., 99

Ochsner, A. J., 174
Ogilvie, H. H., 215
Old Nixon, Tex., 62
Orchard, John, 62
Osler, Sir William, 86n, 99, 109; on books, 23–24, 266; in Hopkins "Big Four," 14, 86; as member of Hopkins faculty, 13, 15, 86, 95, 113, 114, 146; Nixon's opinion of, 15, 23, 86–87, 95; philosophy of, 90, 270

Paget's disease, 148
Paine, Linda, 82

University of Pennsylvania Hospital, 19
University of Texas Health Science Center at San Antonio, 25

Vaughn, Victor C., 99
Vest, Cecil Woods, 19
Virginia, University of, 250

Walker, Frances Hamilton, 205 and n
Walker, James Knox, 66 and n
Walker, Mrs. James Knox, 58 and n, 68, 143
Walter Reed Hospital, 250
War Assets Corporation, 235
Wardlaw, Frank, 29, 47, 77
Warrington Dispensary Collection, 14, 146
Warthin, A. S., 99
Washington, D.C., 96, 98–99
Watkins, John M., 200 and n
Watkins, Leon H., 129 and n, 146
Webb, Charles Wallace, 147 and n, 149, 156
Welch, William Henry, 99; described, 87 and n; in Hopkins "Big Four," 14, 86, 87; influence of, on Nixon, 39, 222; as member of Hopkins faculty, 90, 134, 135, 137, 138, 142, 146, 147, 165; and public health, 39, 222

Welland Canal, 173
Wesson, Miley B., 145 and n
Wheeler, William Morton, 78
Whipple, George Hoyt, 14, 138 and n
White, Jack, 244
Wiesender, Arthur James, 120 and n, 145
Williams, John Whitridge, 41, 91
Wilson, Harrison Garrett, 253 and n, 259
Wilson, Homer T., 215 and n, 218
Wilson, Mrs. Harrison Garrett, 51, 253 and n
WOAI radio station, 228, 229
Wolf, William M., 215 and n
women's suffrage movement, 42
women in medicine, 13, 115–116
Wood, Edmund Franklin, 261 and n
Wood, Mrs. Edmund Franklin, 261 and n
Woodward Carriage Company, 198
Wooten, Joe S., 260 and n
Wright, Almroth E., 135
Wyatt, Walter Simrall, 112

YMCA (Young Men's Christian Association), 11, 97–98, 107, 114–129 passim, 134–150 passim, 156, 174, 177, 268
Youmans, Iva Catherine, 112
Young, Hugh Hampton, 14, 189